# THE SON OF SEVEN MOTHERS

A TRUE STORY BY
'CULT SURVIVOR'
## BENJAMIN RISHA

WildBluePress.com

THE SON OF SEVEN MOTHERS published by:
WILDBLUE PRESS
P.O. Box 102440
Denver, Colorado 80250

Publisher Disclaimer: Any opinions, statements of fact or fiction, descriptions, dialogue, and citations found in this book were provided by the author, and are solely those of the author. The publisher makes no claim as to their veracity or accuracy, and assumes no liability for the content.

Copyright 2021 by Benjamin Risha

All rights reserved. No part of this book may be reproduced in any form or by any means without the prior written consent of the Publisher, excepting brief quotes used in reviews.

WILDBLUE PRESS is registered at the U.S. Patent and Trademark Offices.

ISBN 978-1-952225-08-6 Trade Paperback
ISBN 978-1-952225-07-9 eBook

Cover design © 2021 WildBlue Press. All rights reserved.

Interior Formatting/Book Cover Design by Elijah Toten
www.totencreative.com

# THE SON OF SEVEN MOTHERS

*This book is dedicated to the children of the Tony and Susan Alamo Foundation.*

# Table of Contents

| | |
|---|---|
| INTRODUCTION | 7 |
| PROLOGUE | 9 |
| | |
| CHAPTER ONE | 14 |
| CHAPTER TWO | 29 |
| CHAPTER THREE | 53 |
| CHAPTER FOUR | 68 |
| CHAPTER FIVE | 87 |
| CHAPTER SIX | 115 |
| CHAPTER SEVEN | 128 |
| CHAPTER EIGHT | 149 |
| CHAPTER NINE | 160 |
| CHAPTER TEN | 179 |
| CHAPTER ELEVEN | 188 |
| CHAPTER TWELVE | 217 |
| CHAPTER THIRTEEN | 233 |
| CHAPTER FOURTEEN | 245 |
| CHAPTER FIFTEEN | 256 |
| | |
| PHOTOS | 269 |

# INTRODUCTION

29 years elapsed from the time I started writing this book until its publication. As I have matured over the years the reasons for writing this book have also changed. I have told my story to hundreds of people in part because I found relief in knowing that they an understood who I was and what I had been through. I realize now that there is a need to understand cults and high manipulation organizations because many people are effected by them. I hope this book connects with you and with them. At the core of this story is a story about resilience, people and their relationships with each other, and the power they exert over each other to achieve their goals. And, in the end, it's a story about how facts can dismember and mutilate lies.

This story is my story. However, like many stories, it is deeply intertwined with many other lives and experiences. All the names have been changed other than mine, my biological fathers who passed away before this book was published, Tony and Susan Alamo, who are also deceased, and the names of Tony Alamo's other wives. Children (at that time) are referred to only by first names with pseudonyms to protect identity and privacy, or as 'child/a child.' Like the children in this book, I use pseudonyms for the adults. All the events in this book happened to me, to the people in the book, and I have permission from them to share their stories. I have combined smaller scenes to ensure the smoothness of the larger story. Many of the characters' characteristics have also been consolidated for the sake of brevity and to prevent any one person from being identifiable.

Footnotes are provided as attribution for events that different editors, and I, deemed important enough to support with outside sources. Some of the details of this story are horrific and lack explanation on their face value, but later sources that were closer to the events came forward providing details that explained the unexplainable, like the motive for so many child beatings and why state and local authorities never intervened.

I am fortunate to have been given access to so many different people and their histories as it pertains to the timelines involved. Throughout the life of this book, editors have assisted me with constructing the narrative of this book. They have all wondered aloud why the reports of abuse were not reported to government agencies. My response has always been the same: the abuse occurred in a cult where outside authority was not allowed to intervene and who were considered the enemy. I hope by reading this story you will come to understand the reality in which it occurred.

Originally, I titled this book *The Cult Leader Has No Clothes*. It was never published. Rather, the manuscript under this title was placed on this website, which is a nexus of sharing information for former members and cult survivors of the Tony and Susan Alamo Foundation. It was placed there so they could read my story before it was published.[1]

---

1. https://www.tonyalamonews.com/6257/the-cult-leader-has-no-clothes-a-survival-and-escape-story-by-benjamin-risha.php

# PROLOGUE

The dreams I dreamed before I knew not to dream were the sweetest, but the dreams after I knew better were the most real. It was no surprise that it took a lot of shaking to wake me this night.

"Benji, Benji...wake up," Dad Miguel shook me awake. "Papa Tony called the entire congregation to the chapel."

It was 1989, and I was fourteen years old at the time. I was in the middle of a dream with three sisters. They were all within one to three years of my age, and we were playing house.

On this dark October, Arkansas morning, I would have much preferred to return to my dream, but I soon realized how unusual it was to be invited to a midnight sermon with the adults. I hurriedly got dressed. It was common, though, for us kids to be woken up in the middle of the night to report our transgressions to Papa Tony, which ranged from talking back to an adult, play-hitting each other, walking by ourselves, or something much viler such as a boy and girl holding hands or, even worse, kissing. They knew, we all knew, that we were all born in sin and shaped in iniquity because Papa Tony preached this to us all the time. Holding hands and kissing were the pinnacles of iniquity in my world.

Being "put on report" to Papa Tony meant standing in a confession line telling everything that might be a sin or anything we might have done, or even thought about, that Papa Tony might decide was a sin. We all sweated in fear during this process, and some kids would even pee their pants while standing in line. We would shiver in the distress of awaiting the unknown punishment, both physical and emotional, that would be meted out to us. The only sure thing we could expect was pain; the pain of consequence designed to drive our sins from our bodies and our souls. We weren't punished merely for acting out; we were punished for our thoughts. Most of us believed Papa Tony always knew what we were thinking.

He claimed God told him these things, but I thought Papa Tony could read our minds as well. I can't recall a single sermon in which he did not mention thought control or remind us that God judged every thought, no matter how seemingly trivial. We knew we would be judged for every one of them, either down here on earth or up in heaven on Judgment Day. Apparently, God talked to Papa Tony all the time; he often spoke of how he heard the voice of God all day, every day, and he asserted that God told him everything we were thinking.

In 1981, there were a few hundred children living on The Ridge compound and that Christmas, the last Christmas Grandma Susie was alive, we children were required to sing the Christmas song, *Santa Claus is Coming to Town*, to Papa Tony and Grandma Susie. We replaced "Santa" with "Papa Tony and Grandma Susie" ... *they know what you've been thinking. They know when you've been good or bad so be good for goodness' sake.*

On the way to the chapel, I wondered if Papa Tony knew about the dream I had been having. I feared that he would see it in my face. If he did, I would be punished, but if I lied, it would be even worse, so I would have to confess. When we arrived, I saw it was indeed a midnight service with a sermon that was taking place, not a confessional for us children. I relaxed a little bit, but when Papa Tony was angry with us, his sermons were just as scary.

The chapel used to be our grand living room and was converted to a chapel after the IRS said they wanted to confirm we were a church and not a business. Papa Tony had our living room contents removed and hidden in secret storage locations in order to prevent the agents from seeing our wealth. What I believed this evening was that Papa Tony had been in hiding because the one-world government was trying to locate him just for preaching the word of God, so tonight's sermon looked as if it was going to be prerecorded and blared through the media system we had installed just for this purpose when Papa Tony was not present. Large, black speakers sat between the white columns on the pulpit ready to spread Papa Tony's voice over the nervous congregation, most of whom were in their pajamas. Would the sermon be a lashing of our sins or would we hear from the other Papa Tony, the one who could turn this room electric with energy?

Before Papa Tony went into hiding, his sermon voice rumbled through us and his pacing back and forth kept us on our toes. We would be yelling "Hallelujah" and other demands for God to do our bidding. We gyrated, clapped, sang, and prayed with enthusiasm because we knew God could see us and was judging us based on our actions and our thoughts. I hoped it would be that kind of sermon night.

Prerecorded Papa Tony preached about how the one-world government was after him. He proclaimed the evil Catholic Church, through the Pope, was pulling the strings like a master puppeteer, to persecute him and us, just because we loved God, just because we preached against homosexuals, the government, and anyone else who was not part of our church. "The World," as we called any place outside of our property, was an evil place.

I was falling asleep until his rebuke turned to us, his followers.

"You people make me sick. I am reading reports that you want onions and non-moldy bread. You're tired of the moldy bread. Don't you think the starving Hebrew slaves would have eaten moldy bread when they escaped Egypt? How pathetic.

"And, your socks have holes in them, and you want new socks. Boo hoo. I have reports here that your children are fighting at school. And what's this I hear about a peeping Tom among you? Your children should be more like Benji."

That woke me up completely. This was the third time this year he used me as an example of how the other kids should behave. But if he only knew how evil I was he wouldn't have edified me like this.

"He's a God-fearing young man. All of you should look to him as an example. I raised him to fear the Lord and to flee from evil. 'Train up a child in the way he should go and when he is old, he will not depart from it.' He's not like your children. You should all be ashamed.

"The Bible says, 'Suffer the little children to come unto me, and forbid them not, for such is the kingdom of God. Verily I say unto you, whosoever shall not receive the kingdom of God like a little child shall no wise enter therein.' You milk-toast people will not get into heaven! I might have to leave you to teach you all a lesson."

Whenever Papa Tony threatened to leave us, the congregation lamented with each other that they would do better. Pray more, give more, ask for less.

I was Papa Tony's favorite. Papa Tony said I would someday bring salvation through Jesus to those people fighting in the Middle East because I was from Jewish and Arab descent. I held my head up and straightened my back as I looked around and noticed the other children looking at me. *I am a leader. I will lead these people someday.*

That's what Grandma Susie and Papa Tony told me quite often. "Benji," one of them would say, "You must always do the right thing because the eyes of the world are on you. Someday, you will be required to lead many people to God."

Emmanuala, a girl my age, was sitting in the pew in front of me. Her breasts had matured sooner than most of the other girls my age. She turned around and looked directly at me before bending over in front of me, reaching for her hair clip which had fallen behind her pew. I looked right down her shirt looking at the things that mattered to me even more than Papa Tony's sermon.

I started telling myself ... *you are evil. God sees you. The blood of Jesus is against you Satan. The blood of Jesus is against you Satan. The blood of Jesus* ... I feared that God would send me to hell for my thoughts. Even worse, God might tell Papa Tony, he would punish me, and I would fall from his graces. My sexual excitement subsided.

# CHAPTER ONE

## Papa Tony and How it all Began

When Papa Tony walked into the room we stood up. Observing our loyalty, he would exclaim an exaltation into the microphone such as: "Praise the Lord!" or "God is great!" He knew how to get us excited enough to stay on our feet while he paced back and forth giving us his God-inspired message. When he spoke, it seemed like the air was sucked out of the room. His exuberant messages demanded everyone's full attention.

It's not that he was a particularly large man. He had an average build at about 5' 8", but it was how his chest led him around as he paced across the pulpit of our church. His chest seemed to be filled with all the air that never escaped as we held our breath for what he would say next. What did escape him were his words and the way he spoke them. There was an urgency and an eternal importance to them which could not be ignored. We hung our attention on each word waiting for the next one to drop into our ears, filling our minds with what we should do next and how we should think in order to maintain the overall purity of our lives.

We never saw his eyes though. They were covered by his dark-lensed, prescription glasses that only came off when he cleaned the lenses or when he put on regular glasses to read the Bible to us. The dark lenses protected his glaucoma-ridden eyes from us seeing into his soul, but he said it was to protect him from the bright, florescent lights that bathed us.

He always seemed to wear cowboy boots, which made him seem a few inches taller than he was, a big belt buckle, and an outfit comprised of a pair of designer pants and a shirt. Sometimes his face had a beard; other times not. His full black head of hair was always combed back.

Based on the stories he told me, he wasn't always like this. His life was much different before he gave his life to Jesus. It was much different before he met Grandma Susie.

As a child, Papa Tony, né Bernie Lazar Hoffman, suffered the humiliation of walking from farmhouse to farmhouse with his father begging fellow Jews for a few potatoes, some eggs, anything to tide them over. The town's synagogue had been shut down and the Klan went on night raids, leading many to remove the mezuzahs that were affixed to their entryways. Few homes answered the knocks as no one had provisions to spare seeing how they were living in the Great Depression of the 1930s.

Making his life even more difficult, his parents abandoned him when he was young and he was placed in Father Flanagan's Boys' Home, a Catholic boys' home. If he argued with the priests, they strung him up by his arms from the ceiling rafters for hours and beat him. His only permissible utterances were to moan in agony. If he spoke, or said anything against God or God's church, they put him into a small crate and left him there for days without food or water. At least that is what he told me and other children.

Bernie, his name before he changed it to Tony Alamo, left the orphanage in 1952, when he was eighteen. He fled Montana for Los Angeles where he started hustling leather boots on Hollywood Boulevard to gullible teenagers who fancied themselves the next James Dean. At the age of twenty-one, he began calling himself "Tony Alamo" as a nod to the popular Italian singer, Tony Alamo, who sang with Sammy Kaye's band in the 1940s and 1950s, and said good-bye to Bernie, his Jewish heritage, poverty, and the rest of his past.[2]

He ran afoul of the law and in 1955 he was arrested for possession of stolen property. By the age of twenty-one, he was a convicted felon who had racked up charges of statutory rape, theft, and burglary.[3]

In the early to mid-60's, Tony worked as an advertiser, claiming to his followers during almost every church service to have promoted the Beatles and Sonny and Cher to new clients. Tony bragged to the same followers it was during a negotiation for Bobby Jamison, one of his clients, after ingesting LSD, that he had a vision and heard a deep voice tell him, "I am the God of your fathers! I created the heavens and the earth. You must repent of your sins and commit your life to God. Give up the sins of the flesh and accept Jesus as your personal savior. Give up your pride and personal ambition. Tell the people in this room that they also must repent of their sins, or I will strike you down!"

He looked around but did not see anyone else's lips moving. He walked around the room, looking for a recording device that might explain what he heard. He ran his hands along the corners of the walls and then he walked back to the table. The determined voice returned.

"I am the God of your fathers! I created the heavens and the earth. You must repent of your sins and commit your life to God. Give up the sins of the flesh and accept Jesus as your personal savior. Give up your pride and personal ambition. Tell the people in this room that they also must repent of their sins, or I will strike you down!"

Tony repeated what only he could hear.

---

2. https://www.allmusic.com/artist/tony-alamo-mn0001624746/biography

3. https://www.tonyalamonews.com/101/tony-alamos-history-of-rape-burglary-theft-and-receiving-stolen-weapons-charges.php

The director, growing increasingly impatient, furrowed his brow while he stared at Tony. When he'd had enough, he yelled out, "Is this your idea of a joke? You're not getting any more money, if that's what you're after." He then grabbed the phone and dialed his secretary. "Call security right now. Get them up here immediately," he yelled.

As security arrived, Tony regained some of his composure. "I've heard the voice of God. God has told me that I must repent. You all must repent also."

"You're crazy!" the director yelled.

Tony was dragged out of the office by an armed security guard, but he kept yelling, "Repent of your sins."

"Get the fuck out of here!"

He was thrown out onto the sidewalk. Leaving his car behind, he wandered aimlessly for hours, until his feet were sore, and his legs were tired, all the while the voices traversed his mind. He had walked all the way to Hollywood and that is where he saw her: she was standing on the corner of Hollywood and Vine. In that moment, he truly believed her to be an angel.

She wore a bright white wedding gown and gripped a white satin vintage clutch. Her hair was blonde and wavy, which appeared to wave to him as it moved. She was preaching, surrounded by a crowd of young people clad in denim jeans, cutoff military fatigues, summer blouses, short dresses, long beards, and even longer hair.

"You must repent of your sins if you ever want to find peace in your lives. The drugs will not bring you peace, at least not everlasting peace. Jesus Christ is coming back to earth again. You must repent of your sins or perish. Repent or perish," he heard her say.

"I have to speak to you," he said, pushing through the group of people.

"I'm not sure who you are, but I feel compelled to speak with you. My name is Tony Alamo. I am exhausted right now, but I have to speak with you."

Edith Lipowitz looked upon him with pity. "I'll be going into that café soon Tony Alamo," she said pointing to it. "Meet me there in an hour after you get some rest."

He found a bus stop bench where he folded his Armani suit jacket into a pillow and he laid there, checking his wristwatch every fifteen minutes until it was time for them to meet.

In 1939, Edith Lipowitz, née Edith Opel Horn, idolized Aimee Semple McPherson. Aimee's nightly radio sermon was something she never missed. Edith's father was a Nazarene and she had traveled the streets with him listening to his sermons before she left home in Arkansas at age fourteen.

For years afterward she emulated her father, preaching on street corners. People with barely a few pennies to rub together, loitering with no particular purpose and no distinct place to go, were her ideal flock. Haggard, dirty faces, attired in tattered, grimy clothing and worn-out shoes, only outdone by dirtier, greasier, and darker lines in their necks and hands. The homeless, the drunk, the drug-addicted, and the hopeless all looked upon her in awe as she walked fearlessly amongst them.

Years later she married Saul Lipowitz, the muscle for Eddie Cohen. She had a daughter, Christhiaon, and eventually they moved to Hollywood to become a double for actresses. When not acting, she preached on the streets and in the churches around Hollywood and this is where Tony found her: preaching on the streets.[4]

Grandma Susie often bragged to me how she recruited Papa Tony in a café using her extensive knowledge of the Bible to educate him and save his soul. In the café, Edith asked him, "How well do you know the story of how man was created?"

---

4. https://www.tonyalamonews.com/572/the-splc-reports-christhia-on-coie-susan-alamos-daughter-recounts-abuse.php

"Well, I've read Genesis numerous times, if that's what you mean," he answered, sitting next to her in the booth.

"Did you know that the first two chapters have two distinct and unique creation stories?"

"No ... no ... it doesn't," he replied with hesitation in his voice.

"It does and they are quite different. Genesis 1:26 says man was made in the likeness and image of God himself and placed above all else to rule. He is given the power to even name the animals," she explained.

"By contrast, Genesis 2:7 says man was made of the dirt and in the dirt, he will toil for the entirety of his life. In this story, man is condemned to work and to work in the dirt. Like a slave of that time. Do you think someone who works in the dirt can be the same person who can name the animals? I don't."

"I never thought of it that way. I didn't know both of those stories. I always read them as one story. If you're correct, that means some people were meant to lead, and others were meant to serve. It's their destiny to either serve or lead, to be either slaves or to rule the slaves."

"Correct. If you read the Hebrew version of the Bible, it's obvious that there are two different authors telling two different stories about how man came into existence. The question is: which one are you? Are you meant to lead or are you meant to serve?" she posed, leaning back as if playing a spiritual game of chess and uttering the word "Check" with "mate" hinging upon his next move.

"I'm clearly a leader, that is not the question for me," he answered. "The question is, how do I get people to willingly follow me?"

"No!" she interrupted. "The question is: How do you get people to see that you are worthy of being followed?"

"Worthy of being followed?"

She caressed the top of his hand before placing it on her leg.

THE SON OF SEVEN MOTHERS | 19

"Some people are smart. Others not so smart. Making the stupid follow you is easy. They always look for leaders to tell them how to live, what to do, and how to do it. It's the smart ones that you need to have follow you, and then have them convince the dumb ones to follow you. This way you will create a pyramid, with you on the top of the chain of command."

"I Corinthians 1:27 says, 'But God hath chosen the foolish things of the world to confound the wise; and God hath chosen the weak things of the world to confound the things which are mighty.' Use this verse when you meet those smart people and they try to use reason and logic against you."

It reminded Tony of his meeting earlier that afternoon, of laying out his advertising philosophy to those executives. Only this time, he was trying to understand, and she was doing the teaching.

"I see," he responded with uncertainty.

"I'm not sure you do. From what you've told me, you are good at getting people to follow you through the threat of force. Isn't that why you work with those tough guys? To force people to pay if they owe you?"

"That's right. Might makes right."

"Force, to some, is considered an immoral tool. However, the force of God is viewed by many as a moral force that must be used in the world where the devil is perceived to run rampant. Do you follow me?"

"I think so," he answered, putting the pieces together in his mind. "You're saying that I need to cloak myself in God's moral cause and use the force God has granted his leaders. Then I will be perceived as a moral man worthy of following without the use of violence and threats."

"Exactly. Speak how I speak, with authority. Act like you know what is right and know in your heart that you are, and you will be." Checkmate.

They slept together that night, intoxicated by their newfound understanding and anticipating the many things to come. They saw in each other mutual imagination, ambition, and greed. They lay in bed the following morning and ordered breakfast delivered to them.

"You know. Right before we met, God spoke to me. He told me that his Son was coming back to earth and I need to convert the sinners to his work," he explained to her, leaving out the fact that he had ingested LSD before the auditory hallucinations.[5]

"Sounds to me like Saul of Tarsus. He was blinded by God on his way to persecute Christians. I think you found your cloak, Tony," she said. "That is your testimony from here on out. Use your story to convince others that you were called and anointed by God himself."

One thing Edith knew for certain was everyone needed a hook. For her it was her blond mane, her ease among the lost, her authoritative, mob-mother personality, and the gospel she shared. However, beyond the hook, they also needed a purpose.

"You have to remember this one thing above all else," she urged. "The real story of faith is not about building an empire, but rather repairing the world."

Together they began preaching that they were the light for good in a dark and doomed world. Many different types of people were drawn to them. From former military men to intellectuals, musicians to dishwashers, they accepted anyone who would listen to them. They took in the homeless and gave them a home. Some were drug addicts and the message of God cured them from their addictions. They brought hope to the hopeless. Using her natural acting skills to preach and his skills as an advertiser, they gave the people what they wanted to hear.

---

5. A former leader of Psychedelic Movement told me this story. He was the person who gave the LSD to Tony.

Running small cash-generating operations, they paid no taxes, and every cent they earned went toward advertising their ministries while all their energy went toward finding recruits. Kendra was one of their earliest recruits and she came with an established modeling career. When she and Edith met, she spoke deliberately and with care saying, "I crave depth and substance. I can't grow by listening to my friends' drivel about modeling techniques and opportunities in faraway places like Milan and Paris. The runway and after-hour parties are fun, but they aren't emotionally sustaining. Do you know what I mean?"

Edith assured her, "I know exactly what you mean. I am no stranger to fame and the requisite parties. I was a double for Betty Grable. If you want something emotionally sustainable then you need to surround yourself with people who are emotionally stable."

Kendra nodded, affirming what she was hearing, and Edith replied with a saying she used all the time, "Satan has a plan to deceive the world. However, Jesus has a plan to deceive the deceiver. We must find and live our lives with a higher morality that does not involve drugs and parties. My dear, only Jesus' saving grace could sustain you. Are you ready to be saved? For the right person, a person who seriously wants to develop their spiritual side, we have a room available in our home."

During the first week of Kendra's arrival, her daily training was simple: Read a Bible verse, pray for five minutes, and be available each evening for personal conversations. The second and third week, it required daily praying for fifteen minutes a day and read a Bible chapter. By the second month, she had to pray for thirty minutes and read scripture for thirty minutes each day.

As Kendra's responsibilities increased, Edith stripped away her freedom, telling her, "You are no longer allowed to go to the after-hours parties or speak to any modeling friends, unless it's about God and Jesus. Those people will pull you away from your spiritual development."

Kendra was permitted to continue working, but not to socialize with her colleagues, unless for the purpose of recruiting them. Within three months of moving in, she was purchasing and paying for all the groceries, the utilities, and the rent. She was also charged with cleaning the lean-to, named so because its walls leaned due to poor construction. This was all designed to demonstrate her commitment to God. By this time, she prayed three times a day for an hour each time, read the Bible three hours a day, and fasted on Wednesdays.

By 1968, Edith and Tony had inherited a house from an invalid in a nursing home whom Edith had witnessed to and comforted in her dying days. They were repeating their approach with nine new recruits, all of whom worked and turned over their paychecks to them. A few of the recruits had trust funds, which were drawn from soon after joining the group. Others had welfare payments and GI benefits. Once their original recruits were fully trained, Tony and Edith relied on them to recruit others. They moved to Las Vegas to continue growing their ministry, leaving Edith's teen daughter Christhiaon behind.

An attorney in his own right, Dorian Yale was also one of the trust-fund recruits. His monthly contribution of more than $2,000 per month back then was close to an equivalent of $14,000 per month in 2020. He and Kendra loved each other at first sight and later married.

Abandoned Christhiaon formed friendships with other wayward, abandoned souls, including Mack, with whom she eventually had two children. While visiting her mother and Tony one night in Las Vegas, Tony turned an embrace into something unwanted. Christhiaon fought him with all her might but could not stop him. She kicked and screamed, knocked over a vase, and threw things at him.

The commotion woke her mother up and she found Tony naked on top of Christhiaon. It was Christhiaon she yelled at, though, saying, "You whore. You, vicious little whore. You think you can take my man?"

Christhiaon was shaken and crying. She objected to her mother, but she would not listen to her.

Soon after, Edith married Tony and after they were married, they became Tony and Susan Alamo. In 1969, the Tony and Susan Alamo Foundation was incorporated. Dozens of recruits were willing to follow their every whim, including beating up Christhiaon, kidnapping her children, and blackmailing her and her partner Mack.

Christhiaon told her story to the Southern Poverty Law Center years later.[6] In the story she explained how she told her mother that she wanted to leave the newly-formed group after which her mom instructed Tony and some of the followers to beat her until she lost consciousness. The followers then assisted Tony and Susan with the kidnapping of her children by hiding the children in a house while Christhiaon was unconscious.

Kidnapping her children held the potential of a few options for them. They could grow up to become loyal followers, or more immediately the kidnapped children were used as leverage against Christhiaon to prevent her from telling news and law organizations about the financial scams, the blackmail, the attempted rape, and the brainwashing she had seen or experienced firsthand.

Christhiaon called the police after she woke up from the beating to report the assault and kidnapping. She was given a ride to the police station by two police officers where she was going to be giving her statement. However, before she could file a report, her mother called the police station and told Christhiaon she promised to return her children if she

---

6. https://www.splcenter.org/fighting-hate/intelligence-report/2008/christhiaon-coie-speaks-out-about-her-stepfather-tony-alamo

did not go through with filing a report. No report was filed and when she returned home her children were returned to her.

By 1975, Tony and Susie were able to purchase two hundred fifty acres off Georgia Ridge Road between Alma and Dyer, Arkansas. Its natural beauty was inspirational. The property became known as The Ridge to us and offered complete isolation from the world. Green pines and brown oaks rolled over red and brown clay hills. Its history and secrets were revealed after April storms uncovered arrowheads and other tools from indigenous people. These ancient tools glimmered in the sunlight, long before it was occupied by the Alamos. Waterfowl, deer, bear, porcupine, skunk, wild turkey, and wild cats also made the land their home.

Within a year of purchasing the land, Tony and Susie built a thirteen thousand square foot speculation house, we called it the Spec House. It was a speculation house built to resemble the houses we would all receive in what Papa Tony and Grandma Susie called the Cadillac Ministry. It housed antique furniture, fur rugs, a black grand piano and a pearl white baby grand piano, crystal chandeliers, thick, red velvet carpet throughout, and hand-painted murals of lightly clothed cherubs ascending to and descending from heaven. It encompassed a five-car, covered parking structure with spaces intentionally designed to fit their limousines, pink Cadillac, RV, and travel van.

Adjacent to the parking structure was a heart-shaped pool. Opposite it was a fifty-yard-long by ten-yard-wide solarium attached to the mansion, which was home to the most exotic and varied species of plants and flowers in Arkansas. It had numerous orchids, red buckeyes, birds of paradise, lilies of all types, strawberry bushes, large aloe vera plants, several ficus, thornless rosebushes, numerous herbs, irises, a crepe myrtle, an ornamental banana tree, and many others.

No expense was spared, except for when the county inspector came to claim his permits and fees. It was then that Tony claimed, "We don't have the money to pay the fees. This is a place of God. Who are you to tax God?" That evening, Tony would preach of the evils of the tax collector and pass the donation plate around.

As the congregation grew, they knew they needed a bigger message. When Ed, a Lebanese American carpenter, joined their congregation, the Alamos considered him an Arab. The news outside the compound was full of unrest in the Middle East, giving Grandma Susie an idea. "Let's give Beth to Ed. Let's show the world that peace between the Arabs and Jews is possible, but only possible in our church." Beth was a Jewish American who joined the group a year before Ed.

Ed Risha was the youngest of nine Lebanese American children. His father immigrated to Pennsylvania, USA in 1904. At sixteen years old, Ed was stabbed above the heart by thieves wanting his lunch money. His doctors gave him morphine for the pain and Ed became addicted to the pain medicine. After high school, he left his family behind for Detroit, but he did not leave the addiction.

On the streets of Detroit, he found a substitute for morphine: heroin. He smoked it, but never shot up. On the same streets he met a group of people from the Tony and Susan Alamo Foundation. They preached a message of hellfire and damnation for anybody whose soul was not right with God. It wasn't this message that hooked him though; it was the way the group acted with each other. They were close, like family.

Ed was exactly what the church looked for: lost or addicted souls who missed their families. When Ed heard church members call each other "brother" and "sister," he was intrigued. They promised him an eternal, communally based sister and brotherhood and that was all he needed to sign up. He built homes for the growing congregation and within a few years he was approached by Tony and Susan with a plan that would help bring peace to the Middle East and the world.

In 1969, at the age of nineteen, Beth left her family, and their dream for her to marry a wealthy businessman, in Brooklyn. Instead, she drove to Hollywood with friends where they hoped to keep the Woodstock vibe alive. When one of her friends was recruited by the church, she went to the church with the intention of getting him out of the group. Instead, when a tall musician named Randall sang and played guitar on the chapel's stage, she fell in love with him, his music, the long-haired people who surrounded her, and the message of love and salvation she heard during the church service.

Shortly after she joined, she married Randall. They had two children together, but he died from a brain aneurysm six days after their son, their second child, was born. She was a strong-minded woman when she joined the group and remained so afterward. When she did not show signs of yielding to the charged message of fear and damnation that Tony and Susan began preaching, they blamed her, from the pulpit, for her husband's death.

In front of the congregation, they scolded her, "God took him so you could not drag him down to hell." Hoping to break her will and ostracize her from the community, they sent her to the rose fields in Bakersfield where she worked long hours. Tony and Susan would not approve the expense to buy the gloves she needed to protect her skin from the roses' thorns, and she returned each evening with bloody scratches along her hands and arms.

It was decided that marrying Beth off would temper her strong-willed personality as well as benefit the church. "Yes," Papa Tony answered, rising from the sofa and kissing Susan enthusiastically. "We could use this marriage between an Arab and a Jew to show how our church is fulfilling the prophecy, the necessity of peace between the Arabs and the Jews. The second coming of Jesus Christ cannot occur without it."

He laughed and clapped his hands saying, "This could be a very lucrative union in the spiritual sense of the term. We will be the headliner. I can see it now, *Tony and Susan Alamo Bring Peace to the Middle East.*"[7]

Nine months after Beth's husband had died, her spiritual leaders informed her that God told them she was supposed to marry Ed Risha, a man she hardly knew, but she agreed to their proclamation and Beth and Ed had a wedding. The community celebrated the union of an Arab and a Jew and in 1975 they had a darling baby boy. That baby was me.

---

7. The story of Ed and Beth has been pieced together from various sources: primarily Tony and Susan telling me the story, from my father, and from other church/cult members.

# CHAPTER TWO

## Mothers

Tony and Susan capitalized on the Arab-Jewish union of Beth and Ed by bragging in the community that God had made peace between Arabs and Jews under their guidance. A year and a half into their union, Ed returned home to Dyer one morning from being on the night watch, which was an overnight shift he and the other members were required to perform where they either manned the property's gates or drove around on The Ridge looking for intruders. He was greeted by his neighbor Elaine, "She's gone, Ed. Craig took her and the children. She couldn't take it anymore. She said she was drowning and needed to find higher ground."

Craig was a church brother who was friends with Beth and her first husband Randall. Beth had two children with Randall, but he died soon after their second child was born. Craig wanted to marry Beth when he died, but Tony told him he couldn't because he was a gentile.

Ed huffed, scuffing the ground under his boots, then rubbed his hands through his curly hair and chuckled softly. "That seems about right," he said.

He picked me up from the sofa and whispered, "So much for peace between the Arabs and the Jews." While handing me to Elaine, a long-time member of the church, he said,

"He's hungry, I think. I'm usually at work, but I think she feeds him around now. Can you take him?"

Years later, Elaine told me she whispered in my ear at that moment, "You're the child I have been waiting for, Little Prince."

She also told me how my father drove like a madman to the Spec House and how he burst into the mansion, where Papa Tony and Grandma Susie were having vegetable juice for breakfast. "Beth left with Craig and took her two children. They left Benji though."

The two looked at him, but not with astonishment as he expected. Grandma Susie said, "Aren't you glad we told you to spend more time with Benji? That's why I told you to take him on walks. I knew she might try to run away someday, and I didn't want you to regret not being with your boy. And now look at how good that advice was. It saved him from being taken from you."

"Are you saying that you knew she would leave?"

"Ed, she was a bad apple. She is and always will be a backslider and an adulterer. I thought she would leave when we sent you to Arkansas. God told me she would either leave or try to leave. I did not know that she would leave today, but I knew she would leave eventually. She's an adulteress now. She's condemned her soul to hell. Where is Benji now?"

"He's with Elaine," he said, dejectedly.

"Ed, listen carefully to me. If anyone asks what happened, you tell them she left him in the trashcan outside the house and that's where you found him. Crying and in a dirty diaper."

Grandma Susie and Papa Tony returned to their drinks which had been placed on the table next to a set of blueprints. They ran their fingers along various lines, as they discussed proximity and visibility to and from the main house.

"But that's not true. What about our Godly union? And how Jesus cannot return without there being peace between me and Beth, peace between the Arabs and the Jews?" Ed asked, his voice breaking with emotion.

He was not sure what he expected or wanted. Did he want them to chase Beth down and bring her back against her will? No, but if it was God's will that they be together, then what now?

"Ed," Grandma Susie said, annoyed by his sobbing. "Ed, Ed," she said, walking toward him. "Pull it together," she said. "You are a carpenter. You are not Jonah. There is no whale threatening to swallow you whole. You've got Benji and God on your side. There is still a chance he can grow up to fulfill the prophecy. You'll forget all about this backslider as soon as you get busy working. When he gets older you can teach him your craft. I want you to think about the future, not the past."

"Relationships have never been my strong suit with all their subtle messages and signals that change all the time. Why can't they be more like carpentry? When I make a cut it's there, it's real, and I can count on it to be right. Women ..."

He focused on work to keep his mind occupied and off women. Over the next year he built offices for Susan and Tony and started on building the new church. My dad saw me every morning and held me during Sunday church services, but I lived with Elaine and her husband John.

One crisp fall morning in 1976, Elaine put on her reddish-brown faux fur coat after she bundled me in my autumn clothes. We emerged from the Dyer home and she let me down in the grass outside of the church to demonstrate how well I walked. She put her arms out and called my name. I smiled and stomped toward her with hesitant stuttering steps like a drunken soldier.

"Oh, my little prince," Elaine said.

Grandma Susie followed Elaine to the nursery. "You seem so connected to Benji, Elaine."

"He is a gift from God, Susan. I am blessed to have him. John and I love him like he is our own."

"That's great news, Elaine. But he is not yours. You need to focus on your own salvation and not put this child before God. Don't get too attached to him. He's going to move in with Dorian and Kendra Yale. They have little Mia. The two will be great for each other."

"But ... but ... he's my little ..."

"No, I don't want to hear a word. You are clearly more connected to him than you are to God. Why else would you protest like this? Get his things together tonight. He moves tonight."[8]

Grandma Susie's word was the rule of the land, so that night I moved in with my third family. I was not even two years old and was already getting a third mother. Momma Kendra was the first recruit of the church, the ex-model from Hollywood, and she had married the largest financial donor of the group, Dorian Yale. Dorian was a leader in the psychedelic movement and joined the church in 1968. It was Dorian's trust fund which in part provided steady revenue for the church in its early days.

The Yales, their daughter Mia, and I lived in an A-frame house across from the Spec House. One day, after he left home wearing a suit and tie, I asked him when he returned home that evening why he was wearing a suit. He said, "Hey, I'm the cash man. I count the church's cash all day at the bank. If I don't look sharp, they'll think I'm a bum who's trying to steal all the money." Dad Dorian was the unofficial accountant of the church in its early days. Years later he told me about the barrels of gold coins and piles of cash Grandma Susie and Papa Tony had in the attic of Grandma Susie's house in Dyer, Arkansas.

We would go on walks in the morning where he would name the birds that twittered around us. He slept in on the

---

8. This story was told to me by Elaine throughout my childhood.

weekends and stayed up late on weekdays. When he wasn't reading a book, I saw him writing in them.

I loved Momma Kendra too. I often woke up and went to sleep with her cuddling Mia on one side of her and me on the other. She would get goat's milk for us to drink from Mr. Bruce, the man who sold the Georgia Ridge property to us and who continued to own a house on a border of The Ridge.

Mia and I were practically connected at the hips. Where she went, I went. When I slept, she did also. When she was sick, so was I. We slept together in the same crib; I'd cry if Mia was not next to me when I woke up. I potty-trained early because I was in competition with her to potty-train and get my diapers off before her. Mia and I competed on who had the bigger poops and Mom would fake measure them.

On cold nights she would light a fire in the fireplace and wake Mia and me so we could roast marshmallows. Sometimes, before the sun went down, she and Dad Dorian made fires in the fire pit outside. Mia and I would throw pinecones in the fire and yell with glee when they exploded. During the day I played with clay, making animals from the books Momma Kendra and Dad Dorian read to us. I gravitated to dinosaurs and reptiles, so the clay figures I sculpted were often of them. At bedtime she tucked me in and read Aesop's Fables to me. This was home for me. I felt loved, cared for, and protected.

Once, Mia and I were talking about dinosaurs at the church nursery. Mia and I were three years old and not old enough yet for preschool, but we did partake in preschool-type activities, like coloring and drawing. We had been trying to draw dinosaurs when an adult saw them and asked what they were. "They're dinosorbs," I said. We had learned about them by looking at one of Dad's dinosaur books.

The weekend after we drew the dinosaurs, Dad Dorian took a bunch of us kids to a planetarium. He got in trouble from Grandma Susie and Papa Tony for having the dinosaur book and for taking us to the planetarium. I heard them tell him, "What's gotten into your head? We can't have children learning about evolution."

Dad replied, "I don't see an issue with telling the truth. Have you seen some of the brothers around here? They look like great apes if you ask me. Plus, what does the planetarium have to do with evolution?"

"We can't have kids staring off into space wondering what's out there. They need to be staring at their Bibles or praying."

"I want these children to be able to expand their minds. They need to be able to think about how big the universe is and how majestic it can be."

The encounter gave him reason to consider why he was there in the first place. One of his main reasons for staying in the group was because of Kendra, but he also had a profound desire to help people expand their consciousness and self-awareness. He asked himself, "If children spending time at a planetarium looking at the expanse of the universe scared these leaders, then how can I help people expand their minds?"

While the adults spoke and sometimes argued about evolution, Mia and I played outside the A-Frame. We found gopher's holes and put the hose inside hoping to flush them out. We played until we were exhausted and then took a nap. A voice I knew well woke Mia and me from our nap. It was Grandma Dee's voice coming from the living room. I didn't know she was coming to visit, and I was happy to hear her voice.

Grandma Susie was the spiritual mother of the church but, to me, Grandma Dee was the defacto grandmother of everyone. She was not a co-founder of the church or an insider who helped form the canon of this faith. Rather she was a warm and loving woman to whom everyone listened. She coddled people and made them feel accepted and loved.

While I lived with Dorian and Kendra Yale, there were times when I visited and slept over at Grandma Dee's and her husband, Grandpa Montiel's. I called her Grandma and him Grandpa, but they were also like my parents. My biological dad sometimes lived with us, except when Grandma Susie sent him to work on their other properties in California, Tennessee, Florida, or New York.

When Grandma Dee sang, which seemed like all the time, she sounded like an angel. She could hold high octaves like no one else. She had children of her own, one of whom was Nancy who was almost 18 years old now and beautiful. She had blue eyes and golden blonde hair. Nancy was twelve years old when Grandma Dee joined the church. Grandma Dee was in her late thirties or mid-forties when she joined. Her other children did not join and did not live on the church property. They stayed with their dad somewhere in another state completely unaffiliated with the church. Grandma Dee spoke about them as if they were always with us but would get angry when she talked about their dad. "He'll have a hot place in hell," she'd say.

Everyone who lived on the property had to get saved by giving their life to Jesus by doing an altar call, which involved going down to the altar in front of the church on a Sunday and saying the sinner's prayer in front of the congregation. Nancy got saved when she was twelve. She knew at that age that Jesus would be her Lord and savior.

On this day, when I was about four years old, Grandma Dee came to the A-Frame. I heard her ask Momma Kendra, "Is he talking yet?"

Kendra replied, "You know, he talks to the kids but not the adults. He and Mia talk all day, but the moment I walk in the room he shuts up like a clam. The only things he talks to me about are the colors of the foods he eats. He says things like "green" then he points to broccoli or green beans and grunts. He clearly knows squash and bananas are yellow and tomatoes and strawberries are red."

"He's never actually spoken to me either," Grandma Dee expressed. "I am concerned for him. When he wakes up, I want to take him for a walk. Do you mind?"

No amount of love, affection, and security given to me by Momma Kendra, or my other moms, was enough to repair the eternal hurt I felt from my mother leaving me. It could not bridge the gap that was left in its place.

I walked into the living room with Mia trailing behind me. Mia walked over to her mom and hugged her in a sleepy manner. I looked at Mia in her mother's loving embrace and grunted at her, while pointing to my shoes sitting in the corner near the door. Mia looked at the shoes, then at me, before walking over to them. She grabbed them, untied the laces for me, and walked over to where I was standing and handed me the shoes.

I grunted in the direction of Grandma Dee's pants and shirt. Like the shoes, Mia found my pants and shoes and brought them to me. I began to put on my clothes as best I could. When Momma Kendra tried to help me, I resisted by frowning, grunting, and making it clear that I intended to clothe myself by putting on my own pants and shirt.

While I had been napping, a light rain had begun to descend on the asphalt, causing gray steam to rise from the black road producing a smell of dampness mixed with dust. Now, Grandma Dee stood outside coaxing me to go for a walk by smiling at me and holding her arms out to me. Using a singsong voice, she spoke to me, "Benji ... let's walk and sing to the birds. Benji ... Benji ..."

As I reached the front screen door, I felt the coolness and smelled the air. I hesitated before she coaxed me, "Benji ... come here ... give me a big bear hug, Benji ...." I took a few steps toward her and jumped into her arms, squeezing her as hard as I could. She was wearing her favorite green and brown faux fur coat. I burrowed into it feeling safe and loved. It was wet when I hugged her, but the only thing I cared about was her holding me.

Exiting the porch, she held my hand, as I immediately heard the twitter and chirp of the birds all around me. There were birds of all sorts proudly taking flight and playing in the absence of the previous shower. A few minutes into the walk, I said in my deep voice, "Listen to the birdies. They sound so pretty."

She was so startled she dropped my hand. Looking around us to see if another person was walking nearby and could have been the one to speak, but not seeing anyone else, she asked, "Benji, what did you say?"

"Listen to the birdies. They sound so pretty."

Tears dropped from her cheeks knowing that I had broken my silence and decided to trust her enough to talk to her. Her tears of joy quickly turned to tears of sadness as she considered why I was not speaking to adults.

We continued walking until we arrived at the home where some of the single sisters lived and decided to stop there at their front porch to find a place to sit and talk. Once we were settled, Grandma Dee asked me, "Have you ever heard of the boy who cried wolf?"

"No. Why did he cry wolf? He didn't have regular tears? Ha!"

"No, Benji, his tears were not made of wolves. It's a story about a boy who watches over his family's sheep. A big, mean wolf sometimes tries to steal a sheep and the boy is supposed to yell, 'Wolf! Wolf! Wolf!' and the people in the town will come to wherever he is to scare the mean wolf away. Well, this boy got bored one day. Instead of sitting in the hills all alone, he wanted to see the people from his town, so he yelled, 'Wolf! Wolf! Wolf!' And do you know what happened?"

"All the people came to him to help scare the wolf?"

"Yes. But guess what? There was no wolf. The boy lied. The town's people told him not to lie because someday there would be a wolf and if he lied no one would come to scare it away. A few weeks went by and the boy got bored again and he yelled, 'Wolf, wolf, wolf!' And all the town's people came running with sticks and whatever else they had which they could throw at the wolf. But there was no wolf. The boy lied."

"He must have really wanted someone to visit him if he was lying."

"Yes, but he had an important job to do. The town's people told him, 'Don't cry wolf if there is no wolf.' Another few weeks went by and do you know what happened?"

"He cried wolf again?"

"No. A big, mean, snarling wolf came down from the hills and started circling his flock of sheep. The boy started yelling, 'Wolf! Wolf! Wolf!' And do you know what the town's people did?"

"They scared the wolf away."

"No. They sat in their shops and they kept doing whatever they were doing. They heard the boy yelling louder and louder and said to one another, 'He's just crying wolf. There's no wolf up there.' And the wolf took a baby sheep that day. I am telling you this so you understand why you cannot lie. Ever. If you lie, no one will believe you. If you lie, baby sheep might get killed."

"I won't lie, Grandma."

"I believe you. Why did you decide to talk to me today? Is it because you trust me now?"

"No. Just the birdies sounded so pretty."

The next day Grandma Dee scheduled us a lunch with Grandma Susie. We sat next to the heart-shaped pool that overlooked the Arkansas valley, which spread out in a vast view eastward. A shimmer of yellow and gray light danced on the white outdoor table as sunlight sparkled through the crystal pitcher filled with ice-cold lemonade.

"He spoke to me yesterday. His voice is so deep, and he rarely uses it with adults. He's a smart little guy."

Grandma Susie lit a cigarette and scoffed at her as she blew a billow of smoke toward her. "Well, I knew he could speak. His mother sure had vocal cords."

She continued with an informed air, "After his mother left, Elaine did a great job with him. I would have let her keep him, but she and John keep trying to have their own children and she needs to focus on that and her salvation. This little boy has a special mission. It's not too often an Arab-Jewish boy is born into this world."

"He really likes it with the Yales. He and Mia are inseparable. They're so cute. How many months separate them? Two months?" Grandma Dee asked.

"Yeah. They are two months apart, but the church now has about fifty children. He'll have lots of brothers and sisters."

"Is the rumor true that the Yales are planning on leaving?"

"It's true. You and I will have to play mom for now until another family opportunity presents itself. Someday your eldest daughter, Nancy, can be his mother. She's almost eighteen now, isn't she? We'll have to get her married soon."

Grandma Susie removed her hand from underneath Anne-Marie's, placing it on top of her hand, and continued, "Let's move him into the Spec House with me. I want to make sure he knows his mission in this life. The peace of the world and the returning of Jesus might depend on it."

Grandma Dee quietly nodded in compliant agreement as she sipped her lemonade.

The next morning, Mom Kendra and Dad Dorian took me to Grandma Dee's at 3:00 AM. They had spent the night packing a big U-Haul truck while Mia and I slept. When they said good-bye to me, they had tears in their eyes, so I knew I wasn't just spending the night with Grandma Dee. Mia and I held each other until Kendra pried us apart, crying as she did so. I didn't speak to an adult for six months after that.

Grandma Susie was focused and goal oriented. No fake measurements of poop at her house. No exploding pinecones around her. Instead of sitting around a fire, we read the Bible and prayed together. Unlike Momma Kendra, when it was bedtime, she didn't cuddle next to me, tuck me in, or read me Aesop's Fables. Instead, she read me stories about Shadrack, Meshack, Abednego, and Daniel in the lion's den from her chair across the room.

When Grandma Susie joked, I never understood her. The adults always laughed when they heard her jokes, but I just looked at them confused. Once I saw her on TV talking to a reporter. She made a gross bet to the reporter after he asked her if she was profiting from the followers. She said, "They don't have money. Most of them come here with only the clothes on their backs. But I'll make a bet with you. For each recruit that has money I'll eat ten of them with ketchup if you eat one in a hundred that has any money." Papa Tony chuckled. I did not understand why she would eat them if they had money.

Grandma Susie believed in discipline and self-sufficiency. She'd show me how to do something once, such as getting dressed, tying my shoes, brushing my teeth, putting away my train set after I played with it, and then expect me to do it by myself from then on. I had to be careful I didn't break anything. I couldn't wrestle the other children like when I wrestled with Mia, because there were expensive items everywhere.

Grandma Susie and Papa Tony were always traveling, which meant I was always either traveling with them or being babysat in the mansion with the brothers who were answering the phones. Shortly after I moved in with her, Grandma Susie stood in front of the church behind the pulpit while dressed in an all-white dress, which went to her feet and covered her arms. Behind her was a mural the length of the grand church with a painting of John the Baptist when he was about to baptize Jesus. A ray of light shone through the heavens on Jesus while shabbily dressed people looked toward him with longing in their eyes.

Before she started the introductory prayer, she looked at me, frowned, and furrowed her eyebrows. I knew what that meant. *Quit fidgeting and sit up straight.* Her look reminded me of the time a few weeks prior when I tied two girls' ponytails together while I sat behind them in church. Grandma Susie had seen me fidgeting around them and gave me the same look of disapproval.

After the prayer she looked at me and said, "A very special young man is in the audience. Benji, please stand up and say hello to everyone."

I proudly stood on my dad's thigh waving. I smiled quickly, embarrassed that several hundred people were looking at me.

"He's a darling, isn't he? We want you all to know that he lives with Papa Tony and me now. He will be our special little boy. He's here with his father today. His mother is not with us."

She looked at me again and then said, "He's too young to understand what an adulterer is and why his mother left his father for another man. We're going to take care of him and make sure he gets into heaven, unlike his mother."

I was only four years old, but I understood enough to grasp that a woman, not Momma Kendra and not Momma Elaine, who was once my mother, was no longer with us. I did not understand who she was or her significance to me. However, I understood by Grandma Susie's tone, that she did not like this woman at all. I looked to my dad for an explanation, but something about his downcast eyes and sad look told me not to bother him.

The next weekend at the Spec House I sat on a leopard's skin looking at a small statue of a black jockey dressed in a red jacket, white pants, and a colorful cap. I loved that statue. I was the shortest person in the house, but it was smaller than me. I placed him in the middle of the train tracks and drove the train around him imagining him to be a giant who could crush the train at any second.

"Benji?" Grandma Susie yelled from the top of the spiral staircase.

"Yes, Momma," I answered, jumping up and scurrying to the bottom of the staircase.

"Be a dear and go put on your cowboy suit. Velta Fern and Fayette Peeve are here. I want them to see you in your new clothes. When you're ready, meet us near the white piano."

I ran up to my bedroom. It was a forty-square-foot room built specifically for me, adjacent to Papa Tony and Grandma Susie's bedroom. My room was framed with white and gold crown molding in the shape of flowers. Its wallpaper depicted a Crusader's battle scene -- crusader soldiers with long black lances reined in their horses in a majestic battle while foot soldiers stood with drawn swords.

Due to Grandma Susie's constant reminder, I knew to keep my room tidy. "Cleanliness is next to godliness," she would tell me while pointing at items that looked out of place with her wrinkled index finger. I grabbed a brown suede leather jacket, which had fringes dangling across the chest, back, and sleeves. Its collar and sleeves had golden tips on their corners. I also had a cowboy hat with "Benji Alamo" sewn into the label.

I dressed as I was told and went to rejoin them in the living room, passing the massive painting of cherubs ascending to and descending from heaven. My boot heels sank into the thick, blood-red carpeting. When I walked, I had to pull my heels up and out making my steps look unnatural.

Papa Tony sat at the white baby grand piano with Velta Fern next to him. Grandma Susie clapped as I entered the room. Then Papa Tony, Velta Fern, and Fayette joined in the clapping.

"You are more beautiful than the cherubs, Benji," Grandma Susie said, contrasting the painting with me. "Come over here and give us a hug and a kiss."

I ambled over and was soon surrounded by the pawing adults, caressing my jacket and hair, and pinching my blushing cheeks.

"How cute!' exclaimed Velta Fern.

"You're a little cowboy. Don't shoot us!" teased Fayette.

"You look like a little model," said Papa Tony.

I basked in the spotlight, turning around in circles so my leather fringes swirled with my movements, causing myself to get dizzy after only a few spins. Once my head cleared, I noticed Papa Tony's nose hairs and Grandma Susie's caked-on makeup. She had a brown tooth next to her upper big tooth that she would hide by keeping her lip lowered when she smiled. Fayette had bad breath and Velta Fern smelled of breath mints.

Despite all of that, I loved the attention they showered on me. I felt special, unique, and valued. I felt like the entire world revolved around me, but in a grown-up way. It wasn't the same love I felt with Momma Elaine or Momma Kendra. Their love was soft and compassionate. Most of the time when Grandma Susie and I were by ourselves she was rigid and exacting, but when other people were around us, especially when Papa Tony was around us, she was steady, calm, and generous with her instructions.

"Benji, thank you. You are the most precious little thing," Grandma Susie said, grabbing me by the shoulders. "God himself could not have made anything more precious. Do me a favor. In our room, there is gold-looking cart on Grandma's side of the bed. You know where? There's a box on it that has very precious things in it that I want to show to Velta Fern and Fayette. Be a dear and go get the cart for me."

Eager to please and continue the show, I sauntered into Papa Tony and Grandma Susie's bedroom. Their bedroom had thick white carpet, but not as thick as the red carpet in the living room where they were waiting. Their bed was a large king-sized bed with white silk sheets spread across. Clothing littered around the bed. I found the cart behind a pile of clothes. On the cart, there was an old box made of wood with golden knobs attached to the drawers and lid. I tried picking up the jewelry box, but it was too heavy.

Pushing the cart, I tried maneuvering around the clothes and against the thick carpet. It was too difficult, so I moved their clothes and pulled the cart across the room until I reached the brown and white industrial carpet just outside their bedroom door. I glanced inside my room and was tempted to go in and play with my toy soldiers but knew I would get in trouble. I continued pushing the cart until I reached the thick, red carpeting. The wheels sank into its depths, so I began pulling it until I reached the steps of the grand living room.

The grand living room was called that for good reason. That one room outsized the homes where the other church members lived. It was also off limits to them unless they were invited by Papa Tony and Grandma Susie. Only a few people had ever seen its fifty-foot ceiling with red velvet drapes which ran the length of the solarium, sealing off the southern sun.

It contained four distinct sets of living room furniture – creating four distinct seating areas. Each set of furniture featured at least one antique sofa with matching chairs, end tables, and lamps. Each table had ornaments and multi-colored candies, shiny trinkets, exotic vases, and beautiful tapestries sitting on them.

Two living room sets had green and brown leather ottomans that had red-colored wood borders, which stood in the center of their areas. The third had a handmade silk rug from Persia. The fourth featured a bear-skinned rug. All the tables were accented with rainbow-colored stones with gold and silver borders. Paintings and murals that Grandma Susie claimed came from royal palaces and French aristocrats hung on the walls. Each area was set apart by a pair of six-foot gold-plated candelabras with nine yellow light bulbs.

The adults were sitting at the very end corner near the marble gas fireplace looking at some exotic vases.

I began maneuvering the cart carefully down the stairs, struggling with its weight and the thickness of the carpeting. The cart tipped over and its contents spilled out. Gems of red, green, clear, brown, amber, and purple, along with gold and silver chains, spilled out on the carpet. Having lost my footing, I spilled onto the carpet as well.

"What's all the commotion about?" I heard Papa Tony bellow as he approached.

I jumped up, trying to put the gems, rings, and precious metals back in the cart.

"What are you doing?" Papa Tony asked.

Nervous, I stuffed gems into my pockets, trying to conceal the mess I caused.

Papa Tony grabbed me by my left arm and yanked me into the air, dislocating my shoulder.

"We have a little thief in our midst," Papa Tony said looking at Grandma Susie and their guests.

I screamed in pain while dangling in the air. I tried to object, but could only stutter my denial, "N...n...no...n...n...no. I'm not stealing."

"This little brat is stealing your jewelry, Susie. Can you believe this?"

Papa Tony pulled the jewelry from my pockets. "See ... this little worm is stealing?"

Papa Tony carried me to the bathroom of the adjacent room, pulled down my pants and underwear, grabbed me by my dislocated shoulder and slammed me across his lap. He spanked me bare-handed until my butt was burning. My squirming and yelling did not stop the beating. It only increased it.

I didn't understand why I was getting spanked. One moment I was doing what Grandma Susie asked of me and then the next I was hanging by my arm in the air before getting painfully spanked. My Dad Dad would have never done this to me. He would have sat down with me and explained what I had done wrong. He would have given me a second chance, but not Papa Tony. He was quick to judge, quick to act, and his decisions were permanent. He didn't forgive.

I respected my Dad Dad and Dad Dorian, but I was afraid of Papa Tony, especially when he wore his big gold and jewel-studded rings. At the same time, I wanted to make Papa Tony happy. Everyone tried to please him, and no one wanted to make him angry. He was tough and when he walked in the room everyone paid attention to him. I wanted that attention also. I wanted to achieve and be what he wanted me to be: special. But at this moment, I was confused and didn't know what he wanted me to do.

My screams were more than Grandma Susie could bear. She stormed into the bathroom and saw me crying, holding my left shoulder with my free hand. Papa Tony, sitting on the edge of our pink bathtub, grinned while looking at me.

"What have you done to this boy? Why is he crying and screaming?" She was irate.

Papa Tony raised his eyebrows, feigning innocence.

"Why is he holding his arm like that?" She stepped closer to us and, looking down at Papa Tony, raised her index finger to his face as if saying, "Don't move." She fumed and pursed her lips.

"As God as my witness, if this boy is bruised or hurt in any way, I will kill you. You will be pushing up daisies tomorrow. You better hope there is nothing wrong with him. You better hope he doesn't have a single mark on him."

She turned to me and said gently, "You know God sees all. He knows if you were stealing Grandma Susie's stuff. Were you taking my stuff?"

"N...no... I...I wa...was... not stea...ling ...it." I sobbed. A small trickle of blood ran down my nose.

"Hand me that tissue," she demanded of Papa Tony, pointing to the roll on the wall. Dabbing the blood away, she took my hand and applied pressure to my nose leaving my other arm to dangle free.

"Keep pressure on your nose like this and keep your head back." She gently tilted my head back, then turned to Papa Tony.

"He wasn't stealing, you idiot. He was hiding his mistake. He fell and thought he was in trouble for spilling my jewelry, so he wanted to keep it from you. You scared him, you dumb buffoon. Did you just fall off a turnip truck?"

Papa Tony tried to respond, but she wouldn't allow it.

"I am going to say goodbye to our guests. When you come out, excuse yourself and have the brothers take you for a drive. You need to get some air and think about what you did here."

She tried to take my left hand, but I would not let it move.

"What's wrong? Why won't you give Grandma Susie your hand?"

"It hur...hur...hurts," I told her while I focused on not moving it.

She gently moved my shoulder.

"Ahhhh ... n...no... it hurts," I cried in pain.

"Ah, I know, Benji. This is going to hurt too. But it will make it better."

She took my arm, crossed it over my body and pulled quickly, popping the shoulder back into its socket. Then she took my pants and made a sling to hold my arm.

I yelped, removing my other hand from my nose. She picked me up and blood dripped onto us both.

She grabbed more tissue, wiping my tears away, and held my nose with her free hand.

She looked into my eyes and said, "Let's get some ice cream! Would that make you feel better?"

"Yes," I answered, still holding my arm.

She led me back to the grand living room where Velta Fern and Fayette sat quietly with the case of jewelry near them. Velta Fern had a necklace of diamonds and sapphires in her hands.

Grandma Sue greeted them, saying, "That could feed a small country if it was ever sold. Would you like to see some very special pieces? I think I have a Rothschild's heirloom in there somewhere."

Papa Tony waved goodbye as he walked away, head lowered.

"You'll have to excuse me. Thank you for coming. I'm going to get him some ice cream and a more permanent sling for his arm. He must have gotten hurt when he fell," Grandma Susie told them, clearly implying that she intended for them to depart.

After the guests left, she took me to the kitchen and gave me a scoop of ice cream in a bowl. Then she made an ice pack and ace-bandage sling for my shoulder which she put on me, before hugging me and patting my head.

"This will help," she said as she put the sling under my arm and fed me the ice cream with a spoon.

I woke up the next morning to Grandma Susie standing at my doorway singing a gospel song, "Amazing Grace … how sweet the sound … that saved a wretch, like me …"

I was barely able to move my arm and my butt was sore. Grandma Susie stood staring at me, leaning against the open door to my room. She helped me out of my warm bed, turned me around and pulled down my underwear, placing her cold hand on my buttocks. "Does that hurt?"

"Yes, it hurts. And my arm, I can't move it like normal."

Her eyes grew large and her nostrils flared. She closed her eyes and exhaled slow and loud. She pulled up my underwear and helped me dress before leaving my room.

Next door in her bedroom I heard her yelling but could not understand what she was saying. I heard Papa Tony's deep voice and shattering of glass. More yelling by her. A small rebuttal. More yelling. Then there was silence.

She came back to my room.

"He won't touch you again for as long as I live. Come on out. I'll make us some breakfast in the kitchen."

Grandma Susie and I walked to the round kitchen table where she seated me. She tucked a paper towel into the top of my shirt as a bib. At the corner of the solarium near my chair there was a dead mouse. Its neck was snapped by the trap it was crushed in. Its tongue protruded from its mouth, and there was a small splatter of blood on the floor nearby.

Grandma Susie returned a few minutes later with a bowl of Raisin Bran and sliced bananas. On the side of the plate, there was also buttered toast with a dollop of butter.

"Have some breakfast, dear."

I shook my head, indicating I would not eat.

"What's the matter? Aren't you hungry?"

I grunted and pointed to the dead mouse. She leaned over the table and shrieked.

"What's wrong, Susie?" Papa Tony asked, while walking over.

"There's a dead mouse. I thought you were going to have one of the brothers remove those nightly for us?"

"I was. But if you recall, sweet dumpling, we agreed that we wanted our privacy more than we wanted them removed. So, I didn't tell the brothers to remove them."

She turned from me and the mouse to Papa Tony who was gulping down his protein shake. His thick hair was combed straight back. He wore his prescription sunglasses and brown workout clothes.

"Well this current situation will not work. I will not wake up to dead animals in our kitchen. And, while I'm at it, did the brothers get in from L.A. with my groceries?"

"Your truck full of organic fruits and vegetables arrived late last night and the fridge is packed, Love. As for the dead mice, why can't Benji remove them? He's four years old, old enough for chores. He can water the plants in the solarium while he's at it. I can show him how often and how much to water each of them. One of the brothers will show him how to set those traps."

I imagined my fingers getting snapped by the traps like the mouse I had seen. I assumed Grandma Susie would argue against Papa Tony's idea, so I was surprised when she said, "It looks like you have a few chores around here now. Ignore that mouse and hurry up and eat because I have to cut your hair."

I was confused, was she going to protect me or not? I supposed I was happy that she had not rejected his idea entirely; it scared me when they yelled. I was eager to please them both. I wanted to prove myself and contribute to the household, even if I feared the bloody mice as well.

Grandma Susie would not allow me to get up from the table until I was finished with my breakfast. After she rinsed out my cereal bowl, she walked around me with a pair of scissors and a comb. She placed the cereal bowl on my head and trimmed any of my straight, dark brown hair that escaped the bowl. After a long thirty minutes sitting still in the chair, I began to fidget.

"If you keep wiggling, I'll end up cutting off your ear. Sit still now," she said. Making her point clear, the snapping sound of the metal scissors reverberated near my ear.

Small flecks of hair landing on my nose and cheeks made me sneeze. Papa Tony walked over and blew the hair clippings away and looked me in my eyes.

"Can you forgive me for spanking you?" he asked.

I didn't respond.

"I truly thought you were stealing Grandma Susie's stuff. I bet you will think twice before you ever steal. Won't you? You little scamp," he asked me in a higher pitched voice than normal.

I looked down at the hair clippings that fell onto the table before looking up at Papa Tony who had replaced his dark glasses with reading glasses. They magnified his eyeballs, wrinkles, stress, and strain.

"Won't you?" he repeated.

"Benji, Papa Tony asked you to forgive him," Grandma Susie told me with a concerned tone. "When someone asks for forgiveness it means they will never do the thing they are asking forgiveness for, ever again. Look into your heart and forgive him if you believe him. Do you forgive him?" she asked, removing the bowl from my head.

I looked at Papa Tony who had returned to his protein drink. He then turned to Grandma Susie.

"Yes, I forgive him. But if I'm so special, then why did he do that?"

"He sinned, Benji. We all sin, even me and Papa Tony. He was very tired when he did that."

"Well, he should get some sleep then."

"Did you hear that? From the mouths of babes, the word of God is spoken. That's just perfect, darling."

She looked at Papa Tony with squinted eyes and said to him, "You were out of control and even this child can see it."

"Come on, Benji. Let me show you how to water the plants," he said, extending his hand to help me down from the chair.

I was on cloud nine now. My first job was working with Papa Tony in the solarium, not with the mouse traps. He showed me a list that hung on the wall, which had the plants' names, locations, and the frequency and amount of watering. I could not read the list, but he told me what was on it.

When he poured water into the pots, he would say things like, "This plant likes to be dry ... and ... this plant likes lots of water and sun. Do you see this one? It needs fresh mulch. And, this one is delicate. If it gets too much sun it will wilt. That's why it's hiding under this plant. You'll need to dig up some earthworms for this one. It loves worms ... do you like slimy, wiggly worms Benji, huh?"

"Oh, I don't know if I like worms."

When he spoke, it was at my pace so I could understand. He let me feel the leaves and the moisture of the soil. Here in the solarium he wasn't a tough guy. He wasn't the man who beat me and hung me up by my arms. He was humble like what I imagined the prophets to be that he and Grandma Susie always talked about. In the solarium, he and I were gardeners.

# CHAPTER THREE

By a prophet's prophecies, whether they do or do not come to pass, you shall know whether the prophet is of God or of the Devil.
—a Hebrew Proverb

Late in 1979, rumors swirled in the church that Grandma Susie's cancer was so bad the doctors would need to remove some of her organs and transplant new ones into her. The message the congregation received was that she was refusing the new organs and instead relying on the healing power of God to save her.

When we went to church in Dyer on Sunday, I saw cameras and cameramen stationed throughout the church. Grandma Susie led us in song and prayer. "There will be many persecutions in the future, but God will deliver you from them all. You know, I had terminal cancer for over eleven years. I suffered more than anyone could ever know. The only way for you to know is for God to reveal it to you on judgment day. It did not start like it does for most people. It started low in the rib cage and attacked each one of my vital organs, one after another."

I clinched my stomach.

"I knew that I had terminal cancer and knew it was traveling fast ... I knew that I only had one life to give and I wanted to give it to God ... I had an absolute truth ... I knew that God would not let me die. I lived as if each day was the last day of my life and each day, I kept that nail-scarred hand in the palm of my hand. I leaned on him, I trusted him, and I believed in him. It seemed like during the darkest hours of that affliction that I was a walking dead person. Satan heaped every persecution upon me that can be imagined. I don't believe there was a single vile thing that I was not accused of, but it never broke me down nor stopped me. It encouraged me because I knew that Satan would not come after me unless there was a reason."

I looked around for Satan or signs that Satan was present. One of my friends a few yards away had fallen asleep. *It must be Satan making him fall asleep*, I thought. Another was holding his hands in front of his eye, blotting out the bright lights. "And I purposed in my heart that God would heal me, raise me up, and put me back on my feet. Doctors said the cancer traveled to every part of my body and that based on medical science I was nearly dead because nothing, none of my organs, was working. I said to my doctors, 'None of those things are true because Jesus died so I can live.' They gave me less than two hours to live and, even during that time of convalescing, Satan came at me from every side with every persecution and vile attack. But Satan, I want to tell you something. I won! I won! The one thing you overlooked was when Jesus was hanging on the cross he looked up to the heavens and said it is finished. God has healed me and there is victory in Jesus Christ. I have won this battle. You did not get rid of me."

The entire congregation stood with their arms raised and smiles on their faces crying out, "Hallelujah, hallelujah!" repeatedly ... "Praise you Jesus! Praise be to the Most High!" I repeated what they said, "Hallelujah, hallelujah!" repeatedly ... "Praise you Jesus! "Praise be to the Most High!"

Grandma Susie continued, "I am twenty pounds heavier, stronger, and healthier than I have ever been in my life. My faith has never been as deep and my strength in God has never been so strong as right now. I have won through Jesus

Christ because it is the promise of Jesus to me. I want to say to everyone in TV land, the promises in the Bible are yours if you are washed in the blood of the Lamb. He said he will heal you by his stripes."

She lifted her hands in praise and Papa Tony and the choir behind him stood as they began singing, "Lord, I Believe."

We all stood with our arms raised, in worship, some with eyes closed, some looking around for cues as to the proper behavior we should follow, believing, and wanting to believe, that Grandma Susie was healed of cancer.

Later that day, I sat in my Superman undies and T-shirt watching WWF wrestling with Papa Tony. My train and its tracks sat in a pile near the statue of the jockey.

"Is this your favorite shirt, Benji?" he asked while ruffling the hair on my head.

"Yes."

"Grandma Susie and I made sure we got you that. We knew you would like it."

I smiled and hugged my Papa, giving him a kiss on the cheek.

During a commercial, Papa Tony picked up a nearby phone and spoke into it, "Are the brothers and sisters ready to read me their needs list?"

I knew Papa Tony would listen to the needs of the congregation when he had time, but only when he had time. During commercials seemed to be the best time on most days.

I heard a sister's voice on the phone say, "Yes, they are all here."

She began reading a list, "John needs cigarettes, toilet paper, and underwear. Gary needs T-shirts, pants, and a pair of shoes."

"Ok. Did you get their sizes?"

"Yes, sir ... Anne needs tampons ..."

"Tampons? No. No. Tell the sweat hogs to use toilet paper. These sweat hogs don't need tampons and maxi pads.

Do you think the Israelites used tampons and maxi pads? Tell them to use old clothes. They can open bleed."

"Yes, sir. Mary needs a new bra and underwear ...." The sister continued reading the list of needed items for a few minutes before she was interrupted.

"Hold it right there. I have more godly things to do," he announced as the commercial ended, hanging up the phone as the WWF wrestlers began romping around the rink.

"You know ... someday you're going to be as strong as Superman," he told me.

I looked at the wrestlers. One man held another at the top of the ring then both slammed down onto the mat.

"Will I ever be as strong as them?"

"If you read the Bible and pray you will be even stronger because you're a special little guy. Jesus made you a special person. You have the blood of an Arab and a Jew inside you. That is what makes you so special. That blood will make you stronger than other people."

"Will I be strong enough to throw a car on the bad guys?"

"When you are old enough and have the money to buy one."

"I don't have any money. How can I get money?"

"Well, I'll give you this," he said, holding up a shiny fifty-cent coin, "if you rub my feet and use that red thing over there on Papa Tony's head," he said, pointing to a plastic device with a circular pad on the end and rubber nodules used for scalp massage.

I rubbed his feet. Then upon being shown how to use the plastic device, I massaged his scalp. White flecks of dandruff, spun off his now-pink scalp, mixed with his black hair.

Papa Tony sighed in relaxation as the massage continued.

"Press down harder and move it all around, especially in the front." I pressed harder. The white nodules separated the hair and revealed a pinker scalp with specks of blood.

We heard a raucous group of brother's voices in the hallway, causing Papa Tony to jump up and stand behind the bar.

The brothers, Big Jim, Big John, Harry Sand, and my Dad Dad were known as the biggest and hardest working brothers in the church.

"Big Jim ... that all-you-can-eat place didn't stand a chance. Did you see the look in the manager's eyes when he saw us come in? Hahaha ..." my dad chuckled.

"Yeah ... and after we ate all the food at the bar, you ate the butter. Hahahaha ..."

"Hey, I thought that was whipped cream," Big Jim quipped.

The sign outside said, "*All You Can Eat*. So, I ate some of everything they had."

As the group turned the corner, they went silent seeing me standing on the ottoman in my undies holding the scalp massager. They looked at my dad who glanced between Papa Tony and me.

"It looks like you brothers have been having a good time," Papa Tony said, breaking the silence.

"Yes, sir. Big Jim and John literally ate most of everything in the buffet in Little Rock. We got kicked out, but they didn't get our names," Harry answered.

"I'm quite certain they know where you're from. You're wearing a Tony and Susan Alamo T-shirt, Harry. It's doesn't take a genius to read your shirt. Let's hope they didn't call the police. You brothers need to go upstairs. Susan has a list of chores for you to do."

As the men ascended the stairs, my dad followed and looked back at me a few times, appearing to be saddened. I presumed it was because he had to go work. Soon, the sounds of hammers, saws, and drills echoed throughout the large house.

The next day, I heard Grandma Susie say, "Hold it right there, mister!" as I was leaving for the first day of school.

"Make sure you take your lunch from the fridge. Your dad gave you his lunch pail, so you won't have to use paper bags anymore."

"Is it a Hulk lunchbox?" I asked excitedly.

"No, no, it's not. It's the black plastic one."

I pouted because I had really wanted an action hero lunch pail. All the other boys my age had them.

"You should be proud you have it."

"But David has the Hulk one. And two other kids have Spiderman and Superman lunchboxes."

"Benji," she said, pulling me to her side of the bed where she combed her hands through my straight brown hair. "The other kids are not special like you. They might have those pails, but you were made by God for a special purpose, more special than them. You have the blood of royalty running through your veins. You were born to bring peace between two great warring nations. Plus, you have Papa Tony and me."

I still wanted the Hulk lunch pail.

"Someday you will understand. Now tell me the truth, which would you rather be? A special man of God with Papa Tony and me, or a regular boy with a Hulk lunchbox?"

"A special man of God and you," I said, kissing her on the cheek.

Inside the pail was my usual lunch: A Snickers candy bar, an apple, celery sticks filled with peanut butter, some small carrots, a peeled hard-boiled egg in a plastic bag, and a box of apple juice.

One of the brothers walked me to the cafeteria where the adults assigned children to classrooms based on age. My group was the largest with about twenty-five children in the group. I saw Luke, a boy four years older than me, walking alone on the road with a weird limp and a hunch. We were told we were never supposed to walk alone because if the devil attacked there needed to be a witness. However, Luke was the only other Lebanese boy in the church, so I felt an extra closeness to him because of this.

"I'm gonna go see Luke. He's down there. I'll be back," I told the group.

Knowing I wasn't allowed to walk alone, I ran as fast as I could. I kept my head down, thinking it would prevent people from seeing me. When I caught up to him, I saw that he was sad and disturbed in a way I had never seen in him before.

"Luke, what's wrong? Where are you going?" I yelled as I approached.

Luke ignored me for a second then yelled back, "Get out of here, Benji, you'll get in trouble for hanging out with me."

"Why?"

"You wouldn't understand. They would never hurt you like they did me."

Luke pushed me gently to reinforce that he just wanted to be left alone. In return, I pushed him in the back, and he yelped.

"What's the matter?"

Luke was in tears, but managed to say, "Follow me."

I followed him through a thick gathering of trees to the nearby peach orchard where no one could see us. He took off his shirt and turned his back to me. Raised red welts along with purple bruises and a small amount of fresh blood were visible across his back. I put my hand near them and felt heat rising from the wounds.

"Papa Tony beat me. He whipped me."

"What? Why?" I asked, unable to believe what he had just told me. We kids did our best to protect each other, but, like the adults who told on each other, there was always that one kid who could not be trusted to protect what they'd seen or heard. Our ability to trust each other changed depending on the level of fear of the punishment threatened by our parents and Papa Tony. If one of us kids was afraid of the adults, they would run to Papa Tony and put us on report. We could only hope that there wasn't a witness to confirm what they reported. At times we protected only ourselves and at other times we lied to protect each other.

Being put on report was a confusing time. On the one hand, I believed the Bible and believed whatever Papa Tony said was the true word of God, but I also wanted to impress my friends. Faith and friendships sometimes pulled me in opposite directions.

However, when we could, we kids did lie for each other. We sometimes claimed to be in places we were not and to witness things we did not to ensure each of us were not hurt by the adults. I would ask God to forgive me for my lies and promise to read and pray more to make up for my sins. No one had seemed to be there for Luke that day, and I told myself, "I'll do anything for him. I just wish I was there when it happened."

We kids were organized by our age into groups. My group was the largest with about twenty-five children in it. Like all the other groups of kids, in my clique there were cool kids, religious kids, sports and jock kids, nature kids, and kids that didn't fit into any clique. I had friends from all these subgroups within my group. The older boys and girls were always cooler than the younger kids and we younger ones tried to kiss up to them.

Luke continued, "He beat me because I passed a note to a girl. I drew a heart on it and passed it to her. That's all. Papa Tony quoted Matthew 21:12: 'Jesus ran the merchants out of the temple with a whip.' He said I was out of control and that the devil was in me, and he was whipping it out of me. He said he needed to control me and teach me who's in charge."

"Because of a note?" I asked, incredulously.

I had heard of other boys and girls getting beaten. It seemed like the rumors of kids getting beaten had been gradually increasing. Yet, their parents didn't complain nor leave the church. What wasn't changing was the severity of the beatings. What I heard about that remained consistent: bruising, brutal, and terrifying. Now I was seeing evidence of it.

"Yeah," Luke said, struggling to put his shirt on again. "Papa Tony whipped me with a belt. That's why you'll get in trouble if you're caught around me. The devil's just left my body."

I could not understand how the devil was in Luke's body. He was soft-spoken, kind, and funny. The devil was mean, always angry, and deceptive. Luke wasn't any of those things. How could Papa Tony get the devil out by beating and controlling Luke? How did a beating like that help Papa Tony control him?

I imagined the devil holding onto Luke during the beating. With each swat of the belt the devil loosened his grasp. Only when Luke was beaten to the point where he could no longer move did the devil relinquish, accepting finally that his body was not capable of doing evil.

After Luke went home, I was anxious. I had never thought about someone controlling me. I also flirted with girls from time to time. Maybe Papa Tony will know that the devil is in me and trying to control me. I looked at Papa Tony differently after that, wondering what he might do about what he could read in my mind someday. He was always telling me I was special, but I wasn't sure that would protect me from beatings, especially if Grandma Susie or my dad weren't around.

My Dad Dad was sent away to work a lot, but when he returned, and I saw him it was as if the sun shone only on him. His smile radiated toward me, causing me to feel safe. I felt completely at peace in his presence. He was my anchor.

A few months after my fifth birthday, I saw my dad standing next to a bicycle outside the side entrance to the Spec House. Its training wheels had been removed. I ran up to him and jumped into his arms. His hug completely enveloped me while he whispered in my ear asking, "You wanna try to ride without the training wheels?"

I nervously agreed, but only if he would help me. He held me on the bike, then pushed it a few feet and let go. The front tire wobbled briefly then righted itself. My confidence grew with each inch of ground I covered. However, the Spec House parking area was not long enough for an extended ride and I needed to turn before running out of cement. I braked halfway into the turn not knowing how to make a wide enough turn so I would not lose my balance.

"Don't brake" my father yelled, but it was too late as I had already begun to lean toward the turn area, doing so too tightly. Not surprisingly, I fell, skinning my knees and hands. Seeing my own blood didn't scare me because I had seen it before when picking blackberries and after I intentionally cut my finger and mixed my blood with two boys my age to become blood brothers. Thinking maybe I could get strong hands like my dad; I ignored the blood thinking the wounds would toughen me up.

"You need to speed up halfway through the turn. It will pull you through."

I still thought I needed more room and told him so.

"It's the same as with your training wheels but lean into the turn and the bike will pull you through it. You must speed up though. It's hard to balance standing still," my dad told me, helping me to my feet.

His words reassured me, and I got back on the bike while he walked along, holding my bike as I pedaled. With a push from the bottom of the seat, I moved quickly toward another required turn. This time, I eyed the turn's arc and peddled faster halfway through. Before I knew it, I was riding in a straight line toward him again.

"Thatta boy, you got it!" my father yelled gleefully.

I felt free, gliding across the cement like a bird in the air. After a long ride of going around multiple turns, I managed to lay the bike down without scraping my knees and walked up to my dad.

Pointing to the hill that led to the parking area, I said, "I can't wait to ride down that hill. I'll be able to go so fast."

"Let's get you riding a little longer before you try to go down that hill. If you crash going down that, you will crack your head open. I don't want to see that," he said. "Let's go get some lunch with Grandma Susie. I'm sure she would love to hear about your adventure."

My dad made peanut butter and jelly sandwiches and poured us some milk and we sat down at the end of the solarium to enjoy our lunch. A few minutes later, Papa Tony emerged from his bedroom wearing only white boxers. His hair was disheveled, and he wasn't wearing his glasses, so he didn't notice us sitting on the other side of the kitchen. He rubbed his eyes, opened the refrigerator, scratched his butt, took a juice bottle out of the side door, drank from it, and belched a deep burp.

I giggled as we both watched him, somewhat amused.

Papa Tony turned in our direction. Without his glasses, he did not know it was us.

"Who's there?" he demanded. "Is that you Benji?"

"Y-yes, Papa Tony. It's m-m-me and m-my dad," I said timidly. I never stuttered with my dad, only around Papa Tony.

"We just had some lunch sir. Benji rode his bike without training wheels today for the first time."

"Oh, congratulations, Benji! You're becoming quite the young man," he answered.

He walked over to us and whispered. "Don't tell Grandma Susie I drank from the bottle. I'll be in more trouble than a pig in a slaughterhouse."

"I-I w-w-won't say anything," I said.

"Do you promise? Do you pinky promise?"

He bent down to me and held out his pinky. I had never pinky promised someone before and thought it was cool. I intertwined my pinky with his.

"Now we have a bond. You can't break it. If you do, I'll cut off your pinky."

My eyes grew wide in astonishment as I withdrew my pinky into the safety of my palm, pulling my hand to my chest.

"He won't really cut off your pinky. But you cannot tell Grandma Susie. Got it?" my dad reassured me.

"I need to get Grandma Susie up and we—including you—need to get ready for services today. Aren't you walking up Kings Highway today, Benji?"

My eyes filled with excitement and I clapped my hands.

"Y-y-yes Papa Tony. I am going to be ... be ... be behind Marty today."

"If you're marching today that means you must know the song. Make sure you sing it loud enough for God to hear."

"Get him dressed, Ed. After he's dressed go back to fixing the leak in the solarium. This last spring was horrible. We've had buckets catching the rainwater. If you guys built this place right the first time, you wouldn't have to keep fixing it."

Around 2:15 PM, Papa Tony, Grandma Susie, and I loaded into the pink Cadillac where Ryan waited in the driver's seat. Grandma Susie sat in the front passenger seat while Papa Tony and I sat in back. Gray cigarette smoke wafted over the white leather seats as Grandma Susie chain smoked cigarettes. The adults spoke about the news, finances, politics, and the day's sermon. I put the window down to clear the car of the smoke, holding my hand out of the window with my palm facing the wind, positioned like the wing of an airplane, making it ascend and descend with each gust.

"Keep your hands inside the car!" Grandma Susie ordered, exhaling a thick plume of smoke in my direction. "A car passing by could rip it right off."

I pulled my hand in with the speed of a jet.

"If that happens then I won't be able to cut off your pinky," Papa Tony whispered.

I sat in stunned silence and watched the farm pastures roll by, littered with cows and chickens grazing.

"What's the sermon about today, ma'am?" asked Ryan.

"Sue, darling, let me answer that," Papa Tony interrupted. Then he paused and sighed.

"Ryan, Susie is dying of cancer. The doctors gave her six months to live and thanks to the will of God she has lived for seven years past their predictions. But without the prayers of the church that could all end real soon."

If she died, then I would lose another mom, the loss of the person to whom I felt the most respect and revered the most. She was invincible to me.

Papa Tony placed his right hand on her shoulder.

"Darling, today's sermon has to be about how the church needs to pray more. Do more. Give more. And do with less. We need to send God a sign that we want you healed from this disease. Faith without works means nothing. And works without faith is dead."

"That's right," Grandma Susie interrupted. "The church needs to continue making sacrifices. God needs to know we are serious." She took a long inhale from her cigarette, held it for a second, then exhaled it into the cabin of the car filling it with gray smoke.

Ryan was one of my favorite uncles. On that day, he was called to give his testimony after Brother Abner. Abner's testimony always scared me because of the vivid details he gave about how he tortured prostitutes before he got saved. Ryan was not like Abner. He was kind and he stood at the pulpit and said, "I thank and praise the Lord for my salvation. It's been ten years since I was saved. Like Brother Abner,

I was doing some really bad things before Papa Tony and Grandma Susie's witnesses found me. They witnessed to me and showed me how to get on the path to heaven. Before I gave my life to Christ, I was member of the Black Panthers. I wanted to start a war with anyone who crossed me. I served in Vietnam and saw unmentionable things. Jesus saved me from those nightmares and from my sins."

A black panther?

My mind turned to an actual black panther, and I wanted to be one. No one would ever see me; I could hide in the forest. I could climb trees, spy on people, and jump far. Why would he ever change from being a black panther to a human?

More brothers and sisters gave their testimonies. More or less, they were all the same ... they had lived lives of sin. Some were thieves. Some were violent men who committed murder or caused mayhem and destruction. My uncle John, who was Elaine's husband, and my friend Niceah's dad were both former hitmen. They said that they had killed people for money, but it didn't seem scary when they said it because now they were saved.

Some of the women were former prostitutes but some were university graduates. Most had tried drugs, usually marijuana, LSD, or cocaine. They were all found by a witness from the Tony and Susie Alamo Foundation, had said the sinner's prayer, and were saved as a result. Each testimony usually ended with them saying that after they said the prayer, they felt a weight had been lifted off their shoulders or a void had been filled. I wondered what that weight and void was like.

The end of the service neared as the altar call was made. OCs, short for Older Christians, fanned out looking for people who wanted to give their lives to Jesus. Today, there were no new people, but my friend Lonny and I, we were both five years old, had been wanting to get saved so we planned it for that day without the adults knowing.

We walked hand in hand to the altar, not knowing what sins we needed to be forgiven for but knowing that we needed to be saved before it was too late, and we died with sin on our souls. When we knelt, we knew that we had to get saved in order to not burn in hell, being tortured forever and ever by Satan. I was afraid that I would be put in hell without any water for eternity. We closed our eyes and said the prayer. I expected a weight to be lifted and void to be filled and to be a new creature in Christ.

Instead, I felt nothing, and nothing happened. Everything looked and felt the same. We were not new creatures. We were the same children we were before we said the prayer. Absolutely nothing changed.

After we said the prayer, adults and children hugged us until there was no one new to hug us. I loved the affirmation and knew it was contingent on getting saved and on playing my part as a devoted Christian. In turn, I acted the part, behaving as if something tangible had happened by repeatedly saying, "Praise the Lord! Jesus Saves! Praise the Lord! Amen." Even though I was five years old, I knew I had to repeat the phrases I had so often heard the adults say during their testimonies. "I felt a weight lift from my shoulders. The void I had inside has been filled with the Holy Spirit of God. Hallelujah!" No one questioned my declarations.

# CHAPTER FOUR

## The Demise Begins

No matter how much the congregation prayed, Grandma Susie couldn't rid herself of her cancer. In fact, she grew more ill. Chemotherapy didn't help. She looked much skinnier to me with her eyes and cheeks sunken into her face.

She started looking like the people who seemed to be waiting to die that I had seen when I was four years old and Grandma Susie and Papa Tony took me and a few other children to a nursing home where we sang and read the Bible to the dying people. The shriveled people who laid in beds, which appeared much too big for their bodies, smiled at us, some revealing missing teeth and receding gums. Those were the ones that scared me.

Grandma Susie wore a different, shorter wig now because the chemotherapy made her lose her hair. She didn't give me ice cream at night anymore either. She slept all the time when she wasn't being taken to the hospitals.

The nursing home experience taught me that we were all going to die someday and for Grandma Susie that day was fast approaching. However, unlike the other people in the nursing home, Grandma Susie was going to come back after she died. The smells of rot coming from her mouth, her lost hair, the pain she seemed to be in was only temporary, unlike the dying people in the nursing home.

When she tried to cut my hair, her fingers shook more than normal. The sharp point of the scissors crossed in front of my eyes several times, sometimes getting a little too close for comfort and at other times snapping shut without any hair falling from them. Her breath smelled rotten. Her motions were jerky as she stepped around me. A rattling sound came from her robe pockets which I could tell came from bottles of pills that shook as she moved.

Now when she finished cutting my hair, she didn't wash the bowl and give me scoops of vanilla ice cream. Instead, the bowl dropped from her hands and clanked on the tile floor. I wanted to hold her and help her walk. But before I could, indicating my haircut was over, she flatly told me, "Make sure you check the mouse traps before you go to bed."

She staggered into the living room, passing the painting of the cherubs to join Papa Tony.

"I need to rest. These meds are making me nauseous."

"Okay, love. Let me take you to bed," Papa Tony said.

As they walked, she said, "You won't believe what happened this morning. I went to the school to check up on one of the new teachers. Before I went inside, the teacher approached me outside the classroom and told me her daughter Jenny wet her bed again last night and asked me to pray for her."

"Oh," Papa Tony replied.

"Well, when I walked in, all the girls were in the corner oblivious to my entry, so I dragged my nails across those two chalkboards until they couldn't bear it anymore. Then I wrote on the chalkboard, 'Jenny is a bed wetter' and made her come up to the front of the class and had her write it fifty times in a row."

"Ha! Those little brats," Papa Tony said.

"There are some real spoiled little brats in that group. I'm going to need to have a few spanking sessions with them to make sure the 'spoiled' gets beaten out of them. I realized how good those little brats have it. It made me think of where I was when I was their age."

While listening to their conversation, I was afraid for whoever they were going to beat, but I was also torn between my love of my friends and my fear of God because I also thought that maybe God told Grandma Susie and Papa Tony that they needed to beat them. Who was I to contest the will of God?

After listening to the conversation, I found a mouse trap nearby with a mouse in it. I threw it in the garbage compactor. Just as I pressed the compactor's button, Papa Tony and Grandma Susie walked out of the room together holding hands and smiled at me.

"Benji," Papa Tony said, "you don't wet your bed, do you?"

"Nope. Never," I said, without hesitating about my response. It was the first time I lied to him; I did wet the bed occasionally, but I lied to not get beat and hurt. I knew God would judge me later.

"That's good because tomorrow you're going with me to a clothing show. You know all those nice clothes you've got in your closet? We can't have you peeing in them. You're going to show the world what a perfect little model Christian you are."

Grandma Susie put her hand around the back of my head and said, "Do you remember what we talked about, how you have the blood of royalty running through your veins?"

"Yes, I am supposed to be an example to everyone because God and everyone are all watching what I do," I said, clearly recalling my mission.

She put me to bed, and while she prayed, "Now I lay me down to sleep, I pray the Lord my soul to keep ..." I silently prayed, "Heavenly Father in heaven above, forgive me for lying today. I didn't want to get embarrassed like the other children. I didn't want to get beaten either. I hope you understand why I lied."

Although I had a rationale for God, I still laid in bed in fear that night. But nothing happened to me. God did nothing. Papa Tony did nothing. Grandma Susie did nothing. Perhaps God was saving up all my sins for when I died, and then I will be judged. I would need to make sure I did lots of good deeds to make up for my sins.

The next day a caravan of brothers and I began our drive from The Ridge to a hotel in New York near the clothing show in New York's Jacob K. Javits Convention Center. I modeled my new Alamo brand designer clothes that Papa Tony had created. I walked and turned around when Papa Tony told me to. A lot of non-sisters were at the show. They pinched my cheeks and hugged me more than I expected but I loved the attention.

Before Papa Tony left to go back to Arkansas to take care of Grandma Susie, we had been driving around a dark area of New York City in a rented, black limousine with tinted windows. Papa Tony said we were looking for a Chinese restaurant that he said had the best dumplings in the world.

For some reason he had us stop next to some women who were standing on an unlit street. One of the women wore a black fishnet garment. That's all she wore. Her ebony skin was not concealed at all, revealing everything, and I stared at her nipples.

The other women were wearing clothes that revealed their butts and busts. Papa Tony rolled down the window and beckoned to the woman in the fishnet outfit. When she approached the car, Papa Tony handed her something and she kissed his hand.

He touched one of her breasts before she stepped back from the car onto the sidewalk. I thought maybe he was trying to heal that part of her body.

I also remember that I ate Chinese mustard for the first time that night thinking it was regular mustard. You only need to make that mistake once.

When we returned to The Ridge, Grandma Susie and Papa Tony joined the congregation for Christmas dinner. Grandma Susie was decked out in a leopard fur shawl. Grandma Susie's chair read, "Producer" and Papa Tony's read, "Director." I sat with my Dad. Grandma Dee, her daughter Nancy and her husband Miguel, and their two and half-year-old daughter Nicole also sat with us.

Grandma Susie had children come up to where she and Papa Tony were sitting to sing Christmas carols. I confidently took the microphone and sang "Hark the Herald Angel Sings" to them and the congregation. I was proud of that moment as Grandma Susie praised me for my performance. More than the doting and praise, it was the look of pride that she had in her eyes that I loved the most. She was proud of me and that meant the world to me.

A brother with a camera followed Papa Tony around the cafeteria filming the food and all the brothers and sisters, but not before we children, sixty of us aged two to seventeen, stood in our best dress clothes and sang Christmas carols to Papa Tony and Grandma Susie.

One of the songs we sang was the church's version of "Santa Claus is Coming to Town":

*You better watch out,*
*You better not cry.*
*You better not shout*
*I'm telling you why,*
*Grandma Susie and Papa Tony are coming to town.*
*They know when you've been sleeping.*
*They know when you're awake.*
*They know what you've been thinking,*
*so be good for goodness sake.*

For most of my life, all the kids in the church and I believed that Papa Tony and Grandma Susie knew our thoughts, knew everything we did, and knew everything we would eventually do. This belief frightened me and growing up I was always easily startled. My heightened state of vigilance was so well known that a church artist painted a mural in the nursery of a scared boy jumping out of a bush. Behind the boy, he painted a lion with an open mouth, lunging one paw, with claws extended, after the boy. He captioned it, "Eeeek!" Along the bottom of the painting was written: "Benji."

The next day I was looking at a flower in the solarium when I heard Papa Tony yelling for me outside the Spec House. "Benji!"

I went outside and found brothers scrambling near the open trunk of the black limousine, loading clothes inside while Papa Tony monitored the work. "Come on inside you little rascal," he said pinching one of my cheeks in a playful manner. "We're going to Nashville."

I was used to being heralded into a car with little notice and taken on a trip, but I never knew why. Apparently, a few hours before the entourage left for Nashville, a deputy from the Fort Smith Sheriff's Department had called The Ridge office.

"We've got a detective over here looking for a boy named Benjamin Risha. He says his client left him there in 1975. You folks got a boy out there by that name?"

"We'll have to call you back," answered the person taking the call. It's what they always told anyone associated with law enforcement: "We'll have to call you back."

And a few minutes later, Papa Tony rushed out of the house, calling out orders over his shoulder.

"Call them in a few hours, after we've left, and tell them 'No, he's not here.' Tell them to quit harassing us."

Papa Tony, the entourage of brothers, and I left for Nashville and Grandma Susie went to the hospital. While there, we went to another clothing show near our clothing store, The Alamo, in Nashville. As I had done previously in New York and Los Angeles, I modeled Alamo's line of clothing for children. This time it was an assortment of leather jackets and studded denim jeans.

We stayed at the Tine House, which was a two-story wooden house with a large garage and Jacuzzi owned by the church. Inside, there was wall-to-wall carpeting, a large kitchen, and a stone fireplace. Granite counter tops and modern amenities adorned the kitchen. Above the garage there was an apartment where a few brothers lived who maintained the property and ran errands for Papa Tony.

I woke up to loud thumping and pounding coming from the fireplace. Frightened, I ran from the bed, past the fireplace, and turned the corner to the kitchen where I heard Papa Tony.

"Boo!" Papa Tony yelled, leaping from the kitchen just as I turned the corner.

I shrieked and fell back on the carpeting causing Papa Tony to laugh. But I was trembling as I crawled away from him. The pounding from the fireplace continued.

"What is that?"

"That's the big, bad wolf. He's trying to climb down the chimney to get you."

My eyes grew large and welled up with tears and my bottom lip quivered while I watched Papa Tony stand above me making a clawing gesture with his hands above his head. This made me cry even more.

Papa Tony laughed and picked me up and tickled me.

"There's no big, bad wolf up there. If there was, I would have pulled him out, chopped his head off, and made stew out of him. We could make boots from his skin. How about that? Wanna eat some big, bad wolf stew and wear big, bad wolf boots? They would look sharp."

I laughed as Papa Tony continued tickling me and making light of the moment.

"We c-c-can't eat the wolf. He's too hairy. Y-y-you want to eat h-h-hair?"

"No, we won't eat him. Those are just brothers on the roof. They are repairing it. I bet they surprised you when you heard them."

"Y-y-yes, I thought it was a wolf."

We left Nashville and drove to Tulsa, Oklahoma, where Grandma Susie was in the hospital at the Oral Roberts City of Faith Hospital. I was taken to a big house where a sister watched me. Papa Tony went to the hospital with my friend Lonny's dad, Abner. Before they left I asked Abner, "Why is Grandma Susie in the hospital? She said she wasn't going to get any treatments because God would heal her."

"Well Benji, the doctors want to try to take away some of her pain. She is in the best hospital in the area. If the doctors think a treatment can help her, they will give it to her."

They left me at the Tulsa house that evening and returned in the morning to take me to the hospital to see her. I hardly recognized her. She was so thin; her eyes were even more sunken than when I had last seen her. Her face was wrinkled and saggy, and her head was bare of hair. She lay in the bed motionless with a few IVs in her arms.

A doctor came into the room and said, "She's a fighter. She's been here before and managed to find the strength to leave. We're doing the best we can to make her comfortable."

Papa Tony sat next to her bed while Lonny's dad sat on the far end of the room. I was sitting in the corner looking at pictures in a Bible when I heard her voice. "Benji, is that you?"

Papa Tony answered for me, "Yes, darling. He's here. Benji, come over and say hi."

I walked over and looked at her. She struggled to smile and struggled even more to whisper, "God will save me. Be good and listen to Papa Tony. Okay?"

"I will be good," I promised her.

Papa Tony signaled for Abner to take me out of the room and returned to Grandma Susie's side. Abner took me back to the Tulsa home and then I was taken back to The Ridge to sleep at the Vasquez's house. As Grandma Susie's health worsened, I had been spending more and more time with the Vasquezes. Miguel Vasquez, Dad Miguel, was in his mid-twenties. He smiled often and loved playing football and baseball. He loved Mrs. Vasquez, Nancy, even more. She was a beautiful, sandy-blonde woman with sparkling blue eyes.

Grandma Susie was in the hospital for months before she died.[9] Eventually, my belongings were moved from the Spec House mansion to the Vasquez's two-bedroom apartment at the Nine-Plex so I could live with them, rather than merely stay there. I did not want to leave the Spec House. I wanted to stay with Papa Tony, but Nancy Vasquez did her best to make my transition comfortable. She had my stuffed animals on my bed when I arrived.

My birthday was fast approaching. However, because the church was in mourning, a cake was not appropriate, she told me, but after a few months she would bake one for me to celebrate.

The Nine-Plex apartments, like most of the homes in the church, had modest furniture and appliances purchased from the nearby Walmart. The electricity didn't work the first week I slept in my new home, adding to the sense of darkness that enveloped everything around me. We used candles to light the house and had to go to the cafeteria, which had gas-powered stoves and ovens, to cook and eat all our meals. We also took cold showers to get clean.

The church always had a pair of watchmen or guards, who roamed around from sunset to sunrise, in a van or a truck. Their vehicle was equipped with a spotlight. We called them Rover because they roved. It drove by the Nine-Plex this night and they shone their light into my new habitation casting shadows around my room.

---

9. https://www.geni.com/people/Susan-Edith-Opal-Horn-Lipowitz-Alamo/6000000058675882869

We ate all our meals in the communal cafeteria with the rest of the church members and I missed the private breakfasts Grandma Susie and I had in the Spec House. Plus, I knew I wouldn't get a Snickers bar for lunch anymore either.

My dad visited me at the apartment and told me that he had been working on tree crews and had been sleeping on the side of a mountain for a few months. The tree crews were the life blood of the church during the late 1970's and early 80's. When he saw me, he gave me a few colored river stones and said, "You know I planted more than a thousand trees in the last few months. Your dad is one of the leaders of the crews." I felt proud of his accomplishment but asked him why he didn't stay on The Ridge more often. Without replying, he instead looked at me and walked around to the back of his maroon El Camino and pulled a bike from the back of it. He had modified the bicycle with a large spring connecting the rear tire to the frame. He said it would make it easier to go over bumps on the road.

I rode it immediately and realized that the spring made the chain fall off when I went over a pothole. It fell off because the spring didn't have a counter spring to keep the chain taut when the big spring contracted. I was able to fix it by installing a derailleur from an old ten-speed bike and that made the chain taut no matter the actions of the big spring.

The night before Grandma Susie died, I guess she knew her end was near. The cancer had spread through her entire body. Lonny's dad was there in the room before she passed away. After she died, I heard him tell some adults that Grandma Susie called Papa Tony to her side and pulled him down to her and spoke her last words to him.

"When I am gone, disband the church. Let the people all go. You'll ruin them. You'll wreck it all." It was loud enough for Lonny's dad to hear though and it alarmed him.

After the seven years she was in my life, Grandma Susie passed away seventeen days shy of her fifty-seventh birthday. I stood in the back of the chapel with Lonny and her mom, listening to the roar of thunder while Grandma Susie lay dead in a pink coffin. Bouquets of flowers were at each end. Brothers and sisters filed by, crying, as they walked up and looked inside at her. Some dropped to their knees and prayed. Others covered their mouths and looked away, appearing to be unable to believe that she was dead.

Lonny's mom grabbed my hand and I realized it was my turn to say goodbye. She led Lonny and me to the coffin. We were only about four feet tall, barely taller than the coffin and the perch that held it. Our heads were just above where Grandma Susie lay.

Grandma Susie, my mother, my grandmother, the woman I never thought would die, was now dead and lay in front of me. This was the third death I experienced before I was seven years old. There was baby Stacey and Freddie, but they looked so much more natural than Grandma Susie who had on thick beige foundation caked with light brown powder, even though that is how she looked when she slept. I closed my eyes and imagined her soul floating in the stormy sky, looking down on me and on her dead body.

When I opened my eyes, I could have sworn I saw Grandma Susie's eye twitch while she cracked a little smile at the same time.

"Did you see that?" I asked Lonny.

"I did," she answered. "Her right eye moved, and she smiled a little."

"Maybe she's coming back sooner. We better back up," I said, taking Lonny's hand and moving back a few steps.

"What are you two doing?" Lonny's mom asked. "There's a long line of people who need to say goodbye and pay their respects."

"She smiled at us," we both said in unison.

"She's rising up right now," I continued.

"Move on, this isn't funny," she scolded us, pulling both of us by the arm. "She can't move because she was embalmed with a fluid that prevents her from rotting," she said.[10]

"B-b-but ... she just smiled at me," I proclaimed.

After the line dwindled, Papa Tony walked up to the pulpit. The congregation stood at attention. He was clad all in black Italian silk, except for a belt buckle inlaid with turquoise stones. Dark prescription sunglasses concealed his eyes. He removed them, cleaned the lenses with a cloth from his pocket, and put them back on. Moving away from the pulpit, he walked, with his head lowered, across the pulpit in circles.

"Praise the Lord! Hallelujah! Praise be the Most High!" he exclaimed, almost in a prayer-like whisper. "Praise the Lord! Hallelujah! Praise be the Most High!"

"Praise the Lord!" the congregation joined and responded.

He stood, for what seemed like five minutes, staring at the audience. Indignation took the shape of a scowl.

"She died because you lack faith. Every one of you lacks enough faith. Her death is on your hands. You were given a chance to pray for God to heal her and you failed. You did not believe God could perform miracles. Like the Hebrews in the desert, who worshipped the golden calf when Moses went to get the tablets of the Ten Commandments, you all worshiped your own golden calves."

"For some of you, your calf was watching sports, for others it was your bellies and your children. Well, things are about to change around here. Praise be to the Maker of the heavens and the earth! Praise be to the Alpha and the

---

10. https://books.google.com/books?id=iTgkDwAAQBAJ&pg=PT369&lpg=PT369&dq=birgitta+gyllenhammar+and+tony+alamo+divorce&source=bl&ots=W6pncNzDHh&sig=ACfU3U3oyU-UO1AmDHt7IWL2r8-WW1uZddw&hl=en&sa=X&ved=2ahUKEwj-itOap7zpAhU3oHIEHZCYAXkQ6AEwDXoECAwQAQ#v=onepage&q=birgitta%20gyllenhammar%20and%20tony%20alamo%20divorce&f=false

Omega, the beginning and the end, the Son of God! Praise be to Jesus, the Savior of this world! Praise be to the Lamb of God!"

"We bow our heads humbly before you, praying that you, Jesus, come into this holy church and anoint us with your spirit. Heavenly Father, who art in heaven, we ask that you anoint us with your spirit. We are your humble servants."

"Tonight, we mourn the loss of your prophet. Her body is here with us, dear Lord, but her soul is with you. Like when the prophet Elisha raised the Shunamite woman's son from the dead, we ask that you return her soul to her body. The book of Revelations says that the two prophets will be killed in the end times and that they will rise from the dead. She is that prophet and we are those prophets." He said, raising his voice.

"She shall rise from the dead after three days as it is prophesied in the Book of Revelations. It says, 'The two prophets will die and be raised up.' She shall rise up from the dead and it will be your faith and your prayers that will raise her."

Papa Tony's proclamations were like promises to me. The six months leading up to her death, he preached and prophesied about her reawakening. Who can tell God to do something? Only someone who is truly close to Him. Only someone who understands God can command God.

I wasn't the prophet that day. That was Papa Tony's job, but someday I knew I, also, would be able to command God. I needed to learn the Word of God and only then would I be able I tell God to follow his own laws.

"Today is just the beginning," Papa Tony said. His voice boomed through the congregation while thunder rolled outside.

"Today will usher in a new era. When she rises from the dead, three days from today, the whole world will know the power God has anointed on us, his two prophets."

I am going to be that someone like Papa Tony. Someday I will raise the dead. Like all the children in the church I tried to emulate our leader. I tried to walk in his shoes by saying what he said and doing what he said I should do. Like most of the kids in the church, I was a religious leader at the age of seven. But I had something special. I was from Arab and Jewish descent. I had royal blood.

Three days came and went.

Grandma Susie did not rise.

She lay dead, in her makeup, in an open coffin in our former living room where the cherubs in the painting on the wall looked down on her.

At seven years old, I had heard Bible verses and sermons every day of my life and I had read most of it.

I knew this verse in the King James Version of Deuteronomy 18:22 by heart: "When a prophet speaks in the name of the Lord, if the word does not come to pass or come true, that is a word that the Lord has not spoken." On Monday, the fourth day after her death, Grandma Susie still had not risen. In the back of my head, a mixture of anger, confusion, sadness, and fear lingered, which threatened to dispel the hope I originally had. Something even bigger lurked: doubt.

Was Papa Tony a false prophet? Why had he said she would rise from the dead, yet she didn't? Was it possible that Grandma Susie could still rise? Would he know that I had these thoughts? He hadn't seemed to know when I lied about wetting the bed nor about my doubts surrounding the reasons given as to why Luke was beaten. He didn't know that I didn't really feel anything when I got saved either.

*The blood of Jesus is against you Satan. The blood of Jesus ...*

During church services that night, Papa Tony took the microphone from its stand and walked into the center aisle of the church.

"For some reason, God has decided to keep her in heaven longer. We will continue to pray. God will see our vigilance. We shall pray until she rises. Her body will be transported to the chapel on the main property on The Ridge. We will hold twenty-four-hour prayer vigils. Everyone will pray over her. Every hour, every moment, and every second of every day, someone will be at her coffin praying. Everyone will take their turn."

"We're going to pray over her body?" Lonny's mom mouthed to the sister sitting next to her. Other people around me were murmuring also.

"It won't be any different from what we have done for the past year. Have we not held a twenty-four-hours-a-day prayer chain for her to be healed?" Papa Tony asked. "Her death is a sign that we need to be humbler and more vigilant. She shall return."

Sensing the restlessness of the congregation, Papa Tony commanded, "Please stand for a song." He motioned to the band behind him as he began to sing a solemn hymn.

My mind drifted off to a daydream of Grandma Susie sitting in the kitchen of the Spec House wearing a long, white robe, with a large Bible placed on her lap. She called me to her and hugged me, kissed me on the cheek, and patted my head. I sat next to her while she read from the Book of Revelations, reading the story of God's two prophets who would be killed in the end of times, but who would rise from the dead.

When she was done reading, she spoke to me, "I know you must be confused sometimes because of all the different parents you call mom and dad. I know that you are stronger than anyone in this entire church and that you can handle whatever comes your way. Papa Tony will always be Papa Tony, but you need to live with the Vasquezes. And, who knows, maybe someday you will live with yet another family. I want you to always be a good boy. Don't get angry. I know people can be stupid sometimes, but don't let them know that you know that. Remember, everyone struggles in life. Everyone has pain. You need to be the person that helps them take that pain away. I will always be here for you. You just need to pray. I will be in heaven now next to Jesus then I'll come back, just like Jesus."

She stood up and took a few steps away from me then took items from her robe pockets. There were the scissors she used to cut my hair, Snickers bars, celery filled with peanut butter, a single scoop of vanilla ice cream in a bowl, and a newspaper and a quarter—from when she showed me how to operate the newspaper box. Then she pulled out a pack of cigarettes and lit one. She exhaled before looking over at me, appearing smug and resigned.

"If you don't pray for me, I won't come back. So, pray for my return. You are special Benji, but I am what makes you special." She blew a billow of smoke right in my face and threatened to take away my toys if I didn't behave. I coughed and that ended my daydream.

Because of this vision, my hope and optimism spiked through the chapel's roof. When she returned to us, she would have super-powers. I vowed to myself that I would pray more than I ate and slept. She would make money grow on trees, and I'd be able to do anything when I was with her. The streets of The Ridge would be paved with gold.

A couple weeks after her death, Mr. Vasquez came home late after an evening of his shift of praying over Grandma Susie's body. I asked him, "Did she rise up?"

Dad Miguel, seeing the hope in my eyes, paused before speaking.

"Someday, but not today."

It was my turn to pray over her the next day. For the first three to four weeks after her death, the coffin remained open. Seeing Grandma Susie like that was calming because it felt as if her time there was temporary. I saw the prayer warriors, a group of about ten people, praying aloud and yelling to God, throwing their hands toward the ceiling while demanding God to raise her up. Some knelt and silently beseeched God for a miracle.

Some of them began speaking in tongues, which, I was taught, was a gift that the Holy Spirit only gave to certain people. Mocking or laughing at someone who spoke in tongues was said to be the only sin that was unforgivable because it was deemed blasphemous of the Holy Spirit. Their sounds made no sense to me though. I thought they sounded crazy.

The next night I went to the chapel to pray again before her casket. I stood at the entrance, while I waited for my friends to sign the prayer log, confused about everything. Grandma Susie was still lying there, still cold and dead. It seemed either the prayer warriors had failed, or the Holy Spirit wasn't powerful enough to raise her up. I had been sure she was going to come back, but now I was angry because it seemed like she was not coming back, and Papa Tony might have lied to us. All the praying had been for nothing.

The next day I saw Luke in the communal cafeteria, sitting alone in a corner, staring at his food with tears in his eyes.

"Are you sad about Grandma Susie?" I asked.

Luke briefly looked up from his food.

"No, not that. Papa Tony said she would rise; I believe him and so should you."

He returned to staring at his plate and taking small bites.

I sat down next to Luke and whispered, "It's been weeks. H-h-he said she would rise from the dead in three days. Papa Tony's prophecy didn't come true."

Luke glanced up, looking around the room making sure no adults could hear us.

"Just keep praying," he said. "Don't speak badly about Papa Tony."

I took a bite of food before asking him, "She's not coming back, is she?"

Luke pushed his plate of food away and looked around again. "You wanna get beaten? Keep talking. I talked back to Papa Tony this morning and this is what I got."

He lowered his waist band a little bit to reveal belt marks and red welts on his skin. I had never seen such bruising on his back before. The welts were so defined it looked like someone drew the marks on him.

"They accused me of walking alone. No one was there to walk with me after my prayer hour, and I got put on report when all I did was walk home. Papa Tony called me a liar. I told him I wasn't a liar and he had two brothers hold me down while he beat me. He said I was out of control and that he would control me one way or another." As I listened, I watched Luke's tears fall into his mashed potatoes. I questioned why bad things kept happening to Luke? He always seemed good to me. Maybe he didn't pray enough. Maybe the devil really was still somewhere in his body. God spoke to Papa Tony so He must tell him it's all right for him to control and beat Luke. I'm a good kid so I won't get spanked. Plus, when I'm not good I don't get caught.

"He's always beating me," he said. "Don't let anyone hear you say his prophecy did not come true. If he finds out, it won't matter how much he likes you. He'll beat you just like he beat me."

I'm protected though. Luke isn't, and I told him. "I'm his favorite kid. He won't beat me like that."

"Benji," he began, sternly and with certainty, like a child who has learned because he has been forced to endure things most adults could not. "Listen to me and listen well. I'm warning you. Papa Tony is the prophet, right? If he's a false prophet, no one will believe anything he says, and he will burn in hell. If you tell him his prophecies did not come true, you might as well tell him he's going straight to hell. You think being his favorite's gonna save you from that? Do you really?"

The vigil lasted for six months, twenty-four hours a day, seven days a week. Despite all that praying, Grandma Susie never returned to us. I had taken Luke's words to heart and never called Papa Tony a false prophet, but that didn't mean doubt hadn't crept in. Doubt took hold, slowly turning, like a gear in a bicycle chain.

# CHAPTER FIVE

Crushes, Loves, and Girls

In 1983, a year after Grandma Susie's death, Papa Tony interred her body in a specially-built mausoleum with a heart-shaped roof supported by white, Corinthian-styled columns. The end of the heart-shaped roof pointed to the heart-shaped pool that was now nearly empty of water. Algae grew and clung to the sides of the pool turning its white cement varying shades of green. In some ways, the pool reminded me of our church body. Many people left after her death, but there remained hardcore members who clung to the church like the green algae of the pool. They were primarily followers who'd grown and developed as families within the church, now had children, but had no external work experience since joining the church nearly twenty years earlier.

At 4:00 AM, on a rainy April morning in 1983, I was awoken by Mom Nancy from being fast asleep in my bed in the Vasquez's Nine-Plex home. "Papa Tony wants everyone in the chapel in thirty minutes. After you get dress, put your raincoat and boots on. You're going to school after the service."

The congregants were tired, many people were yawning, and some of my friends were dozing off in the pews when

I walked in. The service opened with a prayer followed by a pre-recorded message from Papa Tony. He was often traveling, at his other properties, or in hiding from the one-world government, so he recorded in advance his sermons to be blared from speakers in the chapel.

I could hear the anger in Papa Tony's raspy voice. "Susan is now buried next to the chapel. You can visit her whenever you need to." He paused then he started yelling, "You people make me sick. I imagine you will visit her quite often seeing how you all failed to appeal to God to bring her back. You should be ashamed of yourselves for your lack of faith. I bet you little weasels ate every day since she died. I am sick to my stomach with you reprobates. You all are pathetic. You don't deserve me."

He paused. Everyone in the congregation looked at each other when he said, "You don't deserve me."

He continued, "I am done with you sinners. Moses left the children of Israel in the desert when they sinned. And now, I am leaving you."

It felt like I was punched in the chest when he said he was leaving us. I began crying when it dawned on me that he was not only leaving the church, but that he was leaving me. *How could he leave me? How could he not say he was taking me with him? Maybe he'll call me to go with him. That's what he'll do. He'll come get me.* I wiped my tears from my cheeks and looked around.

Silence rolled from the speakers for a while before the tape recorder was turned off. It was clear that the message was over, and Papa Tony was gone. Some of the adults began to cry. I looked at my friends and the younger kids whose jaws hung wide open in disbelief. I looked over and saw Lonny crying. Adults stood looking at each other in shock. A three-year-old child flipped out of his mother's limp, despondent arms and fell on the floor causing him to erupt screaming.

Some adults began praying loudly, "No, God! Please don't let him leave us!" Others murmured more quietly in prayer. Other adults began talking with each other, asking one another what they would do and where they would go.

We still gathered at the church nightly and listened to older, pre-recorded sermons from Papa Tony, but the congregation seemed deflated. The testimonies became more about hoping Papa Tony would return to us than about how Jesus saved any of us from our wretched lives. We also stayed and prayed longer and later, which for me meant I was tired more often. It seemed like all the adults were tired too, because they walked with their shoulders hunched forward as they left the prayer room.

School continued for us kids and people continued their work on the Ridge and passing out flyers in town, but it was done with less enthusiasm. We were used to Papa Tony being out of town, but he had always kept in touch via his phone calls, listening to reports, approving the Needs List and giving sermons. This time, he had remained silent after declaring he had left us. No matter how we tried to normalize and carry on, everything felt wrong without our leader.

Despite Papa Tony's silence, he maintained strict control over our finances, but groups of brothers and sisters continued to get food and clothing via donations. The cafeteria served decreased portions. Meat and milk were rationed. There was no more money for extras like soda and various other treats we had been accustomed to. We were no longer given food for our fridges at home. The bills for everything ranging from electricity, gas, food, and local taxes went unpaid.

There were a few ways we received food. We had a few gardens on The Ridge: one that the children operated, and a few private gardens at peoples' homes, but they provided enough food for only a few people. Most of our food was donated from grocery stores. When the grocery stores were going to throw away old or bruised food, our brothers and sisters would go pick up the food on what they called Dono

Runs, which was named for donation runs. What could not be provided from the gardens and donations was purchased directly from wholesalers and farmers.

There were many days when I woke up without lights in the house and went to bed without hot water because we did not pay the electric bills. As normal practice, we never went to a doctor unless a child was born, or someone was dying. We never paid our medical bills anyway, so we were not too concerned about racking up hospital debt. This was because Tony and Susie needed large amounts of cash to pay for their lifestyle, which included a house in Malibu, California; numerous properties around the US; parties with politicians; their chauffeurs; limousines; tailored clothes; and the like.

Two years later, Papa Tony contacted us, in person. His limo rolled onto The Ridge property on a sunny July afternoon. He arrived with a new wife, Birgitta Gyllenhammar, a clothing designer who owned two boutiques in Los Angeles. An adult came to my classroom and took me outside to where Papa Tony was waiting in the Limo.

Once I was inside the limo, he said, "Benji, this is Birgitta. She's my Swedish princess."

A woman who looked like a younger version of Grandma Susie was sitting next to him wearing a stylish red dress.

I supposed he replaced Grandma Susie with this woman, meaning Grandma Susie wasn't his favorite anymore. At least I was. He had come back for me.

"I wanted you to know. You're going to come over for dinner tonight at the restaurant. Okay? Now go back to school, you little rascal."

I walked back to my classroom and the kids surrounded me.

"What did you do with Papa Tony?" Lonny asked.

"I'm going to the restaurant with him and his new wife tonight."

"What? He has a new wife?"

"Yeah, I guess she's a princess from Sweden. That's what he said."

The other kids watched from the classroom window as his limousine drove down the hill.

Lonny asked, "What did she look like?"

"She sort of looks like Grandma Susie if she was a lot younger."

One of the kids turned around and asked, "Could it be Grandma Susie?"

Another asked, "Could she have risen up as a younger Grandma Susie?"

"Don't be stupid. That's not the prophecy. Papa Tony said she would rise in three days after she died. It's been two years and three months."

Some of the kids sighed when I said that.

"Benji, you should watch your mouth. God might strike you down if you're wrong," Lonny said.

"I could tell it wasn't her because she doesn't wear as much makeup and she didn't seem to know me." I was not afraid of God striking me down for disagreeing because I knew she was not Grandma Susie. It was evident that she did not rise from the dead. Three days had come and gone a long time ago. That was the only proof I needed.

I also did not think I was speaking against Papa Tony because he had told me, "This is my Swedish Princess." Grandma Susie was Jewish, not Swedish.

That night two OCs brought me to the church-owned restaurant in Alma for dinner. The Princess and Papa Tony sat in a booth. As I walked toward them, I saw her holding his hand and running her finger down the middle of his hand. Her dress was like nothing I had ever seen. Its material looked like ruby red velvet with sparkling diamonds sprinkled throughout the fabric. Her skin was flawless, and she smelled like a rose. She had makeup on, but nothing like Grandma Susie wore. Hers accentuated her features instead of hiding them.

"Come on you little rascal," Papa Tony teased when he saw me staring at her. "Come say 'Hi' to my new princess."

I thought she was tall because her head was higher than Papa Tony's. She was way younger and far more beautiful than Grandma Susie.

I climbed into the booth next to her. She turned to me, put one hand on the top of my head and the other on the back of it.

"You have a square head," she said in a thick Swedish accent. She rolled her 'r' when she said 'square' and her pronouncement of 'head' sounded funny to me.

"Why do I have a square head? What does that mean?"

"You just do." And that was that. She didn't say anything else to me during dinner. She simply turned back to Papa Tony and kept rubbing his hand.

Papa Tony kissed her then turned to me, "Are you hungry? Why don't you get a hamburger?"

As I ate my burger, I silently contemplated her powers. *Does she know my sins like Grandma Susie? Can she also read my thoughts? Maybe this is her replacement. Maybe I'll get to go back home with him instead of living with the Vasquezes. I'll be Papa Tony's son again. I will get some awesome new clothes and go on more modeling tours. No more cold showers. I'll have food in the fridge that won't go bad because the electricity does not work.*

But, instead of telling me he would take me home with him and his new wife, he asked me, "How do you like living with the Vasquezes? Do you have everything you need?"

"I like them. They take good care of me," I said, hesitating.

I wanted to tell him that I wanted to live with him, but I felt embarrassed to say it. It didn't feel like I had much of an opportunity to do so as most of the evening I had watched him hold her hands and look deeply into her eyes. I felt out of place just sitting there, looking at him and his new wife. Something was different about him now. He was no longer folding my hand or pinching my cheeks. I was no longer his focus.

"I bet you and little Nicole are good friends. Are you making lots of friends in school?" he asked.

"Yes, sir. I am. I'm one of the popular kids," I said with a big smile.

"Well, that's really good to know," he said. "You make sure to tell me if there is anything you need. Okay? I won't be staying on The Ridge all the time. You probably heard that I have been staying in California. My princess has a business in California, so I'll be out there quite a bit," he said as he took his dark glasses off and huffed onto the lenses before wiping them clean.

"Are you going to stay on The Ridge sometimes?" I asked, hoping he would say "Yes."

"You bet I will. I want my princess to see what a wonderful place we have," he said, turning to her and kissing her hand. "Now finish your burger so you can have some ice cream for dessert."

I was happy to know he would be living on The Ridge, at least sometimes. I thought about my potential future visits and the attention he would give me. The attention my Dad Dad gave me was like a spotlight, but Papa Tony's was like a floodlight, I believed to be backed up by God himself. I thought about the admiration I would receive from the kids when they heard I was staying with him again. However, I knew he would have to ask for me to visit him, not the other way around. It wasn't like when Grandma Susie was alive and I could tell an adult that I wanted to see them, and within a day or two I'd be with them. With Birgitta in his life, I somehow knew that had changed.

In the fall of 1984, I went to the Spec House to see Papa Tony and Birgitta. In the corner of the entrance I saw a stack of three-foot by five-foot posters. On the poster there were six photos. One photo was of Papa Tony in a fur coat. Other photos were of Michael Jackson, Bruce Springsteen, and a few other famous entertainers. I overheard some adults talking while they smoked cigarettes near the front door.

"I heard he recorded a musical album and shopped it around Hollywood, but apparently it didn't do well. Plus, somebody said he entered the American DJ Association's Entertainer of the Year contest and rigged the test results to help him win."

"How did he do that?"

"He found a loophole in how they validated the winners and he mass-mailed voting pamphlets to followers and friends of the church. It was supposed to be only DJs who voted. He claimed he won the award—beating out Julio Iglesias, Michael Jackson, and Bruce Springsteen among others—but it was obviously contested."

I could not believe my ears. Papa Tony had already told me he was a world-famous singer, promoter, and businessman, but now I was hearing he wasn't so popular after all. It was hard for me to hear of him swindling others this way too.

Beginning that night, Papa Tony began reviewing the reports list very late in the evening and early in the morning. The reports list was the list of people who were being reported to him for committing sins. At 2:00 and 3:00 AM each day, he selected children ranging in ages from eight to seventeen from the list, and requested they be awakened. I was often in the room because I was either invited by Papa Tony or ordered to show up when the children filed in because I was somehow involved in the incidents. They entered the office in the basement of the Spec House confused and tired and were required to stand in front of a telephone where they could only hear his voice over the speakerphone. I witnessed this more times than I can remember. It seemed like most of my life either one of my friends or I was on report late at night.

The conversations were always one-sided, regardless of the facts. One child did not want to eat soggy eggs one morning, so the cook put her on report. Papa Tony proclaimed the child "argued with the cook" and he then proceeded to say that God told him to give her thirty lashes with the belt. He then ordered the adult accompanying the child to bend her over the couch and lash her and call him when it was over.

The ten-year-old wasn't allowed to defend herself. Papa Tony had made up his mind. The same thing happened night after night. Sometimes with the same children and at other times with whole groups of children. They were all beaten before Papa Tony went to bed.

Many years later I learned from Carey Miller, who was a former member and who spoke with Birgitta after she and Papa Tony separated, that before Papa Tony had the children beaten, the situation was always the same in his bedroom. He tried to have a sexual interaction with Birgitta but could not get an erection. His solution was to have young children beaten while he masturbated while listening to the beatings, the screams, and the crying of the children.

The romance between him and Birgitta soured over a short period of time. Rumors in the church were that Papa Tony beat her, bruising several ribs and even bruising her back.[11] When a brother interrupted him beating her, she told the brother that Papa Tony had complained that she wasn't young enough. The marriage was never legally terminated. Instead of going to court to sign divorce documents, Papa Tony sent her a telegram saying that he divorced her.[12] The news outlets ran stories that claimed Papa Tony borrowed a vast amount of money from Birgitta and had never repaid it. He was also accused of taking her clothing designs and claiming them as his own. We knew they were lies because

---

11. https://www.tonyalamonews.com/58/03-06-1986.php
12. https://www.tonyalamonews.com/wp-content/uploads/2007/02/1986-03-06-press-argus-courier-alamos-second-wife-says-theyre-not-divorced.jpg

Papa Tony said they were. The news and media were always lying.

It wasn't long after that Papa Tony met Elizabeth Amrhein and he quickly married her. She had two children from a previous marriage, Nicholas, a few years older than me, and Amanda, who was ten years old, my age. She was my first crush.

We first met in Nashville at the Tine house during the end of summer. She had sandy brown hair and blue eyes. She was cute, smart, confident, spirited, and funny. She smiled easily and was full of energy. She dressed in new clothes and had a freedom and carefree attitude. Much different than the church sisters I knew.

Amanda walked up to me, looking me up and down, and smacked me on the shoulder.

"Tag! You're it!" she said, before running off. I ran after her. I was the second fastest boy in the church, so it was easy to catch up to her.

"So, your dad is my dad now," she declared, catching her breath.

"And your mom is my mom. I guess that makes us brother and sister."

"No!" she exclaimed, "We're stepbrother and stepsister."

My feelings for her were immediate, but I was forbidden to act on it publicly because Papa Tony taught that the Bible said that desiring a woman outside of marriage was a sin. Papa Tony reminded us, all the time, that thinking about a woman's beauty is lust and considered to be fornication in the mind. I did not want to fornicate with my mind. Fornicators had a special place in hell where their private parts were tortured for eternity. I knew that Satan would burn my privates, tear at them, melt them, and stomp on them because that's what Papa Tony had already told us.

I still had hope though. I could wait for eight years then marry her.

Papa Tony returned to The Ridge with his new family and told the Vasquezes to pack a bag of clothes so I could stay at the Spec House while he was in town. When we were out of sight of an adult, Amanda and I held hands. We let our bodies glide into each other's when we were walking next to each other. We looked into each other's eyes when we had nothing else to do. We were inseparable.

After a few weeks of bliss with Amanda, Papa Tony and Elizabeth pulled up in the limo while we were playing hide-and-seek. They called to Amanda from the limo. Her brother was already sitting in the backseat.

"I have to go. We're going on a cruise with Papa Tony. I'll see you after the cruise," she said, hugging me and kissing me on the cheek.

*Why didn't Papa Tony invite me? Was I no longer his son?*

I learned years later that the cruise was a ruse by Elizabeth to relocate to Europe in order to avoid a heated custody battle with her ex-husband. However, her husband already suspected she might attempt to flee and had contacted the State Department. The Feds flagged her passport and arrested Elizabeth when she tried to board the cruise ship. Amanda and Nicholas were taken and given into their father's custody.

I never saw Amanda again, so I never had a chance to say goodbye.

However, like with Birgitta, Papa Tony and Elizabeth had problems in the bedroom. Birgitta never engaged in the sadism of children, but Elizabeth took the opportunity to have children beaten to a different level. She could be heard by numerous adults and by Mr. Cantwell.

Mr. Cantwell was a middle-aged man who was a singer and a devoted Christian. He joined the group in the early 70s after riding his motorcycle across the country so he could get involved in the Peace and Love Movement that was sweeping the West Coast. His son, Shane, was one year younger than me and when the Vasquezes would go out of town I would stay at the Cantwell's home, which was the first duplex on The Ridge. There we would eat peanut butter and banana sandwiches because Shane never seemed to be able to gain weight. There was a black walnut tree outside their home, which Shane fell out of when he climbed it one day. Fortunately, Nijah, one of our friends, caught him a few branches above the ground, saving him.

Mr. Cantwell had to answer to Papa Tony as to why Shane was climbing a tree this day. When we walked into the room, Mr. Cantwell told me years later, he heard Elizabeth over the loudspeaker yelling to Papa Tony, "Bring in another kid. We need to make sure the devil is not in him also."

Papa Tony obliged by saying, "Who else is on report? Get them in here now."

When the child arrived, Elizabeth's voice rose with her excitement. "I don't know about you, Papa Tony, but the Lord is telling me this kid has a lot of the devil in him. Beat him too."

Papa Tony would order another beating.

The next day, after Amanda left with her mom, my lips, hands, and shoulders were tight with rage as I walked to school. A girl, a few years younger than me, ran up and smiled at me as she walked alongside me.

"What are you looking at, freckle face?" I asked her, unkindly.

The girl wasn't too happy about that and ran off and told the teacher.

"She does have freckles. I was not calling her a name. Just saying what I was seeing," I argued with the teacher.

Momma Nancy was in the kitchen at the Nine-Plex mixing up a cake mix when I got home. At the sound of the screen door slamming shut, she turned off the mixer and looked to me.

"I already know what you did. Your punishment this time is to read an entire book in the Bible. Go get your Bible. I want you to start at the beginning of Proverbs and read until you finish the book."

The mixer started up after I opened the Bible and began reading. Dad Miguel came home, spoke with mom, and sat down in front of the TV with a plate of food she had prepared. Soon the rest of the family sat watching TV while I was restricted to reading the Bible. Wanting to join them, I first skipped a line then a paragraph at a time. No one seemed to notice I was not reading the entire chapters, so I defiantly skimmed the rest and closed the book. The sound of the book smacking shut prompted Mom to ask, "Well, what did you learn?"

"I learned that a crooked path cannot be made straight."

Over time my heartbreak over Amanda mended with the help of Chelsea, one of the Holler sisters. Chelsea was a year older than me; Abigail was two years older, and Chandra was my age. I had been in love with Chelsea for as long as I could remember being alive. Her mom was Lebanese so there was always a closeness I had with her and her family. Chelsea liked me too. Once she went to Canada to see her grandma and asked me if I wanted her to bring me back anything. I could only think of bubble gum. When she returned, we spent an hour competing as to which of us could blow the biggest bubbles.

During a game of hide-and-seek, I crept way back into the forest in the direction of a tree fort I had made. I knew the forest well and began looking for any place Chelsea could be hiding. When I got to my tree fort, I looked up and there she was. From down below I made a frog croaking sound and she peered over the edge.

"You know that's a boy's-only fort?" I questioned her.

"Yeah, well, it's a girl's-only fort now!" she declared.

I climbed up the tree ladder to find her standing in the middle of the fort with her arms crossed. She was wearing a pink, fluorescent tank top and white shorts, and the moon's rays shown through the treetop contrasting her tanned skin with her clothes.

"I told you this was a girl's only-fort!" she playfully snapped at me, as I crested the platform.

"I dare you to throw me out of it!" I quipped and tapped her on her bare shoulder saying, "Tag! You're it!"

She smiled and coyly said, "I dare you to do that again!"

I loved touching her, so I promptly tapped her bare shoulder again and ran my finger down her arm to her elbow. She grabbed my finger and bent it down, demanding, "Say Uncle!"

Her hand was moist from sweat, but she maintained a good grip on my index finger. The pain was increasing, but not to the point where I would cave and say it. She bent my finger more and right before I cried "Uncle" we heard my mom yell, "Playtime is over! Come inside!"

She let go and I lent my hand to her in assistance as she tried to find the tree ladder.

That night the girls slept on the living room floor with pillows and a large sheet. I slept on the living room floor too, but on the other side of the room, separated by the living room couch. I found Chelsea awake after the other girls were asleep. I moved close to her and touched her shoulder. It aroused me. My touch changed to light caressing and that's when my sister Nicole woke up.

She looked at me then at Chelsea. She got up and went to mom and dad's bedroom. She returned a minute later and went back to sleep without saying anything to either of us.

The next morning mom approached me. She said, "I'm not even going to ask you about what happened last night. When your dad gets back in town, I'll let him sort it out with you."

This scared me because I had to wait for an undetermined amount of time for Dad Miguel to return while the guilt continued to stay with me. I could ask God for forgiveness so the guilt would subside, but it wouldn't erase the fear of an unknown punishment which hung over my head. It was like a weight that pulled me down throughout the day.

When I wasn't in trouble, I loved it when Dad Miguel was in town. We played lots of catch with the football and baseball. I loved the summer months with him because he would take me on road trips in the big trucks he drove. He organized football and baseball games with all the boys.

However, Dad Miguel was gone again, this time for a few months. Like my Dad Dad and a lot of my friends' dads, Dad Miguel was often gone on a church mission. Papa Tony was always sending the dads on random missions which they were never allowed to talk about.

By the time he returned a month later, Mom either forgot about it or chose not to tell him. When he arrived, she smothered him in kisses and pulled him from the door to his recliner. She went into the kitchen and began boiling water for spaghetti and emptied a jar of marinara sauce into another pan. He was Sicilian and ate so much marinara sauce it probably flowed through his veins.

"Papa Tony and your dad are going to be on TV tonight," Dad Miguel told me as he sat down. "Turn on the TV and adjust the antenna while you're at it."

The five o'clock news had just started. Papa Tony, my Dad Dad, and Uncle Harry Sand were dressed in suits walking away from what the headline called the "steps of the courthouse."

"Why is my dad there?"

"He's there to protect Papa Tony. Just in case any sinners try to hurt him, Papa Tony always has the strongest brothers with him. Your dad is *fumalackachucka*." That was a name the church members used to describe a church member who was on fire for the Lord or doing the most for the church. My dad, as a bodyguard, attained that value according to Dad Miguel.

"Is he stronger than you?"

"Yes, he is, but he's not a faster runner than me. With Halloween around the corner you might need to run away from the devil. We all might need to flee to the mountains. You'll need to run fast and I can outrun him."

When he said that my dad was stronger, I felt proud. Some people said my dad was one of the strongest brothers in the church. I didn't mind that he wasn't faster though. I was one of the fastest kids in the church. So, when we had to flee to the mountains, we would make a good team. I could outrun the government while he could lift heavy rocks and trees to make barriers.

After the news and dinner, Mom told me to start reading the Book of Revelation. By the time I got to chapter nine I was tired, but I finished reading it. I fell asleep thinking about the devil chasing me.

Before Halloween in 1985, Papa Tony held a mandatory, late-night church service. For us kids, Halloween was a terrifying time because it was the devil's birthday. He had an urgent message all members needed to hear right away. "The Federal Government, crooked Ronald Reagan, and the Catholic Church have upped their harassment against us. The Department of Labor has sued us saying that you are all employees and not followers of God.[13] They claim that you are not allowed to give your time to God and that when you work you must be paid. Who are they to tell us what we can or cannot give to Jesus?" Papa Tony asked the congregation.

Some people in the congregation huffed and puffed in anger. Others began praying loudly telling God to "Fight our battle for us," and "Destroy the Antichrist."

"We need to fight this unholy assault. Everyone must make sacrifices. There will be no more bucks for any of you, and there will be smaller food portions. Everyone will need to work, possibly on the outside," Papa Tony ordered.

---

13. https://supreme.justia.com/cases/federal/us/471/290/

"Bucks" were what people received for being part of the congregation. It was money they could use to spend on whatever they wanted if it wasn't a prohibited item like alcohol or drugs. Approximately ten dollars per month for each adult and five dollars each month for each child in the family was given out in long queues. Bucks were only available when Papa Tony deemed it okay, which meant he considered the church to be bringing in more money than it had going out. And, we would have already heard a sermon about it before the bucks were made available. It was rare to get bucks more than six months in a row. It was normal for me to have less than twenty dollars in my piggy bank all year long.

The Vasquezes received an extra twenty dollars per month for rearing me. They saved the bucks and used them to get little things that we could not, or should not, ask for on the needs list, like shoe polish, mouthwash, or Betty Crocker cake mix. Without bucks, it meant no new toys and no new clothes for Christmas. It meant I had to make sure the tubes on my bike did not pop and the chain did not break. If I lost a lure while fishing, I knew it was not going to get replaced for a long time. While no bucks had its impact, we were also taught to not value physical possessions. Doing so would doom us to hell. Whenever Papa Tony wanted to justify eliminating something tangible from our lives, he quoted the Bible verse Matthew 19:24 that says, "It is easier for a camel to enter through the eye of a needle than for a rich man to enter into the kingdom of God."

Those who were not praying with zeal sat as fluorescent light illuminated their disheveled hair and slumped shoulders. Many of us were still in our pajamas. A bulb flickered above, bouncing light and dark across the many tired faces of the congregants. I nodded off several times during the sermon.

"I Timothy 5:19 says: 'Do not entertain an accusation against an elder unless it is brought by two or three witnesses.' This means, you cannot, I repeat cannot, accuse me of anything. I am the elder in this church. Unless two or three of you witness me sinning then keep your traps shut."

He continued, "Proverbs 3:5 says: 'Trust in the Lord and lean not on your own understanding.' What more do I have to say here? Don't think for yourselves because it will lead to your destruction. Your brains are not strong enough to think on your own. Trust in the Lord, and I am the Lord's representative here on Earth. I know what God wants ... not you. If you don't follow God's word you will be cast into hell for eternity. Your souls will be burned, tortured, and starved forever. Satan will torture you."

This woke me up. Was he speaking directly to me? Did he know that I had thoughts about him being a false prophet?

"You will not have any water. You will thirst throughout eternity. No matter how thirsty you get, you will not be given a single drop of water. No matter your hunger, you will not have a morsel of food. This is the word of God."

"For those who do not listen, the suffering will be unimaginable. God watches you and records everything you do, everything you think, and he never forgets. I might not see what you do, but God does. He will not be mocked," he said.

It was almost as if Papa Tony hated us. All the recent messages were about how we were all failures. He even threatened to leave us.

"If the Department of Labor thinks I owe you money and thinks you are all my employees, then let's see them tell that to Jesus' disciples who followed him around. They are violating our freedom of religion."

When the family got home that night, instead of tucking me in, giving me a teaspoon of cod liver oil and a vitamin C chewable, or at least giving me a peck on the forehead and praying with me, Momma Nancy admonished me.

"You were sleeping in church tonight. I saw you," Momma Nancy said. "You are on restriction for three days.

There will be no playing with your friends, and you will go to bed early. I'm ashamed of you. Now get to sleep."

While she admonished me, I could hear Lonny's voice in my head, telling me a few weeks earlier, "My mom says that Nancy treats you second best to Nicole. You're not her real child and she regrets that she has to take care of you."

"You're crazy," I told Lonny. But then Lonny listed the times when Nicole got to do things I didn't get to do, like going to movie night or getting extra dessert. She also pointed out how I was always the one in trouble.

"When you lived with Grandma Susie were you in trouble this much?" Lonny asked.

I didn't answer her because I realized she might be correct. I thought about my Dad Dad and wished he was there with me. He would have protected me.

That night, Nancy's damnation added to a night terror. Grind, grind, grind my teeth. Grind, grind, grind. Calcium molecules crumbled into alkaline. It gained momentum with the swoosh of saliva and transformed into emulsifying acids in my stomach. It was a nightly occurrence for me, but it was worse this evening.

As I slept, I saw a red and black glowing demon dressed in a black cloak with fiery limbs. It came after me that night as it had many nights before and would come nights after. Its fiery hands beckoned me toward a vast dark expanse of red-hot rock formations where I saw the outline of naked humans: some old, some my age, but they were all writhing in perpetual agony. Their blistered skin paled in comparison to their thirsty faces. They all held their hands out to me with their mouths wide open, begging and pleading for just one drop of water. The demon moved closer to me. Grind, grind, grind, the sound of my grinding teeth got louder.

I tried to hide my anxiety from the adults because sickness and disorders were attributed to the work of the devil, which could only be cured through prayer, fasting, beatings, a miracle, or a combination of them all. Once I saw my friend Carrie, a girl with epilepsy, get beaten during a seizure. Papa Tony ordered her to be beaten numerous times.

"Is the devil still in her?" he yelled over the speakerphone.

The man beating her with a belt told him, "She's frothing at the mouth, sir."

"Keep going until she stops."

Men in the room held her down while they whipped her with a long, black leather belt. She writhed in pain and escaped their grasps, but the man kept whipping her with the long belt. At times it looked like she was in control of her limbs because she crawled toward her mother, but her mother pushed her away and the beating continued.

I winced each time the belt smacked her. I wished I could make it stop. I knew, all the kids knew, that she had a disease, not a demon. It was a confusing moment for me because initially I thought I had a clear idea of what a disease or an illness was versus having a demon inside of you. Now my understanding was very blurred.

I woke up the next morning covered in sweat and stayed awake until it was time for breakfast. When I went to school that day, two of the teachers, who like all the teachers were unlicensed and were appointed by Papa Tony, were in their respective classrooms. They ordered several groups of children to assemble outside on the school lawn.

"Papa Tony has ordered that we all fast to show God that we are sincere and really want to win this battle against the Department of Labor. Children under the age of eight can eat dinner each day, but they must fast all day until dinner. Children ages nine and up must fast for all meals for at least two weeks," one of the adults communicated.

"Water only! No eating starting today!" the other teacher belted out. "Any questions?"

"We won't be having school today either. Everyone is supposed to go to the chapel where we will be praying all day. Let's go!" the first teacher ordered and began walking toward the chapel.

Inside the chapel the lights were off. Small rays of light snuck through the draped windows providing just enough light to not trip over those who were already praying, on their knees rocking back and forth. Others stood with their hands raised, imploring God to "Show this evil government who rules the world! You rule it!" Others sat quietly with their eyes closed murmuring well-rehearsed invocations and appeals.

The adults silently directed children to different areas of the chapel by pointing to specific areas. They separated the boys and the girls as well as separating the boys from their friends. I was pointed to the front of the chapel where a mural of a white Jesus with outstretched arms descending from the heavens looked over me.

I began praying, "Heavenly Father, God in heaven above, I know that you know my thoughts and that you know what I'm gonna say before I say it. You know all my actions and you see me here today. I'm here because your Holy Word, the Bible, says that faith without works is dead and I must show my faith by my actions. Well, I come to you with a humble heart and broken body. Today I am beginning a fast to show you that I can deny the pleasures of the flesh. I am fasting to show you that I am more humble than normal. The entire church is fasting and your word, the Holy Bible, says that a threefold cord is not quickly broken. Well, we are a one-thousand-fold cord and we will not be denied. I demand that you deliver us. I will not be denied."

I was ten years old and it wasn't the first time I made demands of God. I heard Grandma Susie and Papa Tony doing it. Adults also made demands to God all the time when they prayed. Praying was the only time someone could tell God to do something and that was because we were in a humbled state and God respected that enough to allow it. Now, I was demanding God listen to me.

Yelling almost at the top of my lungs, I said, "You said if I ask you will answer. I am asking you to help us. No! I am demanding that you help us! We need a miracle. The forces of darkness are surrounding us. I am demanding that you push them off us and deliver to us a victory in the court. I am seeking you because we need you to lift this unfair burden."

"Your Holy Word the Bible says that you will never give a burden to someone that they cannot bear. Well, we cannot bear this burden. Lift this burden from off our shoulders. The one-world government is seeking to destroy us and only you can deliver us from this evil. Like David, Lord Jesus, who fought Goliath. Right now, we are fighting a Goliath. Give us a stone that will slay these evil doers. Like Jonah was delivered from the whale, deliver us from this whale."

"Deliver us oh Lord through the power of Jesus ... Praise-you-Jesus-thank-you-Jesus-Praise-you-Jesus-thank-you-Jesus-Praise-you-Jesus-thank-you-Jesus-Praise-you-Jesus-thank-you-Jesus-Praise-you-Jesus-thank-you-Jesus-Praise-you-Jesus-thank-you-Jesus-Praise-you-Jesus-thank-you-Jesus-Praise-you-Jesus-thank-you-Jesus ... "

Two of the girls and three of the boys in the back area of the chapel also began praying louder than they had before. Possibly stirred by my zeal, they stood up and walked up behind me and began praying in the same style: loud, demanding, determined, and expectant. When the spirit moved us, no adult could keep the boys and girls apart. It was as if our gender didn't really matter because we were communicating with God. We were now holy beings, not dirty humans. If it was not for this communication, we would not have been allowed to pray in proximity.

I began crying, "You said if I seek then I shall find. I am seeking you. I am seeking your light. How can you let us lose? You won't. You will not abandon us because we are pure and have been washed in the blood of the lamb. Your Son, Jesus Christ, walks in our midst. You said you would never leave him again and if he is with us then how can you leave us? You can't, and you won't."

My crying turned to a rapid and loud prayer, "Praise-you-Jesus-thank-you-Jesus-Praise-you-Jesus-thank-you-Jesus-Praise-you-Jesus-thank-you-Jesus-Praise-you-Jesus-thank-you-Jesus-Praise-you-Jesus-thank-you-Jesus-Praise-you-Jesus-thank-you-Jesus-Praise-you-Jesus-thank-you-Jesus…"

The words melded together into an incoherent babble and the children who were praying loudly behind me matched my babble. We believed this was speaking in tongues and that the Holy Ghost had descended upon us. Other areas of the chapel, which were previously silent, erupted in loud prayer. We young prayer warriors were now in full communion with God. Believing we were speaking in tongues, the practice described in the New Testament book of Corinthians, we babbled incoherent sounds as we reached our hands toward heaven. That night I knew that my prayers had ascended all the way to heaven. I felt it in my entire body.

Each child was taught that they had a special gift that God gave them. For some it was their ability to sing, for others it was to play instruments, and others were meant to be leaders in ways God would show them as they grew up. It wasn't the first time that I provided leadership to my peers, but it was the first grand and public time I did so. I felt like a warrior as we stormed the gates of heaven and knew God would intervene for us.

That day I did not eat. I remained in the chapel for four hours. When I got home early in the afternoon, I held my chest out and proclaimed, "We're going to win this."

Six-year-old Nicole was at the kitchen table eating scrambled eggs with ketchup on them.

"So gross! I'll be in my room reading and praying. We have a war to win," I told her.

The next day in school, groups of children paired off according to their piety: The holy roller kids in one area, and the cool kids in another area. The kids that straddled both groups were in various areas of the school lawn. The holy roller kids were respected by the adults because they adhered to the faith we were taught. However, the opposite was true for the cool kids. They were usually kids that were in trouble a lot because they broke the rules and the commandments. Most of the kids though, of which I was one, fell somewhere in the middle of following the faith to the letter of the law, as Papa Tony preached it, and following their instincts to have fun.

As I walked by the groups, I heard them talking about how long they would go without eating. "I'm doing the entire two weeks," I heard Zeph say.

Niceah, in a group with Gregory and other boys with little piety, yelled out, "I'll make sure to show you all the food I secretly eat. Ha!"

Lonny was in one of the more devout groups. She promised each girl, "I will not eat any food for the entire fast. Jesus went thirty days without food and water. The least I can do is go fourteen days. Will you all do the same?"

The girls hugged and promised to support each other.

The school day dragged on, but for lunchtime we children played four-square in front of the cafeteria and ping pong inside. Games helped the time go by when we would normally eat and socialize.

When it was dinner time, Niceah and Gregory volunteered to work in the cafeteria. Their job was to unload the trucks that brought the food from the day's donation activities. Most of the time, donos brought in fresh chicken. Alma and The Ridge were in the chicken capital of Arkansas, at least it seemed that way to me because there were so many chicken farms up and down the roads. Each Thanksgiving and Christmas, we got hundreds of pounds of frozen turkeys from the donos and in May, near Cinco de Mayo, we always had lots of tortilla and salsa.

When Niceah and Gregory opened the trucks doors they were blessed with seeing stacks of Hostess Twinkies and cupcakes whose expiration dates had expired a day prior.

Wearing aprons over their clothes, they unloaded, sorted and stocked the food. They stuffed as many of the cakes into their aprons as they could, while also hiding cakes all over the cafeteria in hidden niches.

When the two boys saw Zeph that evening, he was reading the Bible outside the cafeteria. They walked up to him and held their hands piously together as if in prayer.

"Brother Zeph," Niceah pleaded with a smirk on his face, nearly repeating what Jesus prayed to God while on the cross, "Please forgive us for we know not what we do." Except Jesus prayed for forgiveness for those who were killing him, whereas Niceah and Gregory prayed for themselves when they knew what they were doing.

Gregory repeated after Niceah, "Yes, forgive us for we know not what we do." Then they stuffed Twinkies and cupcakes in their mouths as if they were at an eating contest.

Zeph chuckled and replied, "God sees you. I am not offended, but I am concerned for your souls."

Niceah, barely able to speak due to a mouth full of chocolate cake crumbs, retorted, "If God sees this then why doesn't he do anything? May he strike me down if he is displeased with me." He peered up into the sky, waiting for a second then mouthed, "Nothing ... just like I thought. He doesn't care at all. May his will be done on earth as it is in heaven. Amen and amen." He made the sign of the cross, which was a Catholic thing we were never supposed to do. After all, we were taught that the Catholic Church was part of the one-world government that was making a smokescreen to hide all their evil.

"I can't speak for God, but with Halloween around the corner it doesn't surprise me to see Satan doing his work in you two."

The eighth day of my fasting was a Monday. I sat in the classroom desk struggling to stay awake. I fell asleep and woke to the sound of the teacher's yard stick slapping my desk.

"If you fall asleep again, you're getting demerits Benji."

Her yard stick was still on my desk. I pulled my foot-long ruler from my desk and said, "On guard!" while pointing it at her. She laughed and smacked my ruler aside. I parried her stick. We did this for a few seconds and the class laughed.

I was awake now and sat up in my desk doing my best to remain that way. I blinked my eyes repeatedly and smacked my cheeks and forehead a few times. The next thing I knew the teacher was dragging me out of my desk because I had fallen asleep again.

"Stand in the corner until the end of the class," she said.

One hundred twenty-six, one hundred twenty-seven, one hundred twenty-eight … I looked up at the ceiling trying to count the black specks on the white ceiling tiles. My eyes blurred, the ceiling went in and out of focus, and I passed out. The fasting had taken its toll.

The next thing I remembered, I was being carried face up and out of the school by four people. After that, I woke up in my bed. Mom Nancy was sitting by my bed with a bowl of chicken broth and crackers.

A few months later Papa Tony ordered another week-long fast, but it wasn't without a rebuke.

"After the last fast you all went back to eating and complaining about not having onions in the cafeteria."

When he said onions, he said it with a "huh" sound in front of the word as a mockery of the people who asked for onions.

"You want hunions … I want hunions. Oh me, oh my … do you think the children of Israel complained about not having hunions when they left the bondage of Egypt? Huh? No! God would have smitten them with boils if they complained and here you are … you know who you are! Complaining that there are no hunions! Well this time we're fasting a week and there won't be any hunions at the end of it. The good news is that your fasting and praying are making a difference. God has told me that we're going to win this case, but we need to keep showing God that we are willing to do without."

I had once overheard two teachers say that we already lost the case in the US Court of Appeals and that Papa Tony appealed the ruling to the Supreme Court. He ended up losing again and the Supreme Court ruled that the foundation's businesses constituted an enterprise and the foundation's associates were employees who were each to be paid nearly two hundred dollars per week.[14]

The church owned an assortment of enterprises in Arkansas including the Alamo Restaurant, the Alamo Kerr McGee service station, and the Alamo Auto Repair shop. There were also the Alamo DX and Alamo Exxon gas stations. The church also owned the Alamo Discount grocery, Alamo Ready Mix concrete, Fort Smith Mobile Nursery, Alamo Shoppers Emporium, Alamo Candy Company, Alamo Construction, Alamo Telegraph, Alamo Freight, North American Leasing, Southwest Business Management, Basco Feed and Farm Equipment, Tempe Towers, the Alamo Pig Farm. and a wide collection of real estate.

There were also clothing, media, and entertainment operations in Nashville, Tennessee, and California: Alamo of Nashville, the Alma Clothing store, Alamo Bandito clothing, the Alamo Record Company, Hartford Advertising, Nashville Today distribution, and Tennessee Boy distribution.

Members' contributions of time alone accounted for an estimated nine hundred thousand to one million five hundred thousand dollars per month profit in 1970. When extrapolated to 2020 earnings, it represents approximately eight to nine million dollars per month income, yet Papa Tony refused to pay the mandated two hundred dollars per individual, which amounted to a few hundred thousand per month. He claimed that the disciples of Christ would never have accepted payment from Jesus. He said we were the

---

14. https://supreme.justia.com/cases/federal/us/471/290/

same and that receiving payment would void our religion. The government was waging war on faith and we were the spearhead to stop it.

# CHAPTER SIX

## Dads Come and Go

The fair was held in the large grass field across from the school. When school got out, the students, who had been looking out the classroom windows all day watching delivery trucks and vans, flooded across the street surrounding the adults who were still setting up.

"Look, clowns!" a child in the crowd yelled out. The children ran to them in pandemonium. The ten-foot-tall clowns took slow, methodical giant steps forward. The children surrounded them and asked how they got so tall, until they revealed the stilts under their pants. After the novelty of the giant clowns wore off, an impromptu petting zoo with a llama, a few sheep, some goats, three nervous ponies, and some penned geese drew an audience while the animals were led into the fenced-off area.

Across from it was a tug-of-war area marked by a thick hemp rope with a yellow ribbon tied in the middle between boundary lines. A pile of potato sacks for a sack race lay at the other end. Barrels filled with apples bobbed nearby. Filled balloons for a water balloon toss awaited in buckets. Strands of rope were laid in a pile for the three-legged foot race next to volleyballs and a rolled-up volleyball net.

Orange Igloos filled with ice water sat next to red plastic cups on white plastic tables with black and brown folding chairs positioned behind them. Colorful pies, cakes, and other sweets from the cafeteria were arranged neatly on tables along with lemonade and bottled soda.

I saw my dad's maroon El Camino pull up and park on a dirt berm between the event and the school. My dad walked slowly, but I ran to him. He swept me up, giving me an extended bear hug.

"The three-legged race is about to start. We must get tied together and get in line. Come on!" I said excitedly, pulling him by the hand to the end of the line.

We raced and took second place for which we were given a yellow ribbon. I waved the ribbon in the air making sure everyone saw it. Our legs still tied together, we walked over to the tables to eat sweets and drink soda.

I noticed my dad wasn't smiling and he was also avoiding eye contact with me. He wasn't talking to any of the other adults either. I wondered if he was in some sort of trouble.

After we finished snacking, my dad untied the ropes, took my hand, and walked me away from the event to the passenger side of the El Camino. He spoke to me slowly with tears in his eyes.

I had never seen my dad cry.

"Benji, I have to leave now, and I am not sure when I will come back. I'm not sure I will ever come back."

"Okay, dad. When you come back will you bring me some bubble gum? You always bring me that red, spicy gum, but really my favorite gum is Juicy Fruit. Can you bring me some of that? Please …" His words were so incompatible that my brain hadn't even picked up on what he'd just said.

"No, I … this isn't like the other times I've left for work. This time I'm not coming back. I have to go. I don't want to live here anymore, and I can't take you with me. You'll be better off here, son."

I tried to make sense of what he told me, as the words spun around in my mind, but I could not grasp the meaning of his words. I was used to him leaving for long periods of time, but then always returning, so I could not understand that the returning part wasn't going to happen this time. Even as my father got into the driver's seat of the car, backed up, and drove away, I felt as if I would see him again. The words had not settled in yet.

My dad's El Camino disappeared behind the arc of the asphalt hill. I later learned that when he got to the guarded gates one of the brothers manning the gate asked him, "Where are you going? Why don't you have a rider with you? Do you have permission to leave on your own?"

"If you don't lift the gate, I'll take that gate and shove it up your ass," my dad warned.

The brother ran to the phone to call the Spec House. As one of the brothers began relaying what my dad had just told him, my dad proceeded to smash the gate lock with a hammer, lifted the gate on his own, and sped away, revving the engine.

Time seemed to stop for me. I tuned out the noise and activities of the events behind me. Even as the fair shut down and streams of families walked past me, I waited out there several hours for his car to return for me.

Mom Nancy had been summoned to the Spec House and told of my dad's departure. She went looking for me and found me alone where I sat, forlornly staring over the hills beyond the borders of the property.

"Benji!" she yelled when she saw me, hugging me close.

"He'll come back," I muttered, in reassurance to myself.

"Oh Benji, Sweetheart. He's gone, Honey. He's not coming back."

She stroked my hair.

"No ... he's coming back."

She held me closer, but then suddenly I knew this time was different. In an instant I was flooded with Dad memories.

I knew that I would no longer be able to learn how to build houses from him or have candid conversations with him about what I learned in school, who my friends were, and what I loved about life in the church. There would be no more rides on his shoulders, no more spicy bubble gum, no more colored river rocks, no more piggyback rides, just no more of my dad.

I remembered myself as a small child atop his shoulders walking around the Dyer property before he went to work. I saw the small, glass figurines and the Mickey Mouse watch he gave me for my third birthday ... shooting a plastic rocket across the railroad tracks in Dyer ... working at a job site where he explained what a 'header' and 'joist' were ... first bike ride I had without training wheels ... him telling jokes to his friends ... him sitting in his maroon colored El Camino full of tools in the back and him waving goodbye to me. I reminisced about all the bear hugs he gave me each time he left and returned to me. Then it hit me, there would be no more bear hugs from my dad. And not only would his presence in my life be gone, so would his humor and gentle nature.

Upon comprehending my new world, I arched my back against Momma Nancy's arms. I wiggled out of her arms and fell to the ground, kicking, screaming, and sobbing. Children circled around Mom and me, attempting to console me.

"It's okay, Benji."

"You can have some of my cake. Will that make you stop crying?" one of my friends asked.

"Why are you crying? You won a ribbon!" another exclaimed.

My weeping continued throughout the night and into the morning. I refused my breakfast. I slept from late morning to late lunch and cried throughout the following day and night. Finally, I collapsed from exhaustion on my parents' bed.

I emerged from the bedroom around noon the next day, having missed two days of school from all the crying. The front yard of the Nine-Plex was empty except for a robin perched on a tree branch about ten feet from my front door. I eyed the bird angrily before running to my bedroom and retrieving my bow and arrow. The arrow was tipped with a small red suction cup. I slowly opened the door, keeping it wedged open with my foot, and shot the robin off the branch. The bird fell to the ground, ruffled its feathers, squawked, but flew away. I had mixed feelings when the bird hit the ground: I felt empowered to shoot something, but sad that I shot an innocent bird.

Except for the occasional car that drove up or down the Nine-Plex hill, it was usually quiet. The day I emerged from my room, I sat in the corner of the yard waiting for the El Camino to drive up the road. Each car that drove up brought nothing but increased disappointment.

I spent the entire day watching, waiting, and hoping. I learned how to identify cars by their sound in order to know if it was my dad. Then the gray-colored school bus came up the road, carrying the church's children from school.

Jerry, my seven-year-old friend and next-door neighbor, exited first and ran up to me smiling. He was a small Native American boy, from Blackfoot and Sioux tribes.

We both had wild imaginations and were obsessed with cowboys and Indians. Normally, we made bows and arrows out of tree branches and rope. We would pretend to hunt in the forest and often caught lizards, rabbits, and the occasional small bird. We once set a trap using a sapling, which we made by pulling the tip of the young tree down, making a loop with it and pinned it to the forest floor.

None of that mattered now. I was enraged by my friend's smile. This rage was stronger than anything I had ever felt before in my life. Unlike the time I called the girl freckle face and the time I shot the robin out of the tree; this was new to me. It was anger mixed with frenzy and confusion.

This new feeling started behind my eyes, moved down my neck to my shoulders, and shot through my arms and hands. With a sudden surge, I shoved him to the ground then sprinted off into the nearby forest. I found a familiar forest path and followed it deep inside the forest to where there was a granite outcropping. It was there that I sat on the mound and cried some more.

I felt betrayed by my father, the only blood relative I had in my life. I couldn't form clear thoughts to control myself; blinding anger consumed me. A red and gray feeling stayed in the forefront of my head.

The tears were mixed with anger for much of that year. As a ten-year-old boy, it was much more acceptable to show anger than to be called a crybaby. I was accused by kids and adults of being filled with a contentious spirit more times that year than I could remember.

We had been told that everyone who left the compound either died and went to hell or was on their way to hell for leaving. How could my dad choose to go to hell? How could he choose to leave me? The devil must have taken over his soul. He must be lost, and I didn't want to be in hell with him. I finally decided God had given me Papa Tony and Dad Miguel. I didn't need Ed Risha.

That summer Dad Miguel drove one of the Alamo Trucking Company semi-trailer trucks across country, and I got to ride with him. We drove and delivered food each day. On the road we listened to Papa Tony's sermons and the Bible on tape. When we had enough of those, we listened to professional baseball and basketball games as we traversed the country. I asked him once why so many more black guys seemed to have the talent and skills to compete in college and pro-sports than white guys. He told me, "Black people have an extra-long tendon in their legs that help them jump higher and run faster."

"Then why can I run faster than most of the black kids in the church?"

"I don't know why. Maybe God is helping you."

His voice inflected with irritation making him sound confused, but something in his response told me he was also angry. I wondered if he was disappointed because he was never a professional football player.

When we arrived at a restaurant in the evening, we were given the customary waiver to get our free meals. We always unloaded the food and stocked it into their freezers, which freed up their employees to run their business. Restaurant owners gave us this waiver as a way of saying thank you for delivering and stocking their much-needed frozen food. Ordinarily, we didn't eat all day until we arrived at the evening destination because we didn't have extra money to buy food and we relied on this free meal. Papa Tony only approved gas money and we could not use it for food or drinks. It was considered as a time of fasting and I considered fasting to be a sign of commitment to God and a way to get forgiven for all my sins.

We took our place at the end of the queue for the buffet, but the line didn't seem to be moving. Hunger drove me as I ran to the front of the line where a tall, dark-haired man in a white dress shirt, black slacks, and black dress shoes stood talking to the gentleman who sliced the beef and ham. With a furrowed brow and pursed lips, I tugged on the man's shirt sleeve. He ignored me and kept talking, preventing the meat carver from serving the waiting customers. The growl in my stomach grew and rumbled. I tugged at the man's shirt sleeve again, and I was again ignored.

Finally, I grew so frustrated that I kicked the man in the leg and informed him, "We're hungry, and you're holding up the line!"

Before I knew it, Dad Miguel grabbed me by the ear and pulled me away from the line and into the restroom. "What's wrong with you? You know better than to kick people. What got into your head?"

"He was talking and talking and kept ignoring me. He can't ignore me."

What I didn't tell him was how angry I was at being brushed aside as if I didn't matter. It felt like when my dad left me all over again. He brushed me aside as if I didn't matter, and that made me feel ignored. I thought if I didn't matter, then he shouldn't matter. That's why I kicked him. Do unto others as you would have them do unto you. That's the golden rule. He clearly wanted me to kick him because he just kicked my feelings, I told myself.

However, inside I knew I was misbehaving and manipulated the golden rule to justify my bad behavior. Unlike misbehaving at the church, I knew I wouldn't get beaten in a public place. Maybe later, but it wouldn't be as bad as if I had done this at the church in front of everyone there.

He opened the bathroom door and shooed me outside, telling me, "Go to the truck and wait there for me. Go!"

I walked to the truck with my head low, kicking the ground as I walked. *I didn't do anything. That stupid man was the one doing something wrong.* I was hungry ... and in full-blown denial about my behavior.

How could Dad Miguel take his side? He's supposed to be my dad. My real dad is a sinner and in hell now that he left the church, so Dad Miguel needed to step up in there. I thought Papa Tony would have punched that guy in the mouth if he ignored me like that. I wished he was here.

I sat in the truck and looked through the bug-splattered windshield at a line of green dumpsters at the end of the parking lot. A few scraggly cats sat on the edges of an open container. Some of our food came from dumpsters just like that. I didn't want to have to sort through rotten potatoes or scrape green mold off white loaves of bread and maggots off discolored meat. But I was starving. Dry heaving, I pushed opened the truck door in case I vomited.

I envisioned the smorgasbord and Sunday dinners at home, which were always my favorite. I could skip church in exchange for kitchen service. I liked the mashed potato station most of all. My second favorite station was meatloaf unless Mr. Vasquez was making taco salad. I liked dipping the flour tortillas in the ten-gallon metal vats of hot oil, pushing them into the oil with a strainer causing the tortillas to take the shape of a strainer.

I inhaled, imagining buttery mashed potatoes.

Finally, my dad opened the driver's side door, startling me. He stared at me and shook his head.

"You have no idea the problem you just caused," he said.

"I'm sorry. I just wanted to eat. He was holding up the line. Can I go back in and apologize?"

"No. I apologized for you."

My dad handed me a Styrofoam container and started up the truck.

"I got you some chicken and mashed potatoes."

I nearly inhaled the food and, when I was done, let out a loud belch.

"My compliments to the chef ... mmmm ..."

My dad looked at me and shook his head with a smile.

"You have any idea who you just kicked? Do you? That was Bill Clinton."

"Who? Who is Bill Clinton?"

"You kicked the Governor of the State of Arkansas, Benji."

"The Governor. Isn't that sort of like the President of Arkansas?" I asked.

"Yeah, sort of."

"Am I in trouble? Did I get the church in trouble?"

"No. I won't tell anyone about this. He's just a man like everyone else who needs salvation. That's why I went back in there: to make sure he knew that God had a plan for him. Plus, when I told him where we're from he said he knew who we were, and that Papa Tony looked like Roy Orbison on speed."[15]

Along with delivering food, one of our main responsibilities was to distribute religious brochures. The Fort Smith Walmart was a well-known target for our tracts, and, on this day, I had two hundred tracts I had to pass out. I knew the drill: take the tracts, in this instance the tract was named, "The Pope's Secrets," and put them on car windshields throughout the parking lot. Do it fast and don't be seen. If someone says something to you, start preaching to them. On my thirtieth car, a young man dressed in camouflage pants and a hunter's bright orange jacket ran toward me yelling with a southern twang, "Hey … what ya doin'? Don't you touch my truck!"

With the certainty of gravity, I stood between the vehicles and began my sermon, "Sir, are you aware that the world is coming to an end and your soul, your everlasting soul, will burn in hell forever if you don't accept God into your life? Are you?"

"Look son, I don't want any trouble. I just don't want whatever yer sellin'."

"I'm not selling anything sir. God gave us his only begotten son so that you could have everlasting life. How does it feel to know that Jesus came down to earth, took all the sins of mankind and went to hell for three days where he buried those sins so that you could have eternal life in heaven? I am not selling you anything. I am here to help you find your way to heaven. Have you accepted Jesus Christ as your personal savior?"

The man stood like a deer in headlights not believing what I was saying to him, or maybe in disbelief at who was saying it. I am not sure which.

---

15. https://www.tonyalamonews.com/299/bill-clinton-mentions-tony-alamo-in-his-book-he-looked-like-roy-orbison-on-speed.php

"Have you sir? Do you lead a godly life, or do you allow sin to enter your heart?"

"Young man," he said with respect and caution. "I am a Baptist. I go to church on the weekends and …"

"A Baptist? The prophet of God, Tony Alamo, says the Baptist believe in sinning and asking for forgiveness like the Catholics! Is that what you think living a godly life is all about? Sinning and then going to church on Sundays to get forgiveness? I have news for you, sir. God is watching you and recording all that you do, say, and think. If you think that on the Judgment Day, you will be rewarded for your current lifestyle with everlasting life in heaven, then you might need to think again. Are you willing to bet your eternal soul that your actions as a Baptist will get you eternal life?"

"Well, I never thought of it that way, young man."

"Well, the first thing you need to do is kneel down with me right here, right now, and say a prayer. This prayer is the sinner's prayer and the blood of Jesus will wash away your sins after you say it. Would you like to have your sins washed away and learn how to live a life without sin?"

We said the sinner's prayer together and I asked him, "Now do you want the tract I was trying to put on your car? It has the address of our church where you can live with like-minded people who live each moment for God. Would you like it?"

He took the brochure saying, "Thanks, kid."

After that experience, my confidence level was sky high. I had led somebody to Christ! I had prayed the sinner's prayer with somebody! I felt like I could walk on water like Jesus or even raise the dead if I needed.

When we returned that evening, we reported to the Spec House office. When I walked by Grandma Susie's grave, I thought about trying to raise her up, but was distracted by the urgency of Papa Tony's request to speak with us. The adults who oversaw passing out tracts surrounded the desk where Papa Tony's three spiritual wives were tending to the phones.

Papa Tony's voice boomed over the speaker phone. "Fort Smith, how many did you pass out?"

"About 1,500, sir," one of his spiritual wives replied looking at a list with the tallies on them.

"That's it? Your quota was 5,000. Why don't you take a few days without food and let's see if that motivates you to save more souls?" He paused for a minute before continuing, "With the lazy Fort Smith crew, what was our tally for the week with all crews reporting?"

I interjected saying, "Papa Tony, this is Benji. I want you to know that I said the sinner's prayer with a man and saved his soul today."

"Benji, great job! You're a light in the darkness. That's what I wish everyone was doing."

"At first, he didn't want to take a brochure, but after I told him how his soul was at risk of burning in hell, he was happy to get saved."

"Well, Benji, you don't have to fast then. As a reward for your hard work you can have some ice cream sent to your house. Tell the cafeteria I said it's ok."

I was excited and elated that Papa Tony recognized my special skills. He knew I was focused on my mission. I turned to the group of people, looking for an area to stand away from them. I felt like I was better than the rest of them at that moment.

His wife replied, "Sir, the grand total of tracts passed out this week is 15,000, sir."

"15,000 …15,000 souls saved. You see, we saved 15,000 souls this week," Papa Tony declared.

In Papa Tony's presence we were confident that for each brochure passed out the person reading it would call us to say the sinner's prayer and give their life to God. Our membership in Arkansas was about five hundred to seven hundred people. In California, there were a few hundred more followers. Adding in all our smaller outposts, there might have been a hundred more followers. We still had nearly thirty church-owned and operated businesses, which generated millions of dollars per year, but the number of actual followers had been slowly declining.

A few weeks later I overheard some adults talk about Papa Tony's recent trip to Amsterdam.

"Apparently, Tony went to Amsterdam's red-light district to preach to the hookers and didn't come back for three days. When he finally came back, he had alcohol on his breath, he had used condom wrappers, cocaine, and weed in his pant pockets. The brothers found them after he passed out in the hotel. That's why Ed Risha left. He was tired of working eighteen hours a day for a two-bit disappointment and liar who lived only for himself whoring, drinking, and doing drugs. I don't blame him."

"Careful, brother. You might be partaking in gossip. We were not there and do not know for sure if that happened," the other brother cautioned.

Why would Papa Tony be drunk when he claimed being a drunkard was a fast way to hell? And the drugs? Maybe he took the drugs from the people he had tried to save. Or maybe, like Jesus whose first miracle was turning water to wine, Papa Tony did the same thing. Maybe he performed a miracle and these adults don't know it. Dad wouldn't have left from the hard work, he never complained about that. No one did. These adults must be wrong. They didn't know what they were talking about.

# CHAPTER SEVEN

## Price of Being Special

Papa Tony's sermon this evening began focusing on the "limp wristed faggots in the Catholic Church." Our mission was to recruit the sinners and save them from the molestations and atrocities of these "limp wristed" priests and the Pope. He also ordered that the children have a daily children's church service bringing the number of daily services we children were required to attend to three per day, seven days a week.

In today's service, Veronica, Niceah's mom, started the children's church service with a prayer, followed by testimonies. Several children testified that they were saved from drugs, lives of violence, and prostitution. The only drug they had ever seen was Aspirin and the only violence was whatever beatings they endured at the direction of Papa Tony. But we learned about other sins, even if we didn't understand them, from the adults and replicated their testimonies.

Our testimonies were opportunities for us to compete with each other on how much we were saved from drug use, lives of murder, burglary, theft, drug dealing, mayhem, arson, prostitution, pimping, torture, rape, molestation, and a whole host of other crimes. Although none of this was true, no adult ever challenged us and that just made us try harder to outdo each other.

Veronica called out over the microphone, "Benji Risha. Come on up and give your testimony."

Risha? No, she didn't say that. She knows my last name is Vasquez or Alamo. What is wrong with her?

It was common knowledge that everyone who left the church was either on drugs, which would result in them dying and going to hell, or they were faggots, which was even worse than being on drugs. Or, they would go crazy and end up in hell when they died. I certainly did not want to be affiliated with my sinner of a father who was clearly either in, or soon to be going to, hell.

I walked up to the pulpit and whispered in her ear, "I'm Benji Vasquez, not Benji Risha." I gave my testimony, based on Papa Tony's recent sermon, about how I would fight faggots wherever they were.

The next day during breakfast I saw Louden's mom talking with my mom. The two made eye contact with me and my mom pointed at me with her index finger pulling it toward herself, beckoning me to come to her.

When I got within arm's reach, she grabbed my ear and whispered into it, "You thought you would get away with this just because your Dad Miguel is out of town right now. Well, you're going to apologize."

I looked at her and rolled my eyes. I knew what she was talking about, I had called Louden a faggot, but she hadn't fully expressed it. I wasn't afraid of her. She never spanked me, but she could take away my privileges. I was afraid of what Dad Miguel would do, but I had Papa Tony's own words to use right now. I felt empowered and knew I could stand my ground.

"What are you talking about? Papa Tony said people who were limp-wristed were faggots. I was just repeating what he said."

"Yeah ... well you're not the prophet of God, are you? What he says is because God guides him to say it. You're just a silly little boy," she admonished.

"I am special, and you know it," I retorted.

I was the future leader born to lead the Jews and the Arabs. Who was she to challenge me? According to the Bible and Papa Tony, faggots have no place in heaven.

I was dragged over to Louden, past a table where girls my age were sitting. The shock I saw in their eyes was expected, but Angie, a golden haired, blue-eyed girl my age, who I had a crush on for as long as I could remember, looked at me with pity. My state of mind flipped like a switch from confidence to insecurity. The pressure to perform and to be in control was too much for me. I knew I had failed when I saw Angie's eyes. She saw a silly little boy, not a leader, not a cool kid who had it all.

I began crying from the embarrassment, tears dripping down my face.

"Go on. Apologize for calling him a faggot!" Mom said letting go of my ear.

Out of frustration and embarrassment, I stuttered, "I'm s-s-ssorry f-f-for calling you a-a-a- faggot."

Louden stood up and raised his arm in preparation to shake my hand.

But I refused to shake his limp-wristed hand. I looked at mom and her eyes communicated approval. The apology was enough for her. She could tell I had learned my lesson and a handshake would not make me learn my lesson anymore.

I ran away to where my friend Enoch Junior was waiting in line for lunch. Enoch's family was one of eight or nine African American families living in the church. I slid my tray to Mr. Brown, who served alone that day. I asked for a sandwich and chips. Tears were still in my eyes.

"Benji," Mr. Brown said to me in a gentle voice. "Do you know how unique and special you are? You're the only person I know, maybe the only person on earth, who literally has a war going on inside of him. You're an Arab-Jew."

"I know I'm Jewish and an Arab, but why do you say there is a war going on inside me?"

"Those two groups have been fighting for a long time. You have both inside you. You're waging a war on the inside."

"I don't understand. Does that mean I get to fight people?"

I was upset. First, I had to apologize, but now I have the right to wage war? People were always telling me that I had a war going on inside of me. I never understood what that meant. I thought about a few fights I had in the swimming pool where I dunked a few different kids into the water. I thought about the times during long foot races where I'd trip the runner in front of me. I thought about the bike races where I'd kick the rear tire of the racer in front of me. All of this so I could win. I loved winning at any cost, if I was not caught. Even though numerous adults told me I had a war going on inside of me because of my Jewish and Arab ancestry, I didn't realize that another type of war also raged: kindness over cruelty, good over bad, wild over subdued, and Christ-like devotion to others over self-centeredness.

"No, no. You're a Christian and must behave. What I mean is that you have the potential to make a huge impact. You'll understand when you get older."

Another adult from behind the food line came up to me.

"Benji," she said, "I overheard your conversation. The Jews are the chosen people and the Arabs, their brothers, are fighting them because they believe in different things. What Mr. Brown means is that someday you can bring peace to both sides by showing them that they have more in common with each other than they have differences. Sometimes that's how wars are won."

"I don't really care about that. I just want to eat," I said. For some reason I had started thinking about when Mom and

Dad said they were leaving again. It became clear to me how they treated Nicole like a princess and me like a vagabond.

"You're being rude, Benji," Junior said to me. "You can't behave like that."

Junior and I walked toward the table where we always sat. "I have a war inside me Junior," I said with a smile on my face. "Don't mess with me lest I might smite thee."

"You smite me. I will cast the Arab demon out of you," he said.

We laughed and pushed each other, until we reached the corner tables. Sitting in the corner seats were three six-year-old boys and Louden. With no adults watching me I knew I wouldn't get into trouble. I stood at the edge of the table and cleared my throat. Three of the boys promptly stood up, took their food, and moved to another table.

Louden objected.

"I'm not going anywhere. You don't own this table. I was here first."

Kai and Nimrod, two boys my age, walked up to the table and stood behind Junior and me.

I licked my index finger and stuck it into Loudens sandwich.

"Are you going to eat that?" I asked, laughing.

His face turned red. He looked around at the other boys who were sitting with their friends. None of his friends were in our group and he knew that I knew that. What I didn't know then was how I was hurting these boys emotionally. I didn't comprehend how I was using my entitlement to bully them and how, each time I did so, I was taking a piece of their inner self-worth, their self-esteem, and I was smashing it to smithereens.

My group of friends included the boys who had one proverbial foot in the cool category and the other foot in the holy roller category. We were better at sports, stronger, older, and dressed better than most of the kids. The age of my group benefited from the handful of older kids who had come before us. And, because my group was the biggest, we were positioned perfectly to learn from within the group and from those who came before us. We used our knowledge to our advantage. One of those advantages was that we had quicker replies using Bible verses when other kids challenged us with Bible verses for why we were misbehaving.

For example, if I pushed a boy to the ground and he replied, "The Bible says to lay your hands on no man," I might respond by saying, "You are not a man," or "That's true, but the Bible also says to cast out demons from the evil, and I thought you had a demon in you so I pushed you real hard trying to get the demon out."

Our authority was absolute around the other kids, but only if we had the numbers. If one of us got reported without a friend, then there was a high chance we would get beaten. But when we were together, we were unstoppable, unless two or more adults witnessed our tomfoolery.

We nearly surrounded Louden's table. Picking up his plate, he ran off to join his friends at their table.

Louden returned to the serving bar where Mr. Brown stood smiling. His friends followed.

"Nimrod, loosen the cap on their saltshaker," I commanded.

Nimrod snuck over to their table and crouched while loosening the cap before the boys were able to see him. When they returned, Louden tried to salt his vegetables and salt poured out all over his food. Our table erupted in laughter.

Over the years, we sat at that table and imagined all sorts of scenarios and gadgets we could create. We imagined an invisible shield that would protect us from bombs that would land at the end of days, and a device that would go get our food for us and take food from our enemies, who were really just the kids we did not like, and even a device that cloned us. We could use our clones to go to church, prayer hours, and foot washings while we played sports, fished, and hiked.

"I'm telling," Louden yelled, standing up to find an adult.

"Follow me," I said to Kai.

Kai knew what to do. He grabbed Louden by the neck and pushed him back into the seat while I blocked the view from adults.

"Hold him still."

I turned to him and pinched the muscle between his neck and shoulders until he let out a scream. I covered his mouth and continued applying pressure to the soft muscle. I was trying to make him cry, but he just wouldn't cry.

"Don't ever sit in our seats. Do you understand?"

"'Mmm hmm …," he muttered.

"All of you started this by sitting in our seats. Next time it won't just be him. It will be all out war on all of you," I warned the others at Louden's table.

After lunch, we chased Louden's brother, Gregory, on our bikes. I caught up to him first and caused him to fishtail by hitting his rear tire with my front tire. He slid into a pile of dirt. One of the boys in my group retrieved the bike and pedaled away. I rode my bike around him, mocking and teasing him.

"How's the dirt taste, Gregory? It looks like your new shoes are ruined. Ha … you have a hole in your pants now. Idiot!"

When I finally turned to ride away, Gregory ran over to a pile of sticks and brush. He pulled out a long, straight tree branch and heaved it like an expert javelin thrower. The stick went through my front tire causing me to flip over the front wheel and onto the pavement. I stood up with skin peeling from my hands and knees.

Gregory laughed hysterically. "I saw what you did to my brother in the cafeteria. You really think you can get away with that?"

"I don't know what you're talking about. I am going to tell Papa Tony what you just did."

"Go ahead and tell Papa Tony," he said.

I rode to the Spec House to find Papa Tony in the back room of the Spec House surrounded by brothers. There were clothing designs and parts of leather jackets strewn about.

"What happened to you?" Papa Tony asked.

"Gregory threw a stick into the spokes of my bike, and I flew off onto the cement."

"Go get Gregory," Papa Tony barked at one of the brothers.

Five minutes later, Gregory and I stood next to each other facing Papa Tony.

"Tell me what happened. He threw a stick into your bike wheel and you flew off?" Papa Tony prompted.

"Yes, and when I told him I was going to tell you, he said he didn't care."

"That's not what I said. I said, 'Go ahead and tell Papa Tony,'" Gregory replied.

Papa Tony backhanded him immediately with his ringed hand. Gregory hit the orange carpeted floor with a thump and tried to hold his mouth. It was bloodied from either the rings or the impact. Papa Tony growled and kicked him with this steel-toed cowboy boots as he rolled around the floor, trying to get away. Next, Papa Tony stomped him in the stomach. It left Gregory breathless, then convulsing.

My stomach clinched at the same time his boot made contact. I watched the violence in silence while Gregory moaned in pain. I stepped backward to get away from it, until I hit the wall behind me.

At the time, I didn't speak up because I had mixed thoughts as I watched. On the one hand he was being evil and on the other hand he was a friend. I'm sure I had an emotional response to this, but we were never allowed to express them. Without freedom of expression, the ability to identify and express emotions dies like a plant starved of sunlight.

"Get me the board of education," Papa Tony ordered. When I heard that, my body temperature rose producing a slight headache. The board of education was a wooden paddle, four feet long, six inches wide, and two inches thick. It had holes in it to make it move faster while swinging and an inscription which read: "Spare the rod, spoil the child."

My nose began to bleed from the stress-induced headache.

"Give me the paddle. Hurry up and hold this little devil over that couch over there."

As I watched the brothers hold him down across a brown-colored armchair, my emotions flooded me. I felt my power over him as they held him down. I imagined my power flowing through the brother's arms. I felt powerful knowing that Papa Tony and I were on the same side against evil. Revenge felt satisfying.

Papa Tony beat him until his arm was tired. He handed the board to a man named Harry Sand. Harry was another big brother. He looked like a giant to me.

At first, I was happy to feel I had the power to exact revenge, but my happiness quickly dissipated as I saw the pain inflicted upon him. His eight-year-old face showed agony and misery; emotions which I did not know how to process. As I realized his helplessness and hurt, I felt a rushing feeling in my forehead. I began to feel remorse for reporting him and shame swallowed me.

My nose began to bleed. I caught the blood that dripped from my nose before it landed on the carpet for fear I would get beaten next. I tried to act like I wasn't nervous.

I was nervous. It was as if I had a wall of Papa Tony's words enveloping a place around my heart and that wall cast a shadow over my feelings. Sometimes the sun would slowly start to shine over the wall but mostly, at that point, self-protection reigned paramount. One slip-up and I would be in Gregory's place. If I spoke up or challenged what was going on, I was afraid I would not survive.

"Benji," Papa Tony said. "It's a good thing you reported this little devil. I think I beat it out of him. Harry will make sure though."

Harry swung at least another twenty times before Papa Tony interrupted him.

"That's enough. Who's next? Who else is on report?" he asked excitedly.

An OC sister, which was an abbreviation for older Christian, escorted a mom along with her nine-year-old son to the room. Both looked around the place as if they did not belong there. Gregory was lying on the ground crying as Harry stood over him.

The mother's and son's eyes darted back and forth from person to person and object to object. The mother shivered as she stared at the paddle in Harry's hand.

"What's this all about?" Papa Tony inquired.

The OC explained that the mother believed there was more than one story in the Bible detailing King Saul's death. She taught her son that one story said that Saul fell on his sword and another story said an Amalekite killed him in battle.

Papa Tony laughed.

"You're a usurper of authority, you little weasel. You're what I like to call a sweat hog. You, from the dregs of society, what would you know about interpreting the Bible? Are you a Jew or a Hebrew like me? Huh? No, you are not. My people wrote the Bible, so I have the right to interpret it. Not you." Papa Tony yelled.

He grabbed the paddle from Harry's hand waving it wildly in the air. "I'm the apple of God's eye. Not you. Do you understand? You little swine! You sweat hog. It's me ... I am God's messenger, not you."

Harry leaned the paddle against the wall.

"Come here, son. Your mother is a sinner. She is a blasphemous swine and needs to be woken up. Go smack her in the face as hard as you can. Tell her, 'Wake up swine!'" Papa Tony ordered.

"Go on! Do it!"

The boy walked to his mom and looked her in the eyes. His arms and body shook in fear. His eyes darted back and forth in search for some sort of escape. Papa Tony continued to yell, "Hit her! Hit her now!"

The boy wept as he softly smacked his mother.

"Wake up, swine," he mumbled beneath his weeping.

"No … smack her as hard as you can. If you don't, I will," Papa Tony said as he picked up the paddle.

"Lean forward, you swine, so your son can smack your lying face."

She leaned over, and the boy smacked her hard.

"Wake up, swine!" he yelled.

"Are you going to make me do this?" Papa Tony chastised.

"If I do it, it won't be like this. Do it again and find the anger you have against the devil. The anger is inside you. She tried to lead you astray. She tried to lead you to hell by misinterpreting God's Holy Word. Do you want to go to hell? Hit her as if you are trying to stay out of hell. Go, do it now. Do it now!"

He smacked his mother again. This time saliva flew from her mouth.

"Wake up, swine!" he yelled.

Her tears flowed and Papa Tony smiled.

"Those better be tears of joy," he said, walking toward her.

"Tell me how thankful you are that I corrected you, you sweat hog!"

She held the side of her mouth where her son smacked her.

"Tha-Tha-thank you, sir."

She cried as she walked out with her son lagging her.

With each smack in the face, I felt her pain and her fear. I found myself switching between fear and excitement. My face got warm as her face got red. I began to wince and shield my face as the blows landed on her. I also felt the boy's pain as my own anxiety burned in my chest. He was torn between fear of Papa Tony and God and the life-long love he had for his mother. Like the fear I felt from my father leaving, I thought this boy was experiencing something similar.

But then I gave myself over to being excited. That part of me knew Papa Tony was guided by God and that knowledge was enthralling. Deep inside I was happy to see her punishment. I was happy to know that she needed to be hit like this because the punishment was a way for her to atone for her sins. It was intriguing to watch the boy let go of his love for his mother and accept the guidance of God through Papa Tony. I saw the moment he let go. It's like he made a mental calculation. After that, I saw the expression on his face turned from sad and angry, to angry and determined.

Could I ever hit Momma Nancy? Could I beat one of my friends how Papa Tony just beat Gregory? No way. It was too much pain. I lost my breath when he lost his. I winced when he was hit in the face with Papa Tony's ring hand. I felt his pain. But then the excitement returned, and I realized that I could hurt my friend if the adrenaline part of me took over.

There is nothing normal about delighting in the suffering of others. To want to increase someone else's suffering is a greater sin than all the seven deadly sins. I am not proud that I was infected with the sadism of Tony Alamo and see the infection as the beginning of development toward psychopathology and/or sociopathy, neither of which I want as a pathology which describes me.

On April 5, 1986, my eleventh birthday, I woke up early to go fishing. After an OC found me in the cafeteria eating breakfast, he handed me a card and told me to go see Papa

Tony at the Spec House. I opened it and a crisp twenty-dollar bill fell onto the table. I pocketed it and read the card.

> *Benji,*
> *Today you became a man. Congratulations!*
> *God has a plan for you.*
> *You will do great things in His Name.*
> *I'm proud of your success as a Christian.*
> *Love, Papa Tony*

I felt pride, honor, and thought myself elevated above my peers to be called by Papa Tony on my birthday. The world stopped when he spoke. The world changed when he ordered it changed. Being a part of his world was better than being completely in mine.

When I got to the house, the speakerphone in the lower room bellowed with Papa Tony's voice. "Hi Benji! How does it feel to be a man? Do you feel any older?"

I could tell he was smiling by the way he said my name. How do I feel? I feel normal. It's not like I got taller or stronger overnight.

"I feel a little bit older," I said. However, my thoughts jumped to the new freedoms I would be given someday as a man. I'll get to choose different types of work I want to do. I can travel with Papa Tony and model his clothing line in fun places around the world. If I want to be a carpenter like my Dad Dad, I can do that, or if I want to drive semi-trucks like Dad Miguel, I can do that. Maybe Papa Tony would send me on missions to different churches around the world to convert their followers to the real way of God.

I'll be able to live in the brothers' dorms. I'll be able to start driving. I'll get an increase in the bucks, when they are available. I'll be trusted to go into the world more often. Best of all, I'll be allowed to marry one of the sisters when I get a little bit older.

"Do you know what God loves more than anything? A person who works for him, and we need to get you working. I understand Grandpa Montiel might be able to use an extra hand at the mechanic's shop. How does that sound?"

It was customary that every boy who was eleven years old or older work a job. Papa Tony always preached, "It says in II Thessalonians 3:10, 'if you don't work, you don't eat.'" There were times when some of the brothers and sisters got sick and couldn't work. They had to fast until they healed. I did not want to be like them. Many of the newly recognized child-men or child-women worked in the same professions as their parents. The church had twenty-four businesses in Arkansas alone so there were plenty of options.

If I could have any job, it would be with Grandpa Montiel. There was something noble about the silent and respectful distance he gave the people with whom he interacted. It was fun and relaxing to be around him. Plus, he was predictable. Even though I loved Papa Tony, I didn't have much fun around him. He was always punishing people and I could never predict his behavior, so it was unsettling.

As the chief mechanic for the church, Grandpa Montiel smelled of grease. When I stayed with him and Grandma Dee, he let me help him use heavy equipment: the backhoe to dig a trench, the Caterpillar to scrape the side of a hill, and the bulldozer to fill a dump truck with dirt. It was exciting to shape the earth with the huge machines.

That's not what I told Papa Tony though. "Whatever the Lord wants me to do, I'll do," I told him, trying to conceal my excitement and to impress him with my commitment to the faith and his will.

"That's a true Christian attitude. Go work with him in your free time. Make sure to keep reading the Bible and doing your daily prayers."

I found Grandpa waiting for me and opening the shop door even before I knocked. The shop was a mess. The yellow, fluorescent lighting inside flickered which illuminated greasy motors, gray transmissions, spare auto parts, and randomly placed tires. At the back of the shop there was a large driveway. At its center, there were four piles of dirt. The piles of dirt reminded me of the cement culvert in front of the cafeteria where all the kids used to jump their bikes.

"If I bring my bike, can I jump them?" I said, pointing at them.

"I don't see why not, but I might have something better for you here than a bike," Grandpa Montiel said, twisting his salt and pepper handlebar mustache.

Grandpa Montiel slammed the door behind me as we walked in. The rickety, metal door shut out the natural light. Then he walked up to me, pausing, as he chewed on a toothpick, resting one hand casually on his hips. With the other, he wiped his bald head.

"Go get changed into some overalls. When you're ready I'll show you something ten times better than a bike. There's a pair of overalls I made into shorts for when it's hot. You can use them."

When I returned, he pulled a black plastic sheet off a pile of parts. "I need you to put those motors on these dune buggy frames. I'll show you how to do it, but only the one time, so pay attention. Once you're done with that, you'll do it on your own for the second dune buggy."

He gave me a toolbox and then showed me how to ready and install the small motors. There were a few bolts to attach, a hose for the fuel, and a few wires that needed connections.

I loved the clear, concise instructions necessary for the task. There was no room for interpretation or mistakes when building the dune buggy. Mechanics would never be like the boy who had to smack his own mother for misinterpreting the Bible. With mechanics there was only one way to do the project because many parts and assemblies were designed to be installed one way: the right way. In the end, either the machine works, or it does not.

"Do you see this notch right here?" Grandpa Montiel asked me as he pointed out a spot on a part for the motor. "This prevents the part from being put on backwards. This gear can only be installed one way and can only be secured by turning the bolt counterclockwise. Do you see that? Putting the dune buggies together is a test for your future job."

Knowing that my job was crucial in making sure all the vehicles operated provided me a boost of pride. It took me all morning to get the dune buggies operational. At noon, Grandpa came over to inspect them. He nodded his head in silent approval and made a few adjustments.

"Go ahead. Turn it over," he said.

I pulled the starter cord and the yellow buggy roared to life. I jumped in and Grandpa clicked the seat belt.

"Don't go too fast and wreck. You get all banged up and your grandma will kill me. Go on now."

I floored the gas pedal. Rocks and dirt spun under the tires as I drove loops in the parking lot, eventually working up the courage to jump the first of four dirt mounds. I leaped it, easing off the gas upon impact. Soon I flew from one mound to the next. Round and round, I went until the motor sputtered and ran out of gas. The two of us sat on the dirt mounds watching the dust settle.

"You know," Grandpa said taking a can of sardines from a pocket in his trousers, "if you told me ten years ago that me and Grandma would be takin' care of you, I wouldn't have believed it."

"Why not?"

"Well, I reared Nancy, Grandma's eldest daughter. Miguel and she are happily married, but Tory, her youngest, never came to stay with us. Guess, I just thought we were done rearin' young'uns," he said. "But you know what's so good about you?"

"Everything. I'm a peace child and someday I'll go to Israel to make peace?"

"No. Not that nonsense."

"I already know how to make dune buggies?"

"No. That's not it. That's all fine and dandy for some folks. But for me, Grandma won't be so bossy with me no more, that's what."

"What?" I asked.

"When Nancy was around, she had the poor girl waitin' on her hand and foot. Grandma was always tellin' Nancy, 'Fetch me a bath. Clean the house. Wash the walls. Do the laundry. Make my food.' But when Nancy married Miguel, Grandma turned all that on me. With you in the house, you and she'll be the ones doin' all the waitin' on me."

"I don't understand," I scratched my head and tried to skip a pebble across the top of a mound. "Mom's always waiting on my dad like he's a king or something. She makes his food. Gets his slippers. Massages his feet. Rubs his back and irons his clothes. She even makes me move the TV into just the right spot and set it up for him, so he can watch sports when he gets home from work. I'm not really sure what he does though."

Grandpa smiled at me and nodded his head in agreement.

"Sounds about right. That's because she was used to waiting on her mom. But now that you're here, your Grandma will want you to wait on her and won't try to make me do that stuff. How could a grease monkey like me clean the house? I need cleanin'!"

"I'm glad to be here working with you, Grandpa. I could be digging holes and planting trees out in the hot sun like some of my friends. Or even worse, I could be sweeping up in the cafeteria."

"Take a bite of that," he said, using the can's peel-away lid to scoop up a sardine. "You're a good kid. You don't need to be doing that kind of work. You'll be a mechanic yet."

It felt like I had a purpose other than as the messenger of peace to the Middle East or as a preacher to lost souls. It felt good to have a different identity. Plus, the brothers in the mechanic's shop were always looked up to, at least after they got the vehicles operating.

A few days later, I found the time to ponder what to do with the mustache I was growing. At eleven years old, the hair on my lip was soft and dark. The hair under my armpits was the same. I took my dad's yellow Bic razor from the drawer, soaked a washcloth in hot water in the sink and used it to cover my mustache. I looked in the mirror and frowned at my unibrow and decided to take the razor and shave the hair between them. Then I pulled the razor across the middle of my lip, down the left side, and then placed the razor above the right side and began the last stroke of my first shave.

I looked good, so I decided to keep going. I moved to the end of my eyebrows, which fizzled out near the hair on my head. I cleared the left eyebrow and moved over to the right side just when Nicole burst into the bathroom without knocking. My hand slipped and sliced the corner of my eyebrow, leaving a large bald spot and a small cut.

Embarrassed, I ran to my bedroom.

Dad came home early that evening. He found me hiding in my room with bloody tissue paper and missing half an eyebrow.

"I was wondering when this day would come. You finally shaved."

"Yeah, but Nicole scared me and look what happened!" I cried, showing him my eyebrow.

"It looks like you got your mustache taken care of though. You should be happy today. Today is a turning point from being a child to being a man. Your eyebrows will grow back in no time. But, there's only one time you'll ever have your first shave. Hold tight. I have a gift for this special day."

He walked out of my room and returned with his black, leather toiletry bag.

"There's shaving cream and a few new razors inside. I also got you some aftershave."

I always wanted my own Aqua Velvet aftershave. I splashed some on my face and walked out of my room as a man.

The following day I left the house to do my chores for the children's garden. I carried several buckets up the hill and watered a small patch of the garden. On my way back to the pond, Louden came riding by on Speckles, a quarter horse. She stood fifteen to sixteen hands and was, by far, the tallest of our horses. Behind her was Ebony, a big beautiful mare being ridden by Chandra. Behind her was Shadow, a gray and white Appaloosa. Sunny, a Tennessee Walking Horse, was at the rear.

*He's tempting me. How dare he show off like this? I should be riding, not him.* Evil, impure, and jealous thoughts raced through me.

*The blood of Jesus is against you Satan. The blood of Jesus is against you Satan.*

My evil thoughts stopped.

I heard one of the ponies in the nearby field whinny and neigh. About ten feet from me, Speckles reared onto her hind legs. Louden, showing off his riding skills, remained calm on her.

*Who does he think he is? Show off!*

"God is watching me right now, and he knows I am doing more for him than you," I told him.

"Yeah? God is rewarding me for work I've already done. So, I get to ride today. What happened to your face? It looks like you cut off your eyebrow."

I growled under my breath and lumbered back up the hill to finish watering the plants, visualizing Louden getting kicked by Speckles as I went.

*The blood of Jesus is against you Satan. The blood of Jesus is against you Satan.*

Louden and the other riders finally rode off in the direction of Sutton's Pond, which was about a half mile away.

It was near lunch time when I finished watering and walked into the cafeteria. A group of people stood in a large circle in the middle of the table area focused on something in the center. I pushed my way in. There, on several tables pushed together, Louden lay naked, except for the bandages and bloody clothes that covered his face and groin area.

Chandra stood next to him. She discreetly rubbed her arm against me when I appeared and whispered, "After we were done riding, all the boys played capture the flag behind Sutton's Pond. Louden ran into the forest with the flag. I guess he ran into the old rusty fence that surrounded the old Native American site and was lying there for a while. One of the boys saw the flag on the ground and went to get it and saw him lying there. He thought he was dead because he was unconscious.

Then I noticed that Chandra was still holding her arm against mine. The warmth of her body and soft hair was exciting. I looked at her and she cracked a small smile. I pushed a little bit harder into her arm and looked down her shirt. She turned as if she was saying something to Louden, giving me a better view.

I pressed my erection into the table and away from Chandra.

*God sees me. God knows my thoughts. God sees me. God knows my thoughts. The blood of Jesus is against you Satan. The blood of Jesus is against you Satan. The blood of Jesus is against you Satan.*

I spoke up, "Hey, Louden. I'll pray for you, brother. God loves you and when you get better, we'll go riding again. Okay? Jesus loves you, brother. Amen."

Success. My penis retreated, and I began backing away from the table.

"Thanks, brother. Sorry for being mean to you today. I didn't mean it. You know if I didn't act like that, no one would," he said with a partial smile.

I needed to get away from the group in case my erection returned so I ran to the bathroom, but it was locked. I went outside into the nearby forest and my erection came back as soon as I remembered Chandra's body. I imagined Chandra's breasts, or what I had just seen of them, and the look on her face. The curves of her breast consumed me.

I heard someone approaching and quickly tucked my erection back under the elastic band of my underwear and acted like I was praying.

"Hey! Is Jesus answering your prayers?" Chandra said. She had been standing there watching me the entire time.

She had the same look she had in her eyes when we were near Louden. We stared at each other and began to walk toward each other, until her breasts were firmly against my chest. I smelled her breath and her sweet body.

I kissed her, my first kiss, and she kissed me back. Our lips moved around each other until her tongue slipped into my mouth. I returned the favor, and my erection escaped the elastic band of my underwear. She noticed and moved the lower part of her body toward mine.

I pulled away from her, smiling from ear to ear, and ran back toward the garden, high on love.

*God sees me. God knows my thoughts. God sees me. God knows my thoughts. The blood of Jesus is against you Satan. The blood of Jesus is against you Satan. The blood of Jesus is against you Satan.*

My erection subsided again.

# CHAPTER EIGHT

## Who Will Rise up for Me?

While Dad Miguel and I were throwing the ball back and forth one evening, he said, "Denji, I have to go out of town for a few months and I'll need you to be the man of the house while I am away. Listen to you mother and don't give her a hard time. You don't want me to find out that you misbehaved. Capiche?"

I nodded in obedience and agreed, "Capiche."

"After a week, your mom will leave so she can join me. We'll be gone for a few months and then you'll be staying with the Cantwells, okay?"

I knew the drill. Once a year, they would leave to some secret place. The rumor was that this time they were going to spend time with a man named Sammy Dasho. With the financial and spiritual support of the church, Sammy was in hiding in Canada with his children whose mother had been legally awarded custody of them after she called the church a cult on national TV news. The secret of the church, which everyone in the church knew, was that these missions were to help financial donors remain outside the grasp of the law by providing them with cash, rental homes in other people's names, and companionship.

One time when a family went to assist, they returned with Richard Church, known as Jim Walh who they were supposed to be helping.[16] He was wanted for murdering Raymond and Ruth Ann Ritter and brutally beating his girlfriend and her 10-year-old son. Instead of turning him over to law enforcement, he lived on The Ridge with us because he was now saved after saying the sinner's prayer. Some kids said their parents told them to stay away from him. Mine did not.

On a few occasions, I saw Jim walking alone to and from the cafeteria to church services. I walked with him and thought he was a funny guy. He always had his hair combed in a stylish manner and he wore new clothes, something most of the church brothers could not afford. Whenever we walked by a sister, he would look her up and down and say something quietly to himself. Overall, I thought he was a cool guy and I wanted to be like him. I did not know for certain that he was a murderer. Even if I knew he was a murderer, as long as he said the Sinners Prayer, I would have considered him saved from his sins.

Dad Miguel and I walked inside, and I heard Nicole ask, "Mommy, you and Dad will be gone for longer days?"

"Yes, snookums, we'll be gone for longer days, but it won't be for another week before I leave."

Nicole began to pout and cry, so Mom handed me little Miguel, who was born the year before. She coddled and cuddled Nicole while reassuring her, "Think of it like a sleepover. You'll get to sleep over at all your friends' homes, and you'll get to stay up late and eat ice cream. Remember, you're a princess. We are related to King Tut, Ethan Allen, and Michael Landon. And princesses don't cry."

"Will you be back in time for school to start?"

---

16. https://www.tonyalamonews.com/563/tony-alamo-harbors-muderers-within-the-confines-of-his-cult.php

"Yes, and if you don't cry, I'll make sure to buy your favorite Trapper Keeper and the coolest school supplies."

"Do you mean like a Barbie Trapper Keeper, heart-shaped erasers, and pencils?"

"Yes," she said, kissing her.

My jealous thoughts started again. Why does she get new stuff? What about me? My shoes have holes in them. So do all the knees on my pants. I have not received a new shirt in years. All my stuff is whatever Dad does not want any more. As I ruminated on these differences, rage built up until I could not watch the coddling anymore. I ran off into the forest without permission, following a well-worn trail a few boys and I knew well.

Deep in the forest was a bird hunter who I nearly knocked over as I ran by. His double-barrel shotgun, which was pointing at the ground before I startled him, was now pointed toward me in the commotion. I noticed his binoculars and I wondered if he was spying on our church.

"Ya best rin off bou," he said in a twang I had never heard before, using his rifle to point the way he thought I should go. It was back to the Nine-Plex.

During the same summer, the boys judged to be the best behaved in the church, ranging in age from ten to fourteen, were permitted to take a road trip. There were ten of us. We spent a few nights at the Black Canyon exploring its edges and depths before going to Mount Saint Helens. It had exploded six years before, but on this day a gray, wet cloud hovered inside of it. From there we drove to the Grand Canyon.

I climbed one of the pine trees on the south side of the Grand Canyon, and when I placed my face near the bark, I realized it smelled like vanilla. A white-tailed squirrel, a few branches above me, nervously flicked its tail, causing some loose bark to fall into my eyes. I quickly slid down the tree chafing my arms, stomach, and legs.

The next morning, we boys challenged each other to see who could catch the largest fish before noon. In a clear pool, a large trout evaded all our lures. Finally, I dangled a pink and orange jig in front of it, which it gulped down without delay, and I pulled it in. The thrill of victory was short lived though.

Upon returning to our campsite, the two adults in charge of the trip, Mr. Koole, who was Zeph's dad and was a tall, chain-smoking cowboy type, and Abner, Lonny's dad, met us at the entrance to the campsite near our vans. Abner was a round man, six foot six inches tall, and hairy all over, except for his head, and he stood ominously in our way.

While wringing his hands, he breathed heavily as he paced back and forth. "We called you here for two reasons," he said, with his New York accent. "Now, the most urgent thing is we don't have enough money to get back home to Arkansas."

Although it wasn't a common event for field trips to run out of gas or money, it was known to happen. On one occasion, several vans full of children visited the gallows of "Hanging Judge" Parker. Someone forgot to check one of the van's fuel levels causing it to be stranded until Papa Tony approved the twenty dollars necessary for fuel to get back home. Someone had to drive the twenty dollars and a gallon of fuel to the gallows.

I knew of other events where brothers had to walk long distances after their vehicles broke down or ran out of fuel. Brothers once had to sleep in the woods where they were treed by a bear. It wasn't until sunrise that the bear sauntered off. It wasn't that they hadn't planned the trip properly, but rather they were afraid to ask Papa Tony for more money when other legitimate expenses like housing, food, or women's feminine products were needed.

This was different. There was no one to run money and fuel out to us. Instead, Papa Tony rebuked the brothers who arranged the trip and accused them of using the budgeted money to buy cigarettes. We were on our own and had to make do with what he had at hand.

"The second reason is that one of you numbskulls threw their chewing gum out of the window while we were driving. Now there's gum stuck to the side of the van."

He pointed at streaks of different colored gum stuck to the side of the van.

"Which one of you geniuses did this?"

None of us responded. It was quite likely we all, at one point, had thrown our gum out the window during the three-to-four-day cross-country drive.

"Which one of you little punks did this?" Abner repeated impatiently, punching his fists into his hand, reminding me of his testimony when he said he used to tie up prostitutes in his basement and cut their tongues out to prevent them from screaming. He paced back and forth in front of us, punching his fist into the palm of his other hand as he passed by each boy.

My nose began to bleed. I held my head forward causing blood to drip down my hand.

Abner stopped in front of me and smacked me on the top of my head.

"What's your problem? You have something to tell me?"

"No," I answered, attempting to hold my nose back a bit while applying pressure.

"If you think your silence will prevent me from knowing which one of you knuckleheads did this, you're dead wrong," Abner said. "I'll whip each one of you until I get someone to admit it."

He walked to his tent and pulled out a two-inch wide black leather belt. He folded it in two and smacked the leather sides together. We all fidgeted, afraid to look up.

"Who's up first? No, wait. You know what? Everyone turn around and put your hands on the van. Hands on the van! Now!"

We never snitched on each other unless we knew there was overwhelming evidence to prove the accusation. If there was no evidence, or only very little, we protected each other. If we didn't, we would be ostracized by the other kids in the group with whom we were hoping to remain close.

I was surprised to find myself amid the boys who were getting beaten. One at a time, Abner whipped each of us boys on our legs and buttocks until we fell to our knees. If one of us fell too quickly, feigning pain, he continued whipping until he thought that boy had had enough. Laughing and calling us names, he kicked dirt and small pebbles on us as we fell.

"Faggot! Baby! Worthless! Weak! Swine!" Once he got to one of the African American boys he said, "N******s."

It wasn't the first time I had heard someone being called that. I had heard Papa Tony use it on an African American member of the church. I remember seeing Papa Tony beat a boy named Tyrone and made him kneel like a dog while Papa Tony sat comfortably with his feet propped up on Tyrone's back.

"Bark like a dog, n****r! Bark!" he said, while dropping the heel of his boot into Tyrone's back. Tyrone was only 10 or 11 years old at the time. I was only nine years old and did not recognize this as racism, but by the way the adults, who were in the room, were acting I knew that something was amiss.

When I heard the word again, I turned around and stared at Abner trying to channel the energy from the room where Tyrone was being abused. When he got to me, he saw the glare in my eyes. Grabbing my shoulder, he pinned me against the van and struck my legs with the belt until I feigned pain, yelling before I collapsed. It really didn't hurt very much. I had been smacked harder by a fish's tail after it was caught and tried to get away. If my Dad Dad or Papa Tony had been around, Abner would never have done this.

This was a once-in-a-lifetime opportunity for him to beat me.

Finally, Mr. Koole intervened.

"Abner, that's enough. Boys, get up and listen up!" he told us.

"We don't have money for food nor enough gas to get back home. The ones that know how to fish, keep fishing. Whatever you catch is what we eat tonight. The rest of you, comb through campsite garbage cans and collect every soda pop can and glass bottle you see. Go tent to tent, RV to RV, and ask the neighbors if you can have their empty bottles and cans. We will recycle them and hopefully get enough cash to get back home, so don't come back until you each have twenty dollars' worth."

"The rest of you, don't come back until you have enough fish for all of us to eat for dinner. And Benji, I want you back here in an hour. Don't make me come looking for you!" Abner said.

The other boys and I walked back to the stream. I didn't dare look back toward Will and Abner. When we were out of sight of the adults, the other boys surrounded me, laying their hands on my head and shoulders in jest. We were taught that demons, diseases, and sickness could be cast out of people if we laid our hands on them while we prayed. I had prayed over friends, but my prayers never healed them. My friends were not serious about healing my bloody nose or the more worrisome problem of why Abner wanted to see me. They were going to have fun at my expense.

On cue, Nimrod started praying, "God in heaven, please cast the demon out of this boy."

I emphatically told them, "I don't have a demon in me!" but the joking continued.

Nimrod's hand clenched my shoulder tighter the louder he spoke, "Don't make me lash you with this fishing pole. Jesus, you said to lay hands upon the sick and they would be healed. We demand that you heal this poor soul."

Louden chimed in, "Yes, this lost soul clearly is possessed."

"Ah, yes," Augustus Aims resumed with a smile on his face, "God, please reach down into Benji's body and yank his soul out of his body and wash the evil out with the blood of the lamb then rinse it really good."

The boys erupted in laughter and I broke free of their grasp.

"He won't spank me anymore. He already spanked me. He probably just wants to make sure my nose isn't bleeding. That's all."

The other boys looked at me with pity. Augustus Aims said, "Oh, you're going back and he's going to give it to you really good now."

When I returned to the campsite an hour later, my heart sank as I heard Abner call my name from his tent. "Benji! Get over here! Quick!"

I pushed open the tent's door flap and saw Abner lying down with his head propped up using his right hand and elbow. He was shirtless, revealing a huge, hairy belly. The lower portion of his body was covered by a blanket. He patted the pillow next to him.

Nervously, I stood at the entryway. It was unusual for an adult to invite one of us into their private living area while their shirt was off and no other adults around.

"Come in here, come on now. Come over here and lay down. I need to see how badly I spanked you. I hope I didn't hurt you too much."

I just stared at him, not moving from the front of the tent.

"Benji, get in here right now! Don't make me get up!" he ordered.

I climbed in, walking on my knees because the tent was not tall enough for me to stand.

"That's right. Come on over here and let's look."

"Good. Now lay down."

I lay down on my stomach, trying to avoid any physical contact with him.

Abner suddenly pulled my shorts and underwear down, looking at my butt and legs.

"There are no marks on my butt," I said. "You hit me on my legs and back, not on my butt."

I pulled up my shorts and stood up to show him my legs.

"What are those marks?" Abner asked, pointing to the chafe marks on the inside of my legs.

"I was climbing a tree and slid down."

Mr. Koole, having heard the conversation, rushed over and opened the tent's front flap. At that moment, I was kneeling in front of Abner whose head was near my crotch.

"Benji, come here right now," Mr. Koole said in gruff voice. "Get out of here."

Mr. Koole held open the tent and pulled me out.

Abner lay back, smirking as I left.

Outside, I watched Mr. Koole enter the tent. I continued watching the outside of the tent as I watched what must have been punches and kicks to Abner's face and groin. I heard the cries of "Ow!" and "Oh!" coming from Abner.

"You sick bastard! He's just a kid! If Risha was here, he would kill you!" I heard Mr. Koole yell.

"Nothing happened. I never touched him. I just looked at him," Abner laughingly countered. "I was just checking him to make sure he wasn't bruised too much."

Mr. Koole climbed out of the tent and knelt next to me.

"Look at me. I need you to tell me what happened."

I retold the events as they happened.

"Did he touch you? Did he make you touch him?"

"No. He just pulled down my pants and underwear to look at my butt while he was lying down. I showed him my legs. But he did not touch them either. He just looked."

"You're sure he did not touch you?"

"Yes."

"Okay. Go back to the stream and catch us some dinner. Hurry up."

That night we boys caught a few more trout and collected fifty dollars' worth of cans. That was a lot of money for us.

Even when we did have money, there was no store on The Ridge. The few times we had money we were not allowed to spend it by ourselves. We were permitted to go inside Walmart or a thrift store when we went out to recruit or pass out tracts, but we always had to go with several adults, who watched us closely and approved our purchases. Normally, our purchases were small things like candy, fishing lures, or patches for bicycle tubes. Papa Tony once gave all the kids who did not have more than ten demerits one hundred dollars each. It was around the time when Reebok Pumps and Nike Airs came out and I bought a pair of Reebok pumps. Other boys bought Nikes and the girls bought small makeup kits. But that never happened again.

After we arrived back on The Ridge, Mr. Koole gave out awards to the children who collected the most cans and caught the biggest fish. I, being the latter, had the option of a new fishing pole or a gift card to Walmart. I chose the fishing pole.

When I got home, I walked into the kitchen as proud as I could be, having won one of the prizes. I leaned my reward against the counter and poured a glass of water.

"Where did you get that?" Mom Nancy asked, eyeing the new fishing pole.

"I won it by catching the biggest fish. I got to choose between this and a Walmart gift card. But who needs a gift card when I got a brand-new fishing pole?"

"So, let me see if I understand this. You had the choice between this pole and getting your sister a gift, and you chose this?"

Get Nicole a gift? Why would I do that? I earned this. I got whipped for this.

"Umm …"

"You selfishly chose yourself over your little sister. You could have got her any number of things, but instead you thought only of yourself."

I am unkind. I am selfish. I only thought of myself. How could I do that? I only did what made me happy. I am a bad person.

"I can take it back and get her something. I'll do that. I'll get her something," I said rapidly, but also pleading to make it right.

"You know what? I don't want to hear what you're going to do now. It's too late. You showed your true nature. You only think of yourself. I want you to think about that for a while. You're not getting dessert for a long time, not until I think you've learned your lesson."

I stood there looking between my prized fishing pole and Mom. I wished my Dad Dad was there so I could tell him about the trip, about the prize I won, about Abner, and about how much I liked the Grand Canyon. Most of all, I wanted to have him tell her that I wasn't being selfish, at least not in a bad way. I was just a boy who was excited about getting a fishing pole.

# CHAPTER NINE

### Young Love

On the last day of school in June 1987, I was part of a select group of children who got to make sock puppets and marionettes with discarded clothing. The prerequisites to participate were that we had to be current on our prayer hours and volunteer to pass out tracts during the summer. We also had to make and deliver ten food boxes each for the larger families in the church.

The boxes were made up after the evening church service which ended at 9:00 PM. From 9:00 PM to 2:00 AM, we made and delivered the boxes. The boxes had basic food staples like rice, beans, dried potato mix, oatmeal, vegetable oil, salt and pepper. Around Thanksgiving and Christmas time the boxes had a frozen turkey added to them. These families typically had little or no food at home, so these boxes were truly a godsend.

The corner classroom where we were making puppets had several long, cloth-covered desks with individual piles of socks, markers, and cotton stuffing on them. I saw a seat next to Emmanuala and took it. My first kiss was with Chandra. I was infatuated with Amanda. I loved Angela, but I desired Emmanuala. She was cute, athletic, and quick-witted and reminded me of Mary Lou Retton, the Olympic Athlete.

She smiled at me and scooted her chair closer to mine when I sat down. Our bare legs, concealed under the table, touched while we played footsies. I sat upright and spoke as normal as possible to hide the pleasure I was feeling.

"Are you going to the sleepover and pool party tonight?" she asked.

The sleepover groups were arranged by age and gender.

"If the Pope poops in the woods does it make a sound?" I replied. She shot me a look of confusion.

"Where is your group staying?" I asked.

"We'll be at the Will's house," she answered.

"We're in the nursery and Abner is watching us."

The nursery and the Will's house were a quarter mile apart. There were several security lights between the two locations. Rover would be on the lookout to ensure no one was out after hours. Her voice pulled me back into the conversation.

"I'll be sleeping near the window facing the pool. Come say 'Hi' when everyone is asleep."

"I'll find you."

The older boys and I slept in the old nursery while the younger group of boys slept in the new nursery, which were adjacent to each other. With Abner asleep and snoring in the new nursery, I tiptoed passed him. Augustus Aims was in on the plan along with a few of the other older boys. The strategy was to distract Abner if he woke up. I was only supposed to be gone for thirty minutes. Upon my return, I would do the same for him, so they could run off to see their girls. On the way there, I ran under cover of as many shadows as possible and tiptoed to Emmanuala's window.

"Emmanuala, Emmanuala!"

She opened the window and and I could see her soft tanned skin, lit by the glow of the full moon.

"I can't believe you're here. If you get caught, you'll get in so much trouble!" she whispered back.

"You told me to come," I said. "Come on. Let's go to the pool."

"No way. If I get caught with you that will be the end of my life," she whispered, chuckling underneath her breath.

"Come on. The lights are off at the pool. No one will see us. We'll be quiet."

"No way."

She wore a thin T-shirt which I pushed aside to reveal her bare shoulder so that I could caress it.

"No one will see us. It's so hot. Don't you want to cool down?" I asked, as she watched my hand caressing her shoulder.

She smiled and turned to look around the room at the other girls sleeping. A few faked sleeping, waiting for their boyfriends to show up.

"You're so bad, Benji," she said, as she climbed through the window and jumped to the ground.

The rush I felt from knowing that I could get caught, combined with feeling my entire body aroused by Emmanuala's presence, overrode any of my remaining sensibilities. The worst that could happen was two kids would see us, report us, and then I would lie. If Emmanuala lied also, then neither of us would get in trouble. Plus, I had already broken the rules with the Holler sisters and a few other girls and nothing bad happened to me. God hadn't done anything to me.

We held each other close in the shallow end of the pool, quietly kissing. We were careful not to splash, but there was plenty of friction. We grinded against each other with our shorts and underwear on. It came to an end with an explosion between my legs. Not knowing what just happened, we looked at each other, laughing.

"What was that?" she asked.

"Sex, I think. I think we just had sex," I answered.

"Are you sure?" she asked.

I certainly was not sure. The mechanics of sex had never been explained to me, so my understanding of it was limited. Papa Tony said sex should be for reproduction only. The more salacious parts of the Old Testament, like Song of Solomon, spoke of desire in simple words and passages. Solomon was the wisest man on earth and had a thousand wives, and Papa Tony referenced Jesus' mother being a young virgin no older than 12 or 13, my age, when she became pregnant with Jesus, but he seemed to praise these concepts more than explain them. There were occasional moans I heard late at night from my mom and dad's bedroom and a scattering of jokes I overheard the OCs tell each other. My understanding of sex was close to nil, made more confusing by lack of reliable explanation or teaching from a trusted source.

Nevertheless, I looked at her and said, "Yes."

A few weeks later several of us were loaded on a van to go work at the designer jean jacket factory, which produced thousands of Alamo Designs rhinestone jackets. The factory was now in the place of our former restaurant where Bill and Hilary Clinton once dined as they listened to Dolly Parton. Our labor was obscured from the outside world by boarded-up windows which let in no natural light. Instead, we worked by bright florescent lights, accompanied by the sound of humming sewing machines, operated twenty-four hours a day by the children older than ten years old and who were trained by adults who worked in rotating shifts. We had no clocks to refer to in order to know how much longer we had remaining in our shift. Papa Tony's sermons played consistently.

Though we returned exhausted from our factory shifts, on the ride to the factory we boys were alert and excited to be near the girls. At this age, the older kids were coupling. Each girl would sit in the seat in front of the boy she liked and allow the boy to fondle her from the seat behind.

Emmanuala's breasts were perky, full, and merely a seat in front of me. She moved closer to my hand and lifted her arm, creating an opening for my hand on top of her shirt, which she then lifted so I could feel her bare skin. She put her jacket across the front of her shoulders to hide my hand. I didn't fear being caught by the adult in the front of the bus because I knew how to do this without being caught. However, I did fear being tattled on by younger girls and the others who weren't paired off.

As soon as the bus pulled into the factory parking lot, the girls smacked our hands away, straightened their shirts and stood up, almost in unison. I stood up too soon. There was a full-on pitched tent in my denim jeans. I tried lowering my shirt over it and turning to my side. Just then I noticed the female supervisor looking at me.

"Benji, is everything okay?"

My heart was beating fast, wondering if she could see the bulge in my jeans.

"Yes, everything is okay. Why do you ask?" I looked down and away, nowhere in the direction of my jeans.

"I saw you. You can be honest with me," she said. A few smaller children squeezed past us.

I gulped.

"I saw you itching. Down there?" she asked, with pursed lips, raised eyebrows, and quickly glancing at my erection. It didn't help that I spotted the King James Bible visibly sticking out of her purse.

"Do you have a rash down there?" she persisted.

And finally, thankfully, my erection was gone.

"No. No rash. I just had to move it around, it's a bumpy ride," I answered, moving beyond her.

The factory building was divided into two main areas. The lower half was full of sewing machines. The upper half of the building was where most of the children worked. It began with an assembly line of smaller children, aged seven to nine, who were the Swarovski rhinestone setters.

The settings were round metal with sharp, four- and five-pointed spikes, of different diameters all under an eighth of an inch, which held glass and acrylic rhinestone crystals. Although this was basically a labor camp, we did the work happily with the belief that the work we did was going to help save the world. We were told the money earned as a result, which was millions and millions of dollars, was used to spread the gospel of Jesus Christ.

The cool rooms of the factory were where the jackets were airbrushed, painted, and embroidered. Music played from the radio, not sermons and bible verses like elsewhere in the factory. Contemporary music, the type I loved playing on my Walkman, permeated the area. The workers in that part of the factory wore shirts they had designed and painted themselves. Many sported mohawk-style haircuts and it wasn't unusual to see paint residue in their hair. They were artists and free spirits. The people in the cool rooms created the most important, money-making aspects of the jackets. Papa Tony didn't condone their mohawks and radio music, but he didn't preach against it either. This implicit acceptance was enough for them to know they could break the codes of the foundation in exchange for creating masterpieces that made us millions of dollars.

I carried a pile of stone-washed jackets to the airbrush room and peeked inside. Silk-screen crews painted skylines of cities like New York, Los Angeles, and Hollywood on jackets.

I took my place among the rhinestone crimpers, the last step in the denim jean jacket manufacturing process. My work group was made up of experienced adults and teenagers. Carefully, we pressed the set stones with a rhinestone pressing machine. I heard a child crying in the next room, having accidentally pricked his fingers. It was a common occurrence. The art of placing the rhinestones in the sharp settings on particle board rectangles, in columns and rows of fifty by fifty with no spaces between, was often learned through a hard process of repeated punctures and blood.

After a few hours, I felt myself getting bored and my mind wandered to the faint radio music I could hear escaping the closed rooms nearby. I left my workstation to go check out the airbrush room. When I got to the door of the room, a boy named Kiona stood in front of it. He was four years older than me and a foot and half taller. He looked like a basketball player but with the broad shoulders of a football lineman. Plus, his mother Diana had just married Papa Tony.

"Where do you think you are going, little man?" Kiona asked, with an emphasis on "little."

"I'm Benji. I'm going in there."

Kiona raised his eyebrows and looked me up and down.

"So, you're Benji. I've heard a lot of things about you," he said. "But the last time I checked; I oversee who works in the airbrush room. My dad put me in charge."

"Your dad is also my dad, so let me in. Papa Tony said I could airbrush."

"He's not your dad anymore," Kiona said curtly. "He's my dad. My mom married him so that makes him my dad. And you're not getting in here."

Normally I would have wrestled or punched anyone who challenged me, but Kiona's size was overwhelming. Besides, what he had just said hit me harder than any punch he could have ever landed. I walked away, feeling fearful that Papa Tony had told this to Kiona, and that I would find out it was true during one of his sermons. I ruminated over this possibility and the consequences it would have on my popularity, on me being protected, and on my ability to get away with doing things I knew I shouldn't. On the bus ride home, I felt so deflated that I didn't even have enough energy to try to touch Emmanuala's breasts.

I had not been asleep for more than a few hours before I was awakened abruptly by my dad. "Benji, Benji, Rover is here. Papa Tony wants to talk with you." I rolled away acting like I was still asleep.

"Benji, if you don't get up, I will have to pick you up." That got my attention and I sat up, rubbed my eyes, and reluctantly agreed, "Okay, I'm up. Let's go."

I slipped on the slippers at the foot of my bed and a brother, who had been sent to summon me and make sure I went, gently nudged me toward the front door in the quiet, dark house, like a guard escorting a prisoner. Brothers didn't typically enter a home to take us kids to the Spec House, which made this time quite frightening.

As I walked toward the front door, Nicole, Mom, and Dad stood silently as I passed them. Little Miguel was sleeping. Even though I didn't know why I was being called to the Spec House, I resentfully thought about how Nicole was too good to ever be in trouble and that Papa Tony surely liked her. Maybe what Kiona had said was true after all, and I was no longer his favored one.

I did my best to push that concern away and told myself it would be like the other times. Papa Tony would ask me a few questions using the speaker phone then I'd go back home. No punishment for me. Someone else might get spanked, but not me. Besides, I had been extra good lately. No arguing, no fighting, no talking back to my elders.

My mind drifted back to trying to figure out why Papa Tony had summoned me. He had closed the bucks line down a long time ago and I hadn't gotten any bucks for months, but I hadn't complained to anyone. But I was feeling angry because I couldn't buy my family Christmas presents. What if God told him that?

After starting the car's engine, the brother turned the heater on full blast and looked back at me and said, "I hope this helps a little bit. Anyway, I've made about thirty other visits tonight to different houses rounding up your friends and their families. What I can tell you is that all your friends and their families are at the Spec House right now. You are the last one I needed to get."

I was unprepared to hear that. All my friends at the Spec House? This can't be good. If their families are there, then something major is going on. My family never showed up at the Spec House when I was called there. I assumed it was because Papa Tony was my family. Plus, I was rarely in trouble like the rest of the kids. I guess tonight they had to stay with Nicole and baby Miguel, but I wish someone was with me.

When I walked in, Lonny pointedly asked me, "Why aren't your mom and dad with you? Don't they care enough to be here with you like the rest of us?"

"They care about me. They had to watch Nicole and Miguel."

Once at the Spec House, memories flooded me. I walked past the area where I remembered being naked, as a child, playing with my train on the leopard skin near the fireplace. Upstairs was where Grandma Susie gave me ice cream before bedtime and Papa Tony taught me about his plants. This was where I lived like a prince. Now here I was, being summoned just like the rest of the people.

The leather furniture, ottoman, and TV projectors I remembered were gone and in their place were fluorescent lights and worn orange carpet. The antiques had been replaced with items from Walmart. The paintings that had once hung in French palaces were now gone. I was home, but I wasn't.

In the middle of the room was a flagpole displaying the Israeli flag. The flag, which once was a partial symbol of my special mission, seemed to now hang limply. We also used to fly it in front of the main office, near our play field, the chapel, and the cafeteria. It now looked dusty and ignored. Papa Tony's most recent sermons were about the 144,000 Jews that would be saved in the last days. We were taught to remain prepared to flee to the mountains. I kept my fishing pole, fishing gear, and bow and arrows at the ready for when the end of the world came.

We were escorted to the basement where a beige metal desk with a solitary phone on its surface stood in the center of the room. Otherwise, the room was empty of furniture. The walls were covered in wall-to-ceiling mirrors causing each person to see themselves and each other at various angles.

Audio-video recording equipment was stored in a back room which had a long, dark-tinted glass one-way window which looked into the room where we all waited. Ever since Papa Tony had married Birgitta, he used a speaker phone to take reports, so we no longer saw him, only heard him. I knew all too well the significance of the phone that sat on the desk. It was now how every report was given and every punishment was doled out by Papa Tony.

My peers and I sat along the edges of the room with our backs supported by the mirror-lined walls. There had to have been more than sixty people in the room. Some parents tightly held their frightened children as if it was the last time they would see them. The kids' weary eyes held the appearance of having shed many recent tears. I had never seen so many children on report at one time and didn't understand why they looked so sad. Did someone die? That's it. Someone died.

Five of the biggest and toughest men in the church stood in the middle of the room. Harry Sand, who in his testimony had said he was a former cat burglar and a hired hand for the Mob, held the board of education. I had stayed overnight at the Sand's house a few times in the past and remembered seeing the barber's leather strap hung up in his bedroom. He did not have any children of his own, but he was married to a woman who had a girl, Helen, one year older than me, and a boy, Dennis, a few years younger. Helen often missed school and when she showed up, she would have black eyes which she tried to keep hidden by sunglasses. She often sat alone, motionless, as if moving hurt her. In the summer, I saw welts on her legs from being whipped with the strap. I asked her about it, and she told me they were not from Harry, but from her mom. Dennis often had marks on his back and legs and once told me, while showing me the strap, "My dad calls that 'Executor.'"

Try as I might, waiting in that room that night, I could not conjure the scenario that made this night possible. The worst child beaters were all in the same room with all of us children. I was frightened, but still confident that Papa Tony would never hurt me. When my name was called, I got right next to the phone and could hear him breathing heavily on the other end of the line.

"Hi, this is Benji."

"Oh, okay. Finally, it's you, Benji," he said, saying my name like 'Bey-n-gee.' "We've been waiting for you and I don't wait for anyone, not even you." Papa Tony's voice was slow and deliberate with a hint of sarcasm and disappointment.

"How old are you Benji? You've got to be twelve or thirteen years old now. I raised you as my own. You would not lie to me, would you? You won't disappoint me, will you?" he asked, with a lilt in his voice.

"No, Papa Tony. I will not lie to you. I'm thirteen years old now."

"Do you see all of the children in the room? Do you know why they are here, and why you are here?"

"No, I mean, yes, I see them. I don't know why they are all here, though."

"Your school mate Susie-Ann told me that she saw you and the rest of the children holding hands, kissing, and touching each other. You know that's against the rules and more importantly it's against God's commandments. Have you seen any of this happening?"

Why would she do that? I thought she was my friend. What was her problem? No one will talk to her for a year after this. She'll be an outcast like Belvin. Belvin was a boy who ran away after he was beaten. The deputy sheriffs found him and returned him to the church despite the many bruises he had on his body. After he returned, no one talked to him. He was locked up in a house no one could enter, but nobody wanted to anyway.

Papa Tony had shattered the kid code. I wondered, was Susie-Ann his only confidant? How was I going to get out of this?

"Don't lie to me. You know God will tell me the truth. Did you touch any girls?" Papa Tony insistently asked. His voice seemed deeper than usual, almost foreign to me.

The thoughts in my head swirled frantically.

"Did you touch any girl? I'm waiting and I told you I don't wait for anyone!" Papa Tony angrily repeated.

By now, I was feeling lightheaded. I tried weighing the impact of any answer I gave to the questions and considered their ramifications. All the other kids had already been here being questioned for hours. What had they already told him? Did he know about the touching on the buses? Or that I touched Brea Ann during movie night? Had someone seen Emmanuala and me in the pool?

"No, I did not touch any girls," I said assertively, calculating my risk. "Once on the bus, I accidentally fell into Emmanuala and touched her breast. It wasn't on purpose. I never saw anyone else touching each other either."

I lied and hoped others did as well. I saw Emmanuala look at me with disgust while I took a deep breath waiting for Papa Tony's response. The pulse in my head was throbbing and I thought for sure he could hear it, so I took a step back, away from the open phone line.

"That's not what Susie-Ann and Miranda said. You're not lying to me, are you Benji?" Papa Tony asked. "Miranda, come up to the phone," he ordered, without even giving me time to respond.

Miranda? Oh, no. I already knew she had it in for me.

"I'm here, Papa Tony."

"Tell me what you saw Benji doing."

She looked at me sternly as she turned back toward the speakerphone. "During our rides to and from the factory he put his hands between the seats and touched Emmanuala's breasts."

Time froze and my mind suspended all semblance of thought in that moment. I knew I was a goner.

"Emmanuala, come up to the phone," Papa Tony ordered.

She got up, walked to the phone, and looked at me as she rolled her eyes and shook her head in dislike of me. "I'm here."

"Did Benji touch you?"

"Yes, but it was an accident. When the bus driver hit the brakes too fast, his hand slipped between the seats."

Another pause which felt like forever.

"Benji, you will receive twenty swats for that."

Without thinking, I blurted out, forgetting the caution I normally spoke with when on report, "I didn't do anything! Why would you punish me?"

Another long pause.

"Okay, God has spoken to me and said to give you only ten swats." Normally, if another kid challenged Papa Tony the swats would be increased so I felt lucky that they were decreased for me.

I saw John Kolbeck, known as Papa Tony's enforcer, in the corner, take the white notepad out of his back pocket and write something down with a carpenter's pencil.[17] Years later he would go on the run and be one of the FBI's most wanted fugitives for beating several small children.

Papa Tony continued, "Miranda, what did you see Karen do?"

---

17. https://www.tonyalamonews.com/717/111708-fbi-issued-a-warrant-charging-enforcer-kolbeck-with-unlawful-flight-to-avoid-prosecution.php

"Oh, Papa Tony, Karen did the most. She kissed two boys behind the sewing room," she replied while staring at Karen with a half-smile. She got closer to the speakerphone and turned to it as if she was sharing her soul.

"Another time, she played house with three boys and she played the mom and they were her husbands. My cousin told me she saw her letting multiple boys touch her on the bus different days of the week."

"Karen, what do you have to say for yourself?" Papa Tony demanded.

Karen jumped up and briskly walked to the speakerphone. She turned around and looked at her dad whose eyes were focused intently on her. She stood tall, then bent over at the waste to address the speakerphone.

"I did kiss them. I did all of those things," she confessed.

"Who did you kiss?" Papa Tony asked quickly.

She named the boys.

"Who did you play doctor with?"

She named the boys again.

"85 swats for you. God has told me to give you 85 swats. And Miranda you get ten for not telling me sooner."

A gasp went through the room. No one in the history of the church had ever received that many. Karen was a good kid. She was well loved. She was polite to the adults. She was funny. She was happy and beautiful. All the children liked her. No one expected any child to be sentenced to anything more than forty swats. 85 sounded like a death sentence.

During the previous four hours, we were yelled at, accused, and made to feel embarrassed. Parents were told their children were evil, and they too had sinned for allowing unholy desires to take hold in their children. Papa Tony vowed to drive the devil from us children and everyone in the room was powerless to stop it. Some of the mothers held their hands over their mouths as tears streamed down their faces. Children looked up at their parents in disbelief, but Harry and Anna-Sue Sand, Louden Sarrgis, and Ragner Flashmigen smiled. I could not believe my ears. Guilt washed over me now for lying and anger exited each pore of my body.

Papa Tony called Kolbeck to the speakerphone.

"Read the list," he ordered.

"Dorry, thirty. Joyce, twenty. Lonny, ten. Jaxon, forty. Terry, forty. Sharon, thirty. Leah, ten. Layla, forty. Allen, thirty. Tina, thirty. Josiah, twenty. Gary, ten. Leon, forty. Cassandra, twenty. José, forty. Erin, forty. Jeanie, thirty. Jessica, forty. Rita, thirty. Thalia, thirty. Benji, ten. Karen, eighty-five. And Miranda, ten. "

"Start with the girls then do the boys, but spank Karen with the boys. Anna-Sue, you do the girls. Harry, you do the boys. Call me when it's done. Oh, use the board of education on the boys. School is in session. It's time to teach these little weasels who's in charge!"

"Yes, sir," Harry Sand responded.

Joyce got up and ran from the room. Her father ran after her, pulling her back. Two men grabbed her by the arms while two brothers grabbed her by the legs, causing her to fall on her face. Without showing any mercy, they suspended her in the air and walked very close to me in front of the one-way glass. Harry removed his leather belt from his waistband and handed it to his wife, Anna-Sue. She swung the belt like an experienced taskmaster, swiftly, with precise timing so that it snapped onto the girl's buttocks.

Joyce screamed even before the first lash hit her.

Beatings were a regular event for all of us children but being suspended in the air was not. Seeing Joyce suspended in the air like that was unbelievable. Her helplessness in that moment, caused by her total lack of control over her own body, woke something up in me. I could feel the havoc about to be wreaked on her, a small girl, and I began to boil inside.

It was as if a light switch was turned on inside of me and it shone a light on this evil event. With most of the other beatings we could wiggle or move around to make the paddle hit different areas. If our legs were not held down, which was rare that they would be, we could pull our legs up to our butt blocking the paddles for a second of relief. Albeit limited, we had some control over our bodies during the other beatings but being suspended in the air removed all control from us and created a sense of complete helplessness.

"One," Anna-Sue said, delivering the first blow, "two."

Joyce screamed again.

I closed my eyes and put my hands over my ears, to block out the horror of her screams, but it didn't work. Seeing my friend suspended in the air was horrific. Rage and hatred coursed through me. *I won't cry. I won't let them see me cry. I will not break. How dare they hurt my friend!*

"Three, four," ... more screaming ... "five, six."

"No! You hit my back!"

"Then quit squirming!" Anna-Sue ordered.

"Seven ...."

At twenty, I lifted my head to look up at Joyce. Her body was limp. She had either given up or she had passed out from the pain. The four men unceremoniously laid her on the carpet next to her dad for him to take her home.

"Lonny, it's your turn," Anna-Sue ordered next.

"Not my daughter!" Lonny's mom said. "We're leaving. This is child abuse! Lonny, put your jacket on and let's go."

Lonny's mom was respected in the group so when Lonny ran out of the room no one even attempted to stop her. Her mother pulled a set of keys from her jacket and jingled them in front of Anna-Sue and Harry as she departed to follow her daughter. The other parents looked up from staring at their own children. They looked at Anna-Sue and Harry and each other in anticipation, but Harry just furrowed his brow and continued, turning to Kolbeck.

"Who's next?"

"Sharon," Kolbeck replied.

One by one, each girl was called up and cruelly suspended either in the air or over a chair and whipped in front of her parents and friends. Some of the girls were bloody when it was done because the belt had cut into their soft skin. Some even appeared to be unconscious, but others continued screaming even after the beating had concluded, as if something had gone off inside of them which could not be quieted.

When the beating of the girls was over, Harry Sand began warming up for the boys' round by circling his shoulders forward and his neck side to side. He did calf raises by standing on his tiptoes a few times. It was as if he was preparing to run a race, but the race was not with his feet. He twirled the paddle in his hand, appearing to relish the moment.

Boy after boy was suspended while the men came down brutally with the paddle on their butts, backs, and legs. The sound of the paddle was only slightly less horrific than their screams. None of us could stop it from happening, and I was next. My own pain was coming.

When it was my turn, I was determined to not cry. I tightened my buttocks in preparation for each strike of the paddle. At this point, my hatred for the men who beat me and for the friends who had told on me was stronger than the stinging pain of the physical punishment.

There were nearly 20 adults in the room at the time. None of them reported this abuse to the authorities because they did not believe it was abuse. To most of them it was the Word of God being meted out. Like the children, the adults had been exposed to a slow increase in abuse and abusive orders over the years that they executed at the command of Papa Tony, the mouthpiece for the Lord.

Afterward, I stood and glanced around, saying aloud the names of each adult as I looked straight at them. I hardened my heart against every adult in the room. Some of the adults, the adults who were normally kind to me, returned my gaze, the sadness visible in their eyes and on their faces. The adults who believed we deserved the punishment averted their eyes as I stared directly at them.

They were going to hell. I hoped they would burn forever.

It wasn't over.

Karen was beaten last with the belt. I cringed when they called her name, knowing the brutality she was facing. No child was tough enough to endure this, but she still had not cried out as the lashes approached thirty in number. She moaned in agony at lash thirty-five. By lash number forty, I watched her body begin to convulse after she let out a violent, bloody scream. I thought she was going to die. At number forty-six, her body went limp. The four men looked at each other, unsure what to do.

"Put her down," Harry ordered. They laid her on the floor. A few minutes went by before she moved. Gasping for air as if drowning, she tried to crawl toward her dad who turned his back on her by facing the wall.

I was breathing through my nose with anger, seething like a bull, and wanting to charge the adults. No matter what we kids did with each other, I knew deep down inside that this was too much. This was not what the word of God communicated. Jesus taught love, peace, and kindness. These beatings were demonic.

Most of the adults in the room seemed to happily accept the beatings. Some of them even smiled while it happened, but a few adults did cry.

"Take her arms," Harry ordered two of the men.

"Follow me," he added, as two of the men, along with the two who dragged Karen behind them, walked out of the room and into another room. The doors to the room stayed open after they dragged Karen's body into the room and suspended her in the air a second time.

I could hear the belt start back up, hitting her again followed by counting. "Forty-seven," followed by more violent screaming. By the time I heard "sixty-five," the screaming stopped, but the beating continued, as they ruthlessly beat the nearly lifeless body of my thirteen-year-old friend. We no longer heard any sounds of resistance coming from her.

A few minutes later the men brought her down the stairs. I was afraid she was dead. She was completely limp and unmoving, and her pajamas were stained with blood. I wanted to do something to help her, and I wanted to do to them what they had done to her and to the rest of us. Karen's dad took one of her arms while her brother took the other, carrying her away as her legs dragged behind her. She turned her head looking over her shoulder. I saw her struggle to even keep her eyes open. I was relieved to know that she was alive.

This was the last time I ever saw Karen; a persistent memory of her bloody, limp body being carried away. During the time the beating was taking place, Papa Tony had called back and kicked Karen's family out of the church.

The embarrassment and helplessness of that day became a permanent state of being. Yet the pain of the torture and abuse did nothing to remove our natural, God-given desire for social interaction and physical contact with one another. Yes, it was shocking and had made it confusing, and frightening for all of us, but it didn't make the yearnings for a sense of belonging go away.

# CHAPTER TEN

## Tortured

The next day I was numb, couldn't think too well, and had no ability to make jokes. I wanted to be anyone other than me. The silence on The Ridge was deafening. Everyone stayed inside. There was no activity. No cars driving to and from The Ridge. No laughter. No talking. No fellowship. The curtains were closed in all the homes. The winter sun shone down on defrosting leaves and stillness moved throughout the property, but a darkness permeated my insides. It was a darkness I had never felt before and its unfamiliarity confused me.

That Sunday, only the adults went to church. I didn't know how many families had left on their own or were kicked out, but it seemed very likely some of my friends would not be around when normal activities resumed. Papa Tony held a virtual service where he phoned in and set new rules for the boys and the girls, as follows:

- Boys and girls would always be separated
- They could not go to school together
- They could not go to church together
- They could not walk with each other
- They could not talk to each other

- There could be no interaction between boys and girls at all for any reason unless there was an adult present
- There must always be a watcher following boys and girls
- No eye contact between the opposite genders
- No smiling at each other
- No crying around each other
- No communication at all between the boys and girls
- No note writing to each other
- No hand signals toward each other
- No touching each other
- No smelling each other
- Girls and boys were to be fully covered including when swimming
- No sounds were to be made that might cause someone from the opposite sex to look toward the sound
- Whenever possible, boys and girls would be fully segregated in different rooms from one another
- Anyone who defied these rules would be severely punished

Papa Tony now controlled almost every important interaction between the boys and girls. He already controlled our food, our money, where we lived, where we worked and for how long, how often we were supposed to pray, and sometimes even our thoughts. Along with this he was removing any free will the youth had when it came to relationships of the opposite sex. He controlled who among us could marry and who could have children. He groomed young girls for himself by having them come to his house for Bible study and sleepovers. He had three wives that I knew of; one was a legal marriage and two that were considered spiritual. Now he was going to try to dictate how every relationship could occur or not occur.

All of this was to show us who was in charge: him. He was God's messenger, the blessed and the anointed one on Earth.

On Monday, the children would normally be in school. Instead, all the boys my age and I were told to report to a construction site in Dyer. The cement foundation had already been poured and some of the wood framing was complete. Our job was to remove the existing framing. An OC was already there upon our arrival. We walked around silently, with our hands in our pockets, looking at the ground and kicking dirt and pebbles. Most of us were still sore and hurting from the beatings and abuses.

Across the street was Emmanuala's house. I saw her standing in front of it, waiting for her sisters, looking as beautiful as she always did. But there was something different about her too. She no longer looked in my direction, hoping I would notice her. I knew the new rules and I knew the risks, but I couldn't help sneaking peeks. She wore jeans which revealed the curves of her legs and even though she wore a puffy winter jacket, I could still make out the curves of her upper body. I wanted her more than ever, but the forced gulf between us was much wider than the street.

I was terrified, terrified of God and Papa Tony. Terrified of my own thoughts and actions. I wished God had made me blind and made me so that my body could have no way to sin unlike what it was like now: a body of complete sin.

Hell was closer to me. I knew it. I felt it each moment of my life. My life after death was to be one of torture and everlasting suffering. Holding hands was a form of fornication. Thinking of how attractive a girl was, was fornication with the mind. Fornication was only allowed for married people and yet that was all I wanted to do. Also, I wanted to comfort her. I wanted to comfort all the girls with whom I was reared.

Papa Tony knew my thoughts because God knew my thoughts, and since Papa Tony talked to God, consoling my friends was impossible, because my thoughts didn't stop there. I was now filled with a void each time I thought about Emmanuala, in the place where there was once love, affection, and kindness. How could something so beautiful be bad? When I thought about her, I was reminded of the punishment awaiting me in hell due to my sinful thoughts, causing tears to well in my eyes. A fuzzy feeling in the middle of my head, something I had never felt before, began to grow, not permitting me to think clearly. I couldn't escape the endless cycle of thinking about her and then feeling the terror of impending punishment due to my thoughts. It was a prison from which I could not see out due to its darkness.

And yet, I couldn't stop looking at her. My thoughts were scrambled. Nothing made sense. The desire to look at her beauty drove me to short moments of happiness and clarity only to be muddied when she was out of sight. I was depressed and confused, and it caused me to work slowly. With each pull of the hammer, I wondered if I would be beaten for thinking about or looking at a girl. Every time I placed a complete board on the done pile, I saw Karen in my mind, being beaten with it.

"You're working too slow. Hurry up," said the OC.

I threw the hammer down. The last straw.

"Too slow? Too slow … huh? You do it then." I was done following the rules now, and I wanted to make him, and all the adults feel pain. Now my anger was unveiled. No more hiding the side of me I had so carefully kept concealed. The beatings were not fair, and I would no longer play fair either. I figured if Papa Tony could hurt us, then we could hurt him. The Bible says, 'Do unto others as you would have them do unto you.' The adults must have wanted to be hurt because they had hurt us. If Papa Tony could lie about the word of God, then I could lie too.

"I'll put you on report if you don't pick up that hammer and start pulling the nails out of those boards," the OC reprimanded.

"Come on! We just have to get this job done and then we can go home," one of the other boys yelled at me.

I stood up and walked behind a nearby building, out of the adults' field of view. I needed to unscramble my confusion from the thoughts and emotions which consumed me. Trying to not think of girls only made me think of them more. I didn't care about work. I didn't care about the OC. I didn't even care what Papa Tony thought anymore.

That night I was called to the Spec House. Several of the people who had been at the work site were called there as well.

"Is it true you refused to work, Benji?" Papa Tony asked.

"No, it is not. This brother is lying. He called you names, and he's lying about me. He said you were evil for separating the boys and the girls," I answered. When I said this, I felt the heat of guilt mixed with delight. The revenge I wanted temporarily concealed the fear and anger that consumed me because of all the restrictions meant to keep us from having any contact with the girls.

Without even asking the adult if it was true, or allowing him to make any rebuttal, Papa Tony ordered that he be beaten. Two brothers leaned him over the couch and beat him with a belt. The people who had been on the work site had been called to the Spec House as witnesses as to what happened at the work site, but they were not asked to speak. They shook their heads in disbelief after Papa Tony issued his order.

I watched, smirking, while the adult cried in pain.

"Vengeance is mine, sayeth the Lord." I thought to myself, thinking of Emmanuala and Karen, "Vengeance is mine."

When I walked outside, I found Marty waiting for me.

"I couldn't go inside there today," he admitted. "Too many people getting beat."

"If they mess with the anointed one, what do you expect?" I asked.

"You're not the anointed one. You're a liar! You just lied about that brother! What's wrong with you?"

"I don't know what you're talking about," I replied, walking away. "I am the anointed one."

Today I do my best to do no harm to any living being and I am aware of the pain I caused others that I hurt during that time. I know now that the abuse I suffered caused me, in turn, to lash out at and hurt those around me to try to find control in an uncontrollable environment. Even the Bible says, "Raise up a child in the way he should go and when he is old, he will not depart from it." I was raised in such an unstable and frightening environment, that in order to protect myself, I learned to seek revenge and believed I needed to win at all costs. I try to understand my behavior from those days by understanding that I was a child who was not fully responsible for my actions because of the culture in which I was immersed. As an adult, I have had to unlearn these behaviors as I realized I must now own responsibility for my behaviors and the effect they have on others.

A few days later, Lonny found me while I was sweeping the school. "Have you seen this?"

"Seen what?" I asked, without glancing in her direction, continuing to sweep, eager to join my friends outside.

"Benji, stop!" she said, sitting down on a desk. "Stop pushing that thing and get over here."

She held the color photo out in front of me. There was a boy in it who was about two years old, dressed in a pair of yellow and green plaid pants and a matching jacket. He had blonde hair and a soft smile. He appeared to be waving at whoever was behind the camera. A girl with long, dark brown hair, who couldn't have been older than five, stood behind him. She wore a white summer dress with a big yellow ribbon around her waist. She wore a serious expression and seemed focused on the camera.

"They are your brother and sister," Lonny told me.

"So what? You're my sister too. Everyone in the church is my sister and brother," I said. "Who are these kids?"

"They are your blood sister and blood brother," she replied, emphasizing the word blood. I put the broom down and walked toward her, looking first at Lonny then at the photograph.

"What do you mean, blood? Like a blood pact?" I asked.

"You silly nit. You're not listening. You have the same mother."

She paused and then resumed, "The boy is Samuel and the girl is Chelsea. They are your siblings. He is your real brother and she is your real sister."

I snatched the photo from her hand and sat down, looking at it, examining the faces of the children, the clothes they wore, and the boy's smiling face.

"I've seen this photo before," I said. "His clothes. I've seen this before. Where did you get this?"

"My mom had it in her photos, and I asked her who it was. She told me it was your sister and brother. I thought you might want to see it."

"The same mother?" I exclaimed. "I have a ... a mother?"

"Yes doofus. What did you think? The stork dropped you off?"

"Grandma Susie was my mom. Elaine was my mom. Kendra was my mom. Grandma Dee was my mom and now Mom is my mom," I answered, still examining the photo. "I've had so many moms; I never thought I had my own. Not one that I came from anyway."

"You were born just like the rest of us. You have a mom. She carried you in her belly. She probably yelled in pain in childbirth, just like everybody else."

"You know where she is?" I asked.

Before Lonny could answer, Mom walked in.

"What's going on in here? You should have been done a long time ago."

"I'm almost done, but look at this photo," I held it out to her. "Do you know who this is?"

She quickly took it from me, looking at it with one hand on her hip, squinting at us both in disbelief.

"Where'd you get this?" she asked angrily.

"Lonny gave it to me. Her mom gave it to her. That's my brother and sister. We have the same mother."

There was a lingering silence as I realized Mom's eyes had filled with tears. She wiped one as it rolled down her cheek.

"I am your mother now. That mother is dead. She died when she left the church. She was an adulterer, and she's in hell now. You need to forget this photo. Do you hear me? Forget it. Get out of here. I'll finish sweeping."

I slowly stood up, preoccupied with the word adulterer, with the details of the photo, and the concept that I had my own mom. I was thirteen years old, yet it had never occurred to me before this moment that I had a mother who had given birth to me. The children in the photo looked familiar to me, but I couldn't remember from where I knew them.

"Give me the broom."

I walked casually to where I had left the broom, focusing on the pile of debris as I pushed it toward Mom. Why did those children look so familiar? Especially the girl? Her eyes looked like mine.

When I was about two feet from her, I flipped the broom handle to her and looked up as she reached to grab it. She dropped the photo while moving her hand to catch the handle. I saw the handle of the broom hit her on the top of her hand, knocking the diamond from her wedding ring, as if in slow motion. Everything felt like it was in slow motion ever since Lonny told me I had my own mother. I watched the diamond pop into the air and then bounce with a ding off the wooden desktop before finally landing on the hard tile floor.

"You knucklehead!" Mom said furiously. "You knocked the diamond out of my wedding ring. You are grounded all winter, Mister, if I have anything to say about it."

I dropped to the floor to fetch the diamond from where I had seen it fall and stood up holding it triumphantly. "Here it is! Maybe we can glue it back into the ring?" I said, with pleading in my voice.

During this whole diamond incident, Lonny had picked up the photo and backed out of the room without us noticing.

From that moment forward, I didn't forget the photo Lonny showed me. I hadn't forgotten the new-found awareness that I had a real mom of my own, other than all the church moms. I often stayed awake late at night, thinking about her and wondering if she was still alive, what she was like? Was she rich? Would she recognize me? Why did she leave and why did she commit adultery on my dad? Would she want me if I found her? These questions pursued me each night when I went to bed.

I tried to ask Mom about her a few more times, but was always told, "She's an adulterer and in hell. Forget about her."

But how could I forget about my own mother?

# CHAPTER ELEVEN

### The Pool Party

The annual pool party took place just as life was getting more stressful, confusing, and darker by the day. The girls and boys remained segregated and we did our best to not look at each other when our paths crossed so we wouldn't get put on report. I struggled and failed to not look at the girls. I even stared and gawked when an adult was not around or when I thought the girl who was in my sights would not put me on report.

Putting restrictions on my eyesight exceeded all the other restrictions in severity. I knew how to lie about my thoughts in order to get around the restrictions on evil thoughts. I knew how to argue with people and escalate verbal fights to get away with being mean. I merely had to find a Biblical reference for my verbal attack. Even physical fights with other boys could be justified as "just playing around." But when I looked at a girl, everyone could see where my eyes were pointed. The challenge to look, but not get caught looking, pushed me toward other neurotic tendencies like nail biting, more teeth grinding at night, and more fighting.

When it was the girls' time to swim, I watched a girl do a backflip off the diving board while other girls climbed out of the pool using the side ladders. Three girls raced each other from one end to the other while the boys were kept out of the pool, surrounded by adults, about fifty feet away.

It appeared to be a festive and joyful outing. Five barbecues were situated at the end of the pool where chicken, hot dogs, and ground beef patties were being grilled, creating a billowy layer of smoke.

Four picnic tables were topped with fresh watermelon, homemade potato salad, and ample soda. All the adults were laughing and talking with each other. Small children played on the nearby swing set and merry-go-round.

At the center of it all was a tanned boy, about nine years old, with long blonde hair. He wore new clothes, which was an immediate signal to me that he had just joined the church. He strutted out of the circle of kids, legs before torso like an angry bull, but smiling. One boy ran away crying, holding his arm, after the new boy had twisted his arm. The new kid continued smiling as he pinched and twisted the loose skin of another boy's chest. That boy, too, screamed and ran away. The new kid was half their size and completely unfazed by their screams.

I was apprehensive yet intrigued by this new boy who seemed more popular than me. Why was he so cool?

"Who are you?" I asked.

"I'm Sebastian. Who the hell are you?"

I was startled by the word "hell" and looked up and down at the tan, shaggy-haired little kid. Sebastian pushed me aside and continued toward the grills.

How dare he push me aside? He doesn't know who I am yet! I followed, determined to make a point.

"You know you can go to hell for saying that!"

"Saying what?" Sebastian asked.

"Hell, saying hell."

Sebastian continued walking.

"You just said hell three times. Are you going to hell for saying that?" he asked with a chuckle, looking back at me over his shoulder. "That barbecue is hell to that burger. Will I go to hell for saying that?"

I followed him to the grills where we both filled our plates. I had a lot of questions and Sebastian didn't mind answering them. He told me that he was from Miami and that his mother was an epileptic heroin addict. She had a boyfriend who peddled Cuban cocaine. I had seen *Miami Vice* and thought I knew what the Cuban drug dealer's life was like. It was full of parties, girls in bikinis, fast cars, and race boats. It was exciting to be this close to that lifestyle.

I wondered if this was the life my mom lived before she died and went to hell. Did she die from drugs like all the rest of the people who left the church?

Sebastian and his family had lived across the street from one of the church's recruitment outposts, a beachfront house where several married church members and their children lived. As his mother's addiction advanced, Sebastian hustled on the street. He sold her jewelry when he had no other options for food. John Bounty, an OC and a long-time member of the church, approached him one day and offered him free food.

"He didn't have any kids of his own, see? He saw me one day trying to get this bookseller to take some of my mom's old hardbacks. Then, whenever I saw him, he would give me peanut butter and jelly or salami or bologna sandwiches. And apples, oranges, and sodas. He would check on me, you know."

Then one day, federal agents showed up at Sebastian's apartment to question his mom's boyfriend. The boyfriend, in very short order, snitched on his supplier. A few days later those suppliers showed up and beat the boyfriend within an inch of his life. Sebastian saw it all, peeking through the tiny opening of his bedroom door.

"I jumped out of my window and ran to John Bounty's place," Sebastian said while biting into his burger. "It was the only place I had to go."

I admired him now. He had had a tough life like the adults from before they got saved. Yet he managed to live through it all. He really was cool.

I'd never spoken to anyone from the outside world unless it was to preach the word of God with the hope of recruiting them. The newer members never spoke about their old lives unless they were testifying in church. With Sebastian as my friend, I could learn about the outside world without asking an adult. He could tell me things no one else could, or would, tell me.

From then on Sebastian spent more time at the church's beach house than his own home. He ate meals there and played with the other children. Eventually, John Bounty asked Papa Tony for permission to adopt Sebastian. Sebastian's mother happily allowed it, saying, "My son will lead a Christian life."

By the end of Sebastian's story, both of our burgers had been consumed and there was nothing left of our watermelon wedges but green rinds and seeds. Sebastian spooned up the last bit of his potato salad, gulped down half a can of soda then let out a huge belch.

"So, that's how I ended up here. How about you?" he asked smiling.

"Me?" I asked. "How did I end up here? I was born here, dude."

Here was all I had ever known. The faces that surrounded us, the children I grew up with, all my parents, The Ridge, the ponds where I fished, the peach groves. This was it. Most of the children, my friends, like me, were born close to The Ridge or Saugus, California, or another church-owned property.

We're here because Jesus chose us. I am a special person with the blood of royalty flowing through me. He's a kid from the streets. He talked about seeing someone beaten within an inch of their life in his home while in my home I read the Bible an hour a day after school. He talked about cocaine in his house while in mine I was lucky if I watched cartoons on Saturday morning.

Through Sebastian, a glimpse of a new world opened for me. Sebastian became one of my brothers and fished and swam and went to church just like everyone else, except he wasn't like everyone else. He had a lot of questions and wasn't afraid to insert his opinions. While the rest of us just accepted what Papa Tony and the adults told us, Sebastian wanted explanations.

"If the universe is everything that exists, then how can God be outside of it?" he asked an OC during Bible reading time.

"That's a good question, young man. But the universe is not everything, God is. God holds the universe in his hands," the OC responded.

"He he." Sebastian smiled sardonically. "That's crazy. Everything is everything."

The OC put him on report for saying that.

"You are getting twenty swats, so you learn that everything in the Bible is truth and nothing else," Papa Tony bellowed through the speakers late one evening after reviewing the report.

A year later, Sebastian had memorized the Song of Solomon, Chapter 4. He thought it beautiful and sensual, even though it was scripture, so he recited it to a girl.

*Behold, you are beautiful, my love, behold, you are beautiful.*

*Your eyes are doves behind your veil.*

*Your hair is like a flock of goats leaping down the slopes of Gilead.*

*Your teeth are like a flock of shorn ewes that have come up from the washing.*

*All which bear twins, and not one among them has lost its young.*

*Your lips are like a scarlet thread, and your mouth is lovely.*

*Your cheeks are like halves of a pomegranate behind your veil.*

*Your neck is like the tower of David, built in rows of stone,*

*on it hang a thousand shields, all of them shields of warriors.*

"Your two breasts are ...."

The girl he had recited the passage to interrupted him.
"You're not supposed to say that word," she said.
"What word?"
"You know," she said, glancing down at her breasts.
"Breast? I'm not allowed to say that word? It's in the Bible. If it's in the Bible then it's the truth, and I can say it," Sebastian argued.

I loved his attitude, and his confidence in the face of a direct challenge. He made a good argument that I harbored for a long time. If it was in the Bible, then it was true even if the adults said otherwise. The Bible was the word of God, not the word of man. However, the adult reported him, and he was given twenty swats. Again, Papa Tony meted out the punishment via speakerphone. This time it was around 3:00 AM.

"You have to listen to your brothers and sisters! When they tell you that they know what's best, you must listen!" Papa Tony ordered him.

Sebastian tried tempering his behavior but there were so many rules. Also, the religious kids snitching on the cool kids was increasing because Papa Tony was always telling us to report "everything you think might be ungodly."

Sebastian took the precaution of wearing an extra layer of underwear, gym shorts, and sometimes even two extra layers of pants for fear of more beatings.

His dad, John Bounty, was also struggling under Papa Tony's rule. He and his brothers had been gifted some money by their parents which they had used to start a trucking company. After the company proved successful, Papa Tony demanded that John Bounty and his brother give it to the church, and they refused.

Papa Tony kicked them out of the church and took the company by force by having some of the brothers physically take the keys to the trucks and coerce John Bounty's brothers to sign over ownership of their company to the church under threat of physical violence. Once John Bounty left the property, Papa Tony used his spiritual powers to divorce John Bounty from his wife then married her to another member of the church. Papa Tony sent her, her new husband, and Sebastian to Saugus so John Bounty wouldn't know where they lived.

As the sun was setting one evening before they moved to Saugus, John Bounty snuck onto The Ridge and into his former duplex home. His wife was sitting in the living room when he walked through the back door. She screamed when she saw him, and he quickly covered her mouth.

"Love, please don't yell. I've come back to take you away from here." He removed his hand cautiously. "Tony Alamo is a pervert. He is abusing children for his own sexual gratification. You and Sebastian are not safe here."[18]

"What are you talking about?"

"Do you remember when Birgitta accused Tony of stealing her clothing designs and money?"

"Yes."

"Well that's not all. I met her in a bar in Hollywood and she said she sued him for a five-figure, monthly alimony in

---

18. Based on interview with Carey Miller and supporting docs here: https://www.tonyalamonews.com/3424/42210-court-document-nov-2009-custody-appeal-court-affirms-alamo-parents-failed-to-protect-their-children-from-tony-alamos-sexual-abuse-beatings-ordered-fasts-and-underage-marriages.php

the settlement. And get this ... she told me he's the biggest pervert she ever met. He can't get it up unless he listens to or knows that a child is being beaten. She said he'd make a phone call and have some poor kid brought to his house where either he beat him, or he had another man beat the child. Then he'd come back in with a raging hard-on."

"That's child abuse. You have to acknowledge that," John Bounty told her.

He continued, saying that Birgitta stated that Tony justifies it with the Bible, and that Arkansas can be so ass-backward she wasn't sure she'd be able to prove anything. She said she whipped him good plenty of times, saying she used to step on his balls and make him beg for relief. Once she choked him out while making him pray to his dead wife as he gasped for air. She said she could have just killed him, but she's too nice for that. She said he's a really fucked-up, sad little puppy.'"

As soon as John Bounty finished talking, his wife screamed as loud as she could. John Bounty ran out the backdoor just as the neighbors next door walked in the front door.

"Get Rover over here now," she told them. "John Bounty was just here, and he tried to kidnap me."

He escaped, but that wasn't the end of John Bounty.

In Saugus, Sebastian was again put on report. This time it was because he burped and farted in the chapel. After listening to their report, Papa Tony ordered that Sebastian receive seventy swats, and added, "That little punk is a wolf among the sheep. We will definitely beat the devil out of him this time."

One of Papa Tony's spiritual wives was in their bedroom when Papa Tony made the call to punish Sebastian. She told me years later how she made the mistake of objecting to the severity of the punishment. Papa Tony slammed the phone down. He grabbed her by the hair and dragged her to the bed where he brutally beat and raped her. He left her bleeding on the bed. She remembers him saying repeatedly, "Oh, sweet redemption. Another win. Jesus saves."

His fury remained with him. He called the brothers at the Saugus property again.

"Am I on speakerphone?" he asked.

"Yes, sir. We are all here."

"Is it over?"

"Umm ... no sir ... we got to sixteen swats, then Sebastian kept moving on us."

"Start over! Start over! Every time he moves or talks, you start the count all over. Got it?"

The four men took Sebastian to the couch and held him down again. One pulled out a large wooden board. By the fortieth swat, blood oozed from his clothes. By the one hundredth swat, the blood splattered on the faces and clothing of the adults who stood by watching as they counted each swat with zest. In their view, each swat represented one step closer this child would get to God. Their happiness could not be concealed as they rocked back and forth counting in unison until they reach one hundred forty.[19]

The only protection or tactic Sebastian could muster to mitigate the pain from the beating was to lift one butt cheek higher than the other, alternating them with each swat. With each movement though, the beating started again. Many hit his back near his kidneys and his legs as far down to his knees. The people in the room counted fervently and in unison, as if the more the child was beaten, the more righteous they were in the eyes of God. In total, they counted one hundred forty swats but, in truth, Sebastian received more like two hundred.

After the beating was finished, the adults left the room, leaving Sebastian curled up on the floor bleeding. The next day was a school day and Sebastian was still bleeding. Puss

---

19. https://www.tonyalamonews.com/843/12409-doug-christopher-jailed-in-1988-justin-miller-child-abuse-case.php

and blood dripped from his clothes. He bled onto the school seat. The teacher, concerned for his health, sent him home.

Around the same time, John Bounty sued Papa Tony over the trucking business. He hired a private detective and established that his ex-wife and Sebastian were living at Saugus #7. He filed a missing person's report for his son. A few days after the beating, John Bounty arrived at the Saugus property with the local sheriff's department to take custody of Sebastian. Upon seeing Sebastian's injuries, he filed child abuse charges against Papa Tony. A week later, child protective services raided the Saugus, California, property to examine the remaining children. Crime scene investigators located the paddle and Sebastian's bloody clothes, seizing them as evidence of the abuse.[20]

Papa Tony successfully evaded law enforcement for two years during this time. But the brutality of the case and widespread media coverage put him on the radar of the federal government.

After that, the beatings throughout the church changed. Papa Tony ordered parents to beat their children at home. No longer could a stranger beat a child unless both parents were not available. He also ordered less noticeable forms of punishment. Extended fasting, sometimes a week to three weeks at a time, became common. Longer prayer times, which normally were one to two hours, were extended to three to eight hours. The same went for working. We children worked eleven to fourteen hours a day when we were not in school. We would then be given odd jobs in the cafeteria or we were given watch and Rover duty, which lasted all night long. At times we worked with enthusiasm, happy that we could contribute to the cause against the devil, but most of the time we put on a smile for the adults and complained to

---

20. https://www.latimes.com/archives/la-xpm-1991-12-13-me-184-story.html

select, trusted friends about the extra work, the beatings, the fasting, the extra prayer hours, and copious Bible study.

Despite working fourteen hours a day, our hormones still raged and controlled us more than the adults could. At the annual pool party, when it was time for the boys to swim and the girls to leave the pool, I stood on the diving board watching the girls swim in their T-shirts toward the shallow end where they were exiting.

As they exited the water, I happily noticed that their wet T-shirts made all the curves on their bodies appear larger as the material formed around them.

I noticed an erection making a tent in my shorts for the fifth time that day, so I jumped in the pool to conceal it, counting on the cool water to help. I swam underwater to the deep end of the pool and came up for air to find Emmanuala standing on the edge of the pool looking down at me. She was pure curve. My erection sprung back to life as I watched her turn away and run to catch up to the other girls. God sees me. He knows I have an erection. *The blood of Jesus is against you Satan. The blood of Jesus ...* my erection subsided.

On the deck of the pool there stood a particularly zealous adult, Mrs. Krebbs. She pointed at me.

"Benji!" she yelled.

I acted as if I didn't hear her and sunk to the bottom of the pool holding my breath. When I reemerged three minutes later, she was still there, pointing at me. I dropped back to the bottom of the pool and swam its length to the shallow end where the children who could not swim mingled in oversized T-shirts.

She saw me and ran to the edge.

"Get out of there! Let's go! Hurry up!"

When I climbed out of the pool, she grabbed me by the ear.

"I saw you," she whispered. "Do you think you can fornicate with your mind and get away with it? Not on my watch, Mister. Go sit in the gazebo until we leave for evening church service."

At church, the boys and I stood on one side of the chapel while the girls stood on the other. Adults and parents stood between and behind us, keeping watch for turning heads or gestures made toward the opposite sex. I worried about the punishment waiting for me at home while I listened to one of Papa Tony's pre-recorded sermons. The sermon was about how sinful everyone in the church was and that there were sodomites in the church.

"It is ungodly to be a sodomite," Papa Tony proclaimed. "Sex should be for reproduction and reproduction only. God will turn you to salt, like Lot's wife, for sodomizing each other."

I didn't understand what he was talking about. What is sodomizing and who was this sodomite in the church? Do I know them? Is it contagious? Was I sodomizing Emmanuala today? I snapped out of my trance just as the girls exited the chapel. Once the girls and adults were all gone, I saw Niceah, Enoch, and Gregory standing on the girls' side of the pews with smirks on their faces.

"Papa Tony said, 'No smelling the girls.' Watch this!" Gregory said. He leaned over the seats of the pews where the girls' butts had been and sniffed along their length.

Enoch and Niceah laughed.

"That's gross, dude. But watch this!" Enoch said, humping another pew where the girls had been sitting.

Niceah took it to a whole other level by kissing the pews. We watched him in awe.

"Awesome!" we said in unison.

We went to each of the twenty pews, kissing, dry humping, sniffing, drawing messages with our fingers, hugging, and fondling the pews, as if the girls were still sitting in them. We gave each other high fives and started for the exit just as an OC walked in.

"Praise the Lord, Brother!" we each said to the OC in passing.

Once outside, we laughed until our sides hurt.

I made my way home via Rover. My mom was waiting for me with a scowl on her face. When I smiled broadly, it upset her even more.

"Mrs. Krebbs told me all about you today. I hope you had fun," she said.

"I had fun."

"Well, she said you were fornicating today."

"I didn't fornicate. What are you talking about?"

I walked right up to her and looked her in the eyes. I learned this move from seeing Papa Tony corner people when he was about to smite them in his Godly anger. At thirteen, I was as tall as she was and stronger, but I didn't have the audacity to really do anything to her for fear of Dad Miguel.

She didn't move, but she changed the subject. "You've been asking your friends about your mom, wanting to know where she is, and why she is not here. You need to know that she is an adulterer. You need to forget her. Papa Tony has said many times that she is dead and in hell. So just forget her."

My defiance turned to confusion because I suddenly realized her statement seemed to contradict itself. "I don't understand. How can she be dead and an adulterer at the same time?"

"There you go with your smart-aleck attitude. That's going to change tonight. Your dad will be here shortly to make sure of it. Go to your room and wait for him. Don't touch your toys, your guitar, or anything other than your Bible."

The time dragged on as I waited, filling it by wondering and worrying about my punishment. I tried not to think about Emmanuala, but I failed. Mom had given up on controlling me, but Dad would confront me. The knock on the door terrified me and I froze. The knock got more insistent and I opened it up to Dad.

"I heard what you did today," he said.

"What did I do?"

"You were caught staring at Emmanuala when you were swimming. You know the rules."

I stood in silence not knowing how to answer. It felt good to look at her. How could that be wrong?

"Let's go. You know the drill," dad said. He retrieved a three-foot long board from the hall outside the door.

I had expected the one-foot paddle. This was a new paddle. I bent over face-down on the bed with my shorts dropped and only my underwear to protect me.

The board stung much more than the normal paddle, but I did not cry. Upon the tenth and final swat, I was biting my upper lip in agony. I went to bed hating my family, but I also prayed that God would forgive me for lusting after Emmanuala.

A few days later, I was told to watch some toddlers at the nursery. After the toddlers fell asleep for their afternoon nap, I walked to the adjoining old nursery to use the restroom. I left the door ajar, so I could hear if a child cried or woke up.

I heard Dad's voice in the next room. He was talking to Mr. Krebbs.

"Thanks for that paddle. It definitely got him better than those smaller ones."

"Yeah, I made that from some hardwood maple. These kids are getting out of hand," answered Mr. Krebbs. "You should see my boy squirming under it. Ha! Like a little worm!"

I had horrible memories of Mr. and Mrs. Krebbs beating their daughter with a belt. I saw Lonny clawing on the floor, trying to get away while her parents whipped her. Her dad had a paddle and her mom had a belt. Lonny was running around the house and they whipped her like she was a fly trying to escape.

Hearing him brag about beating his son angered and scared me. How could they talk about beating me as if it was a conversation about the recent baseball game? Their insensitive attitude confirmed that even Dad Miguel was becoming hardened like them. I feared for the punishment the next time I got into trouble.

The two men soon left, and I returned to the nursery to attend to a child who I could hear crying. Lonny opened the door to the nursery shortly after I calmed the child. She was ready to take over the next shift. Her shoulders were forward, her head down, and it looked like she was about to cry. I walked over to her.

"What's wrong?" I asked quietly, before any adults could catch us talking.

"You know we can't talk, Benji. Get away!" she said motioning with her hands. Her head was still hanging low.

"No one sees us. Not even God," I said.

"You are so bad," she smiled. "You're an evil little thing, but I love you."

"I know I'm evil. I got beat last night," I replied in a matter-of-fact tone.

"So did I," she said surprised. "An adult told Papa Tony I was looking at Kiona. All I did was glance in his direction. I got thirty swats, Benji."

Tears welled in her eyes and ran down her cheeks. She wiped them away.

"They hurt me, Benji. They hurt me bad," she said, taking in a few shaky breaths as if trying to find the strength to continue. "There were ten of us on report. We all got thirty swats strung up by our arms and legs."

I briefly hugged her, not wanting to get her into more trouble, before running outside. I went to the nearby pond where I watched water moccasins crisscross the pond in search of their dinner. It seemed like everyone was getting beaten all the time now. I felt more anger and confusion at the same time because we kids were doing what we did all the time: we played with each other. We loved each other and shared unique bonds that were being torn apart. We hadn't changed. The adults had, and we were the ones getting whipped.

With the number of abused and beaten children, the charges against Papa Tony and his followers should have swarmed and consumed them. However, in April 1989, only John Bounty's single felony child abuse charge was filed against Papa Tony Alamo. Two months later, a federal warrant was issued, and Papa Tony went into hiding again.

Through his lawyer, Papa Tony claimed to not be affiliated with the Tony and Susan Alamo Christian Church.[21] He claimed he was in no way affiliated with the church bearing his name and legacy.[22] In 1990, the US District Court in Fort Smith, Arkansas, ruled against Papa Tony in absentia for numerous charges.[23]

By 1992 he was discovered again to be in violation of minimum wage laws for not compensating church members who worked at his various enterprises. He owed millions to his followers in back pay and to the federal government in unpaid taxes and penalties.[24] He lived in undisclosed locations throughout the time of the court proceedings. He knew if he was found he would be imprisoned. Instead of facing the charges, he disguised himself by growing a beard, gaining weight, and using the identity of one of his followers to rent a hiding place.

---

21. https://www.tonyalamonews.com/wp-content/uploads/2007/02/1989-10-13-newhall-signal-alamo-changes-mind-says-he-wont-surrender.jpg

22. https://www.tonyalamonews.com/98/tony-alamo-wont-surrender-denies-affiliation-with-the-alamo-ministries-churches.php

23. https://law.justia.com/cases/federal/district-courts/FSupp/748/695/1966881/

24. https://www.tonyalamonews.com/259/alamo-promises-to-pay-5-million-to-satisfy-wages-owed-to-foundation-members.php

Since he was in hiding, this left the church with fines and fees arising from the legal defeat owed to the Department of Labor as well as additional fees which had never been paid to the IRS. IRS agents came to The Ridge and Dyer. They sat in church services, visited the cafeteria, and walked the length of the property performing an informal assessment of the church and its followers. They walked through the Spec House and other buildings looking for valuables.

Papa Tony continued to run the church in absentia, directing his followers to act on his behalf. I thought he could foretell the future because, in a phone sermon a week before the IRS agents arrived, he had ordered that all properties be gutted of anything of value, predicting the IRS would try to take our possessions. My friends and I were pulled out of school to hide all the valuables.

At some point he even ordered that the body of Grandma Susie be removed from her crypt. He had what remained of her body taken to Florida. In 1995 he was ordered to return it after Susan's daughter Christhiaon sued to have it returned.[25]

An OC was assigned to organize the removal of items of value from the church's properties. He stood in front of us teenagers and said, "As all of you know, the IRS and the devil are trying to ruin our church. They want to take our property and give it to sinners," the OC told us. "Papa Tony has ordered that all valuables, the antique furniture in our homes, the grand and baby grand pianos, the paintings, exotic rugs and furs, his wardrobe of leather jackets, fur coats, boots and jewelry, all of it needs to be hidden so these devils can't get it."

"Papa Tony wants the maple tongue-in-groove walls of the church taken down, musical instruments, sewing machines, and construction equipment like the backhoes, bulldozers, and cement mixers. Everything worth more than

---

25. https://www.tonyalamonews.com/306/tony-alamo-has-wifes-stolen-body-returned-to-avoid-more-jail-time.php

a hundred dollars, like the marble floors in the Spec House, needs to be moved and hidden in storage. Papa Tony asked for you six boys by name. We'll have three U-Haul trucks. Two each to a van. Papa Tony is depending upon you to save our church."

We looked at each other, smiled, and nodded in agreement. It was a soldier's mission and we were teenage soldiers. It made me feel honored and responsible for fighting evil. We didn't want Satan taking our stuff and we were the hand of God to prevent it.

It made us feel important and proud that Papa Tony asked for us. I told myself it was redemption for all my sins of the flesh, all the gawking at girls, and all my impure thoughts. I was also happy to be out of school.

I approached the first house and greeted Mrs. Turner who was expecting us.

"Hello, Mrs. Turner," I said. "We're here to take the Ethan Allen writing desk Grandma Susie gave you."

"Come on in boys, it's right there."

The dark brown walnut desk and chair sat in the corner of the room. The desk had a wooden inlay of white Arabian horses prancing in a green field on top. On its side there was a light green field with blue and yellow butterflies. The chair had a pronounced white velvet cushion. I remember it from the grand living room in which I spent my childhood years.

Next door, we removed gold lamps with emerald-colored lamp shades which sat on petite tables we also took, whose tops had cherubs painted on them and whose legs were carved in the shape of angels. Two doors down, we removed an Ethan Allen canopy bed, matching armoire, and love seat. We went to three dozen homes on The Ridge packing the U-Haul truck full of miscellaneous antiques and valuable items, all which were once in the Spec House or in Papa Tony's other houses.

For seven days we worked tirelessly packing item after item onto our truck. After they were packed, we hauled the items to storage units in Arkansas, Oklahoma, and Texas. We worked around the clock for a week.

On the seventh day, while we slept in the back of the truck as it drove between houses and storage units, the driver opened the back of the U-Haul's sliding gate at one of our stops to let in fresh air and sunlight.

"Hey, close that! We're sleeping. We've hardly been able to sleep all week," I grumbled, partially blinded by the light.

"Rise and shine, sunshine!" the OC pronounced. "We've got a few more hauls before we go home."

"They rarely let us sleep, and we only get three hours this time? This is insane," I whispered to a friend sleeping across from me.

"No kidding. I'm not sure I can even walk, I'm so tired," he said. "Other jobs, like passing out tracts or construction, we at least get five hours of sleep."

"It's for a good reason. Can you imagine if they get this stuff?" I asked. "Let's get into the front cab before this guy puts us on report. The last thing we need is Papa Tony thinking we want to sleep instead of work."

"The upside," I surmised, "we know where things worth probably a million dollars are located. How many kids besides us can say that? None!"

All three crews met at a KFC where we ate all the fried chicken we could stomach and washed it down from the endless soda fountain. The OC who organized the project stood at the front of the table.

"We've got one more project before we go home. We need to remove the maple siding in the church. We'll sleep there tonight. We have three days to remove, load, and hide the wood," he told us.

"That wood goes all the way up to the ceilings, and they're like sixty feet high. How are we gonna do that?" I asked.

"We'll have ladders and scaffolds. You afraid of heights?" he asked.

I was afraid of heights, but I remained silent, not wanting to appear weak in front of my friends.

We arrived at the empty church. The grand chandelier light hanging in the center of the room was gone. The base of the tall gray ladders stood on gray, smooth cement. The carpeting was gone. Six ladders extended up brown walls with long red ropes dangling from each.

Seeing the dangling rope reminded me of the Hanging Judges gallows. They looked like empty nooses. The OC gave each of us a tool belt with gloves, screw drivers, a hammer, pliers, and a small crowbar.

"Be careful. Don't break the wood panels. Be careful not to fall. See those ropes?" the OC asked. "Tie yourself to them when you climb the ladder. You get hurt and there won't be anyone to help you. I'll get you guys started. This is how you remove the panels."

He put a crowbar under one, gently pulled on it, and then released it. The panel settled back to its original position and small nails were raised on the side. He used pliers to remove the nails. Once free, he placed it on the floor.

"Stack the undamaged wood four feet high. Make a pile of the damaged ones in the middle of the room. I'll check on your progress tomorrow morning. Get to work!" he ordered.

He walked out, closing and locking the door behind him. One of the boys jiggled the door handle. "We're locked in!" he exclaimed.

"Better to be locked in here than locked in hell," I said, climbing the ladder. "I'll take this wall." Suddenly, the ladder began to slip from underneath me. One of the other boys managed to stop it with his foot before it slid completely to the floor.

"We should nail these ropes to the wall, so the ladders won't slide out from under us," Gregory suggested.

With that, each of us began removing panels, nailing the ropes to the wall as we continued moving up and down the ladders. We worked until we were exhausted. The church had restrooms where we drank water and peed, but we hadn't been left with any food. We slept that night, woke up the next morning, and worked again.

That morning, the OC opened the door and saw us all covered in fine particles of fiberglass insulation. Wood piles were strewn about.

"Hey, what is wrong with you guys? Why is there so much damaged maple wood here? If you knuckleheads followed my instructions, there wouldn't be so much damage!" the OC yelled. The sudden outburst startled Gregory, who was at the top of one of the ladders, causing him to fall off the ladder. Like a cat, in mid-air, he used one of his legs to push off the wall, turning his body as he fell, into a pile of insulation where he disappeared into the pile. When he emerged, we all laughed nervously, relieved he had survived.

A U.S. Court ruled the following February that everything could be seized by federal agents and sold at auction to the highest bidder in order to pay millions in tax liens. Thanks to us boys, there was little left to be taken and sold. But the world and its agents were still out to get us.

One cold morning, my brindle pit bull, Bruno, barked as unmarked police, sheriff, and federal vehicles passed by our home on their way to the Spec House. One van stopped at my house and four masked agents exited in black riot gear with AR-15 semi-automatic rifles in their hands. One approached our front door while the others took up positions around the sides and front of the house.

"Go calm Bruno down. Make him shut up! They'll shoot him if he keeps barking," Mom ordered me.

"What's going on? Why are there men with guns at our house?" It was the first time I had seen a gun up close. We didn't have guns on The Ridge, and I was afraid they would shoot us.

"This is the Beast. These men are part of the one-world order. They are here to persecute us for our beliefs. They want to stop us from preaching the gospel," Mom said.

I opened the back door and saw the agents, masks drawn over their faces, holding their firearms, and remembered the bow and arrows I had stashed in my tree fort. No way my arrows could ever pierce their gear.

"Go shut Bruno up! Go!" Mom barked. "You want him to get shot?"

"Shhhh ... no ... keep quiet," I whispered as I knelt beside him and rubbed the top of his head. "I'm going to let you go. If you keep barking these guys will shoot you. Now go! Make sure you come back for dinner!"

Just as I was getting ready to let go of him, an agent walked around the corner and I froze, still holding onto Bruno's collar, when I saw him.

"Hey boy, that's a good-looking dog you've got there. What's his name?" he asked.

I stood in silence, unable to move by the sight of the black rifle and riot gear. I had never seen such gear.

"What's his name, boy?"

Thankfully, Mom opened the side door at that moment, breaking my trance.

"Get in here," she hissed at me.

Immediately, I pulled Bruno inside with me, where my family was clustered in the living room. Dad went outside and talked to two of the agents. After that, he came back inside and told Mom to make some breakfast.

"It looks like we'll be moving to New York with Grandpa and Grandma," Dad told us while we ate.

"What?" I asked. "Why do we have to go to their house? What's wrong with our house?"

"The government is seizing our land, Benji. We can't stay here. We have just a week to move. You and I need to get up to the Spec House and get the van. It's in our name."

Bundled up in old winter coats and gloves, mine had a few spots where my mom patched and sewed the seams that had ripped, we walked to the Spec House. "Will I be able to see my friends at Grandma and Grandpa's house?" I asked Dad.

"No. They will not be there."

"Where will they be? Where will they go?"

"They'll probably go to their families."

"What about school? Who will teach us? I have homework due tomorrow."

"I'm not sure about that. And since when do you like doing homework? We'll have to figure it all out later," Dad replied. "There are a lot of things we'll have to figure out. What I do know is that our life here is done. God has bigger plans for us, and they do not include us living here anymore."

"So, my friends are gone. My school is gone. My home is gone," I bemoaned. "That seems like a weird plan for God to give us."

"Benji, not another word! You are a man now. You need to start acting like one," Dad scolded me. "*Capiche?*"

He never answered why God would take away our home, friends, church, school, and possessions. I knew he could tell me that God was trying us spiritually, but this didn't feel like we were being tried spiritually. It felt like we were being killed spiritually.

We walked past the soccer and football fields, the pond where I had spent untold hours fishing, and the A-frame and Spec House where my first memories as an infant and a child with Mia were made.

"Soak it in. This will most likely be the last time you'll see this place," Dad said.

I kicked the rocks on the road as we quietly continued our walk.

At the Spec House, agents had set up a de facto office at the entrance of the bottom floor. There, they approved the release of different items to church members as they queued up with receipts and ownership papers in their hands. Dad showed the agents his name on the registration for a beige Dodge van. He let me into the chapel to get my Gibson electric guitar. But when I tried to get in the van with it, an agent stopped me.

"Do you have a receipt for that?" the agent asked, an assault rifle slung over his chest.

I looked mournfully at Dad.

"Sorry Benji," Dad said, shaking his head.

"No, I don't," I told the agent, "but this is my guitar. I've had it my entire life," I argued. "I traded some ivory dominoes for it when I was five."

"If you don't have a receipt, then it stays here. I don't care what you traded for it," the agent retorted. "Put it down, kid!" he commanded, pointing.

I looked in the direction he had pointed, where I saw a pile of odd items like fishing poles, musical instruments in their cases, small bicycles, and a red toolbox. As I gently set my guitar next to the pile, I noticed my favorite guitar pick in the strings. Porter Wagner had given it to me when I was in Nashville, telling me, "This was the pick Elvis used when he played at the Grand Ole Opry."

I quickly pulled it from between the strings and stashed it in my pocket.

*The agent can't make me leave this.*

"Are we going to be taking Bruno with us?" I asked on our drive back to the house.

"There's no way we can do that. We have a long drive ahead and no room for him."

"He'll be good. I'll feed him and clean up after him."

"I'm not sure we will have enough food for us, let alone your dog."

All my life I had been taught that Jesus would provide for us as he always had, so at that moment it struck me as odd that Jesus could provide just enough for us, but not for

Bruno. Then I realized that Bruno might starve to death on his own and I began to cry.

The following days on The Ridge until we left were silent and still. None of my friends said goodbye to me nor did I say goodbye to them. No one walked around. No one even drove anywhere unless they were in the process of leaving. There were no church services. No prayer hours. No more messages from Papa Tony. The only words from him were old cassette tapes that circulated from family to family.

On the seventh day after the raid, I took all the food that remained in the pantry. Mom had already bagged up what goods we could take on our trip. I cooked it all and took it out back and made a big pile of it on top of Bruno's remaining dry dog food. Bruno circled me in anticipation. After I let him off his chain, he quickly lapped it up.

"I have to let you go, boy. I can't take you with me. I must leave you here with everything else I own. Stupid government is taking everything," I told him. "There's lots of food here for you and there are wild animals in the forest."

As if on cue, Bruno ran off into the forest in the direction of a distant rustle.

On the way back inside, I noticed my toolbox, bicycle, and fishing gear. I opened my tackle box and slipped a rubber worm in my pocket next to the guitar pick.

Along with the food Mom had grabbed, each of us packed two bags of clothing. As we boarded the van, I called out to Bruno, but there was no response. I peered through the naked trees, across the frozen ground covered in brown leaves, trying to catch any glimpse of him. I yelled for him some more until Mom told me to be quiet. I got in the van and cried.

When Dad started driving, he yelled at me, "Stop crying, Benji. You need to be a man about this. Remember what we talked about. God is going to try us in ways we never expected. This is one of those trials."

I got distracted by the unfolding events as we drove to the freeway dorm gate where we showed our papers before the sheriff's deputy moved the vehicle blocking our path to the world.

As we entered the world, I questioned how God could allow us to have to vacate our Arkansas property after our members had built it with their own blood, sweat, and tears. If they didn't have families to go to, people were going to have to live on the streets. As my friends streamed off the property to return to their families, wherever they may be, I doubted Papa Tony, who had promised us this day would never come.

How could God, a just God, allow hundreds of lives to be uprooted and changed practically overnight? Many of our people were thrown to the streets because they had no place to go. Children who had grown up together were torn apart and soon would be separated by thousands of miles. Tree forts were left abandoned. Bicycles stood motionless, their colored twirlers flapping aimlessly in the breeze while the cold rain rusted their chains. And, God, through Papa Tony, had allowed all of this.

My parents, Nicole, Miguel Junior, and baby Sal, the newest addition to our family who was born a year before the raid, and I headed toward our new life. I fell asleep and dreamed of a big house, something like the Spec House, built especially for us, and the many new friends I would meet. In my reverie stood a mom, other than Mom Nancy, in the driveway of a beautiful home with a lush, green lawn. She held a set of car keys and pointed to a race car next to her, implying it was mine. Next to her was a beautiful girl I knew was my girlfriend.

My dream shifted to me playing football, baseball, and volleyball on teams that would win awards and be celebrated on TV. I woke up, thinking of Bruno and my BMX bike, skateboards, clothes, train track, race cars, and fishing gear—things that had taken my entire life to acquire and I cried as fantasy could not compete with the hard reality of facts.

"Why are you crying?" Mom asked when she saw me.

I knew that talking about possessions would yield a rebuke but talking about my friends was allowed.

"My friends, will I see them again?"

"I know you didn't have a chance to say goodbye or make plans to keep in touch. None of us did," she answered. "We have to adapt. You'll make new friends. You're in tenth grade now. Maybe we can find a football team for you to play on."

"There are a lot of football teams where we're going, Benji," Dad chimed in.

I was trying to listen, but I wasn't really hearing any of what they were saying.

We drove from Arkansas to Delaware where we stayed with a church family for a month or two. After that, we packed up again and drove in the direction of Georgia before turning north again toward New York. Every four to six hours we stopped for gas and a phone call on a pay phone to Papa Tony. He directed our movements with each phone call.

If we needed to spend the night in a hotel, we couldn't leave the hotel room unless one of our parents was with us. We were instructed to not speak to anyone we saw. "After all, you kids are supposed to be in school right now and if the wrong person sees that you are not then they can take you away from us," Mom reminded us over and over.

"Where are we going?" I asked finally, seeing a "Welcome to West Virginia: Wild and Wonderful" sign.

"We've been talking with Papa Tony on the phone. In case you haven't noticed, we've taken back roads and stayed off the interstates," Dad said softly. "We go where the Lord leads us and he's telling Papa Tony where we should go."

I was sitting up front at this point, while Mom and the kids slept in back. The road was dark, illuminated only by the van's cone-shaped headlights. There were mountains and valleys surrounding us. "We need to make sure no one is following us."

"Are we going to be with Papa Tony? Will my friends be there?" I asked.

Dad did not respond to my questions right away. He sped up and adjusted the rearview mirror, before finally speaking.

"Papa Tony has entrusted us with a very important mission. He doesn't have too many people he can trust, but he trusts us. We're going to Florida to see Papa Tony."

Before reaching Florida, we stopped in South Carolina and stayed in a few motels for another two months. During the day, Nicole and I did homework from the Abeka Book curriculum. Sometimes we went for walks. Little Miguel played with and sometimes kept an eye on Sal when Mom got tired. At night, we watched Nickelodeon until we had to go to sleep then Dad watched HBO and Showtime. He watched adult movies that had nudity, violence, and drug use. Often, I feigned sleep while keeping one eye glued to the TV.

Our homework and TV time was not enough to distract us from the burning questions we had. Where were our friends? When would we see them again? Were they alive? Were they living in houses or did they have to live on the streets and become drug users, gay, or crazy, like Papa Tony always said anyone who left the church would become? Was there a way to connect with them?

Whenever I inquired, mom and dad would tell me to be quiet and to stop thinking about such purposeless pursuits. I couldn't though. The friends with whom I was reared were like the other half of me. Without them I felt empty and lost.

Papa Tony was still guiding our every move though, and he had us moving and driving around in case the Feds were following us. He didn't want us to go to him if we were being followed by them. That's what Dad told me. I understood that we needed to protect Papa Tony, but Dad also left the motel almost every day and would return late at night. He would take the van when he left, leaving us stranded at the motel. Whatever it was he was doing must have been top secret because he never told us and never told Mom.

After staying in South Carolina for a few months we drove to the northern tip of Florida and rented another motel room for a month. Eventually, while we were there, Papa Tony called us on the motel room phone and told us that we were not needed in Florida. Papa Tony told Dad he could always be called upon later and he needed to keep the satellite phone charged and turned on.

# CHAPTER TWELVE

## A New World: Meeting my Grandparents

Since we were not needed in Florida, we were left with only one option: to go stay with my dad's family in New York. The only thing I knew at that point about my grandparents was that I couldn't be in the family when they were around. Once, after living with Mom and Dad at The Ridge for four years, Mom came to my room and announced, "Grandma and Grandpa Vasquez are coming to visit The Ridge next week. They'll be here for one week. You'll go live with another family while they're here. They want to take Dad from the church. We don't want them to know you are living with us because they might try to take you too," she said. "Clean out your room and pack. A van will come by to take your stuff tomorrow."

I knew to expect this, and, to me, it all seemed normal. Like a deck of cards, I was used to being shuffled around.

"Well, what about the photos of me? They'll see them and wonder who I am."

"Nicole will remove any pictures of you from the house. I guess I'll make sure we don't open any of the family photo albums."

The day of their arrival I hid out in the cover of the leafy peach grove, watching from afar, essentially stalking my family. Grandma and Grandpa walked slowly toward the house, while Grandma carefully examined everything around her, but she did not see me hiding in the grove. Grandpa held Nicole's hand and made a few attempts to pick her up, but she ran off toward Dad. As they got closer to the house, she finally let him pick her up. She was only seven back then, but she still had a strong sense of what she wanted.

A week later, they were gone, and I returned home. They had taken a lot of photos and had them laying in a pile on the living room table. I looked through them and saw a photo of Dad Miguel sitting with his father. Behind them was a photo of me, Nicole, and little Miguel. Mom saw me looking at it.

"I think your sister left it on purpose. She talked about you even though she was told not to. They know all about you now."

I bubbled ecstatically knowing they knew about me. By this point in my life, I had had five different families and a few distant grandparents, but none of them had ever acknowledged me because I was not a biological or permanent child in their families. With the Vasquezes, for all intents and purposes, I thought I was now a permanent member of the family, and that these grandparents had chosen to accept me.

And so, it was, that five years after the grandparents' initial visit to the church, and a four-month trek to get there, we pulled up to their Long Island trailer park community on a hot June day in 1991. My grandparents stood, awaiting our arrival, on the steps of their home, an old single-wide trailer with a small, neatly landscaped yard. It didn't have flowers or a white picket fence like some of the other trailers. Instead, only a four-door white car sat parked outside.

I jumped out of the van, happy to stretch my legs, but apprehensive. I stood aside, leaning against the van, twisting the curls above my forehead. I watched Grandpa as he hugged, kissed, cried, and lovingly smacked his prodigal son on the side of the head. Grandma kissed Dad all over his face. It made me think of when Ebony gave birth and cleaned her newborn foal.

Grandpa ushered him inside, but Grandma, in a floral blouse and white pedal pushers, stood on the porch with tears running down her face. She held her arms out, waiting for an embrace, and called out, "Get up here and give me a hug, you rascals!" she playfully ordered. Nicole enthusiastically ran up the steps to be enveloped by her. Mom, holding Sal, was next to be hugged. She looked Grandma in the eyes and tilted her head.

"Thank you. We don't have anywhere to go," she said and went inside.

Grandma cried some more. It seemed her tears were constant, but she kept smiling and wiping them as they poured out of her. She then turned her focus on me. I stared back, lingering, unsure how to approach her. "What are you waiting for? Are you going to give your grandma a hug? Or am I going to have to come down there and grab you?" she asked, in her strong New York accent.

Her smile disarmed me, and I jumped up the steps and grabbed her around the waist. She was soft, warm, and smelled like garlic. I loved her right way because she reminded me of Grandma Dee who always smiled and had a big hug waiting for me whenever I saw her. I felt right at home and her warm reception helped me to forget my losses. She rubbed her hands through my hair then gently turned my face to hers.

"I've heard a lot about you, Mister. You are welcome here for as long as you are alive," she told me, looking directly into my eyes. "Me and Grandpa are your grandparents if you want us to be. We will always love you, no matter what. Is that okay?"

"We don't have a house anymore. They took it," I said.

"I know. It's okay, Benji, this is your home now," she said then turned toward the inside of the home.

"I love you even if you are a knucklehead," she said, looking at Dad. "That's for your dad, not you. I bet you all are hungry. I made spaghetti and meatballs," she said, making her way to her humble kitchen.

As the family sat down, she set a plate of spaghetti, meatballs, and bread in front of me and hugged and kissed the top of my head.

"Eat up. When you're done, go outside to play. There are some neighborhood kids and other family on the way," she said. "They can't wait to meet you."

The meatballs were the best thing I had ever eaten. They were like nothing I had ever eaten. Fresh garlic and parsley mixed with pork and parmesan cheese and egg yolk. Once I was full, I looked through the screen door where I saw four boys out front playing with an insect they found trapped on the hot asphalt road. I stepped outside and one of them greeted me.

"Do you play football?" asked one boy. "Your grandma told us you were coming."

Looking at the boys, I wondered if their souls were saved. Had they accepted Jesus into their hearts? What sins will they commit in my presence?

A boy threw a football to me, but not far enough. It landed on the asphalt. I picked it up and noticed how the fresh asphalt had bubbles. It was dark black and still soft. I pushed my finger into it. In some places, there were seams of twisted tar covering the earth below. Would the seams open to reveal hell below? Would Satan rise from the seams? Were the bubbles concealing the lake of fire? Would the ground open and swallow me alive? Papa Tony had said it would. I began to feel anxious.

I stepped off the tar, to be safe, and onto the grass. I threw the football back to the boy.

"There's a field that way," said another boy, gesturing with his head. "We're gonna play two-hand touch. Wanna play?"

"Sure," I said, walking along the grass until the asphalt ended and the cement began.

We reached a wire fence that marked the boundary of the trailer park. The fence had been cut and twisted into an opening large enough to allow us boys to pass through. As I approached the fence, the fear of being caught breaking the rules shot through me, momentarily paralyzing me.

One of the boys noticed and tried to reassure me.

"No one cares if we use the field," he said. "Besides, no can see you. Come on."

No one can see me. Yeah, right. Papa Tony knew what I was doing because God tells him everything I do. I've committed too many sins and gotten away with most of them. I will be punished for them eventually.

Then, like a light switch being flipped on in my head, my thoughts turned rogue.

No. Papa Tony had lied about Grandma Susie rising from the dead. He must be a false prophet! He beat my friends even though the Bible says to lay hands on no one. Papa Tony broke the golden rule which commands us to do unto others as we would have them do unto us. He wouldn't like it if I had my friends stretch him out by his hands and legs and beat him until his eye rolled to the back of his skull. He wouldn't like it at all. So why did he do that to us? He violated Jesus' commandment that said, "Suffer little children to come unto me, and forbid them not, for of such is the kingdom of heaven." Papa Tony beat us. He didn't bring us to heaven. He brought hell to us. He said looking at girls was evil, but God made all of us in his image, which means girls are holy.

I flipped the switch in my head back and suppressed my thoughts while I wiggled through the fence opening to the other side. I looked toward the sky, pausing for a moment, wondering if I would be struck down, but I wasn't. The boys began to choose teams.

"Hey, you know how to play or what?" someone yelled.

"Yeah!" I yelled back.

Why wasn't God punishing me? I kept thinking maybe he wasn't there or maybe it's all been one big lie.

I ran toward the boys, the grass soft under my feet.

"What position?" one of the boys yelled back.

"Wide receiver!"

A few weeks after arriving in Long Island, a black U.S. government van with tinted windows pulled in front of Grandma and Grandpa's house. A U.S. Marshals agent came to the door and asked to speak with Dad. Wearing a NY Giants football shirt and sweatpants, Dad stepped outside with the man. Through the trailer's open, side window, I strained to hear their conversation. Mostly I could only make out the muffled, indiscernible sounds of an argument, before I heard an agent say, "We know you have the boy with you. We know you have Benji and he's not your son. From the looks of things, you couldn't afford to get wrapped up in court proceedings for child kidnapping, child endangerment, and neglect."

Dad stood silent for a minute, as if considering what the agent said to him.

Why would they say that to him? He's my dad. Papa Tony said the one-world government would try to take me away. That must be why he said that.

"Benji has only us and we love him," Dad replied. "We are providing a home for him. If you take him, where will you put him? In a foster home?"

"It doesn't have to be that way," the agent replied.

"What do you want from me?"

"It's quite simple. What's the phone number to your satellite phone?"

"You came by to ask for my phone number?"

"Yes," the agent said and handed Dad a pen and a piece of paper.

I saw Dad write something on the paper and the agent looked at him and smiled.

"Just keep doing what you're doing. If Alamo calls, you take his call. If he asks you to go somewhere, go. Just keep doing exactly what you have been doing and we won't come after you."

The agents got into their van and drove off, leaving Dad standing in front of the trailer home feeling dumbfounded.

Mom Nancy saw me eavesdropping and told me to get away from the window. I walked away feeling confused and yet excited that someone would fight over me. I had it all. I had a family with the Vasquezes, and now that we were in New York I had the opportunity to meet new people and make new friends.

I remembered the dream I had on the night we left The Ridge. I wondered if I was taken away from the Vasquezes, would I get that sports car? Would I get to play sports and have the pretty girlfriend and big house from the dream?

Later that day, our family went to a large family cookout closer to the city. After the barbecue, the family went back to the trailer home and left me there with Dad's aunt, uncle, and their daughter. Their daughter, Tina, my cousin, was a beautiful sixteen-year-old with long, red hair. She was angelic. She had kind eyes and was gentle when she spoke. She also had a bubbly energy she concealed just beneath her gentle nature.

We talked about my trip to Long Island and my life in the church. I sensed that she was much different than the girls from the church. She wore clothes that revealed some cleavage and she wore tight pants.

It wasn't just that the church girls didn't wear the same types of clothes, but rather Tina had a level of self-confidence that seemed pure and unfiltered. She was comfortable with her body. She sat so close to me on the couch that our legs touched. At one point, her arm rested on mine. At another point, she used my leg as a pillow as we watched MTV. I loved the touching.

She was relaxed and free. I, on the other hand, wanted to be free like her but struggled to be comfortable with my own body. I was fine with her initiating small touches, but I could not initiate it on my own without a lot of internal reassurance. When I got up to get a cup of water and returned to the sofa, I made sure to not touch her as I sat down because touching a girl was sexual to me.

She moved closer to me, asking, "Do you think I'm going to bite you?"

When I told her I did not, she told me to "relax."

She and I were watching R.E.M. sing "Losing my Religion" on MTV in the living room. R.E.M.'s words spoke to me as I realized I had not prayed or read the Bible in months. I was losing my religion with R.E.M. and, yet, nothing bad was happening to me. No devil grabbed me. God didn't open the sky and smite me with lightning. There were no plagues afflicting me. I was experiencing freedom for the first time and there was nothing evil about it.

"You want to go to a party with me?" she asked as she turned to me smiling, raising her eyebrows, and twirling her hair. "There will be lots of cute girls I can introduce you to."

I was uncomfortable with meeting new people. I struggled with what I thought my role was as it pertained to girls. Could I talk to them, or not? Did I have permission to? Would God judge me for talking to girls? Even if it was clear that I could, I didn't know how to be cool with new people. It's like they spoke a foreign language.

"No, I don't want to go," I answered, trying to sound as nonchalant as possible.

Tina's mom stood nearby in the kitchen and overheard the conversation.

"Why don't you want to go with Tina? She's a very popular girl. She knows a lot of people."

"I just don't want to," I answered, jumping off the couch and running to the bathroom. I was self-conscious as I looked at the zits popping up everywhere on my face. I popped a few and then applied a beige-colored zit concealer. I scrutinized my clothes in disgust. They were outdated and made it evident that I was too poor to afford new clothes. It was all too much for me to want to be seen in public. Plus, I had no experience with kids outside in the world. What would I talk about? The Bible? I didn't think so.

When I returned to the living room, Tina was gone.

"I think you hurt her feelings," her mother said. "She thinks you don't like her because you don't want to go to the party with her."

"I have zits. Look. How am I supposed to go to a party looking like this? Plus, I'm from Arkansas. They'll call me a hick."

"You're a handsome young man. I don't think anyone will care where you're from. You should go. Talk to Tina. She's in her room about to cry."

I realized this was the first time a mom saw me as just Benji. I wasn't the special Jewish-Arab or Papa Tony's son. I was just a boy who made a girl cry, and that was not who I wanted to be.

I walked to her room and opened the door without knocking. Looking back on that, I realize I hadn't been taught anything about respecting boundaries. At the time, all I could think was I had to get to Tina before she started crying. Knocking on the door would have simply wasted time. She waved me away while shaking her head "no." With her other hand, she held a phone to her ear. The coiled wire twirled around her index finger.

"No. He's not coming. He just doesn't want to come ... I don't know why. He said he didn't want to. I can't read his mind."

I positioned myself so she could see me shaking my head "yes" as I enunciated "I'll go with you" with my lips. When she became aware, she giggled with enthusiasm.

"Wait! He's coming with me!" She hung up the phone and excitedly jumped up and down while hugging me.

I was still nervous, but said to her, "If you promise not to leave me alone with a bunch of strangers, I'll go."

"I will introduce you to my other girlfriends. Maybe you'll like one of them. They are cute and cool. My friend, Crystal, just got a convertible for her birthday. I think you might be her type."

Her type, I thought. What does that mean? I thought I was friends with all the girls I like. I had no idea what a type was.

I stood there just looking at her, not knowing what my next move should be. Tapping me on the shoulder, she said, "Go take a shower and get cleaned up. We'll leave in forty-five minutes."

The party was at an Italian restaurant. The walls and floor melded together with the same dark red wood. There was a mix of young adults and teens with a few adults chaperoning the event. Everybody was pretty much dressed up, with the girls wearing dresses and the boys were clad in dress pants, buttoned down shirts, and jackets. In my baggy denim jeans, a light blue Ocean Pacific T-shirt with holes in the armpits and dirty Reebok Pump basketball shoes, I felt somewhat out of place as I took it all in. I stuck close to Tina, feeling my usual awkwardness, as she went from group to group kissing and hugging her friends. She introduced them all to me, but I could feel myself lacking in a certain social skill they all seemed to have. I realized that I wasn't cool like them.

Some of the teens talked about the colleges and universities they planned to attend while I thought about how I had not been in school for eight months. I had a stack of homeschooling materials I was supposed to teach myself, but I didn't even understand enough to get started.

The girls congregated at one end of the table, exchanging stories and photographs. The boys talked about the girls at the other end. I did not understand the meaning of some of the words they used.

One boy was "dating" a girl. Another was "seeing" a girl. Another was "sleeping" with a girl and she made him use a "jimmy."

"What is dating?" I asked myself.

I see all girls all the time. Why would it matter if these guys saw those girls? What is that supposed to mean? Why would a girl make this boy bring a guy named Jimmy into their bed? These questions plagued me.

"I never use a jimmy. I like it natural. Know what I mean?" said one cousin, slapping me on the back.

"I hate Jimmy," I responded, trying to act cool. "Wouldn't let that guy anywhere near my girl."

Confused, the cousin furrowed his brow and chuckled.

"Okay, okay, I am going over there," he said and walked away.

I remained seated for what had seemed like an eternity when the cousin who had just walked away came back with two other guys.

"Hey, tell these guys what you told me about jimmy. Go on!"

"I would never let Jimmy near my girl. I'd kick his butt."

They erupted in laughter.

I knew they were laughing at me, but I didn't know why, so I asked, "What's so funny?"

"Nothing, nothing … it's just jimmy is another word for a condom. It's okay if you're a virgin."

"I'm not a virgin!" I shouted.

A few tables over, some of the girls turned to see what the commotion was about.

A little bit quieter, I said, "Yeah, I've done it." I proceeded to tell them the story of me and Emmanuala in the pool. And then of me and Chandra in the church.

"That's not doing it, man," my cousin said. "To do it, you have to stick it all the way in and leave a deposit. Using the jimmy lets you make the deposit without making a deposit.

Know what I mean?" His New York accent made him sound like such a tough guy to me.

I answered, "Yes," even though I really had no clue. I knew nothing of a woman's anatomy. I wished they would tell me more, but I couldn't get useful information from these guys in this place.

I began to sulk, hating each passing moment. The distance between me and the people at the table might as well have been a million miles. I couldn't leverage the backing of Papa Tony here. There was no one here who would do what I wanted because otherwise they knew I could put them on report. No one here knew I was the fastest and one of the strongest boys in my age group. None of them knew I was chosen to bring peace to the Middle East. Even if they did know, they wouldn't have cared. It seemed none of that mattered in the world.

Tina saw me sitting alone and walked over, smiling and tossing her hair over her shoulder.

"Hi, Benji! Aren't you having fun?" she asked.

I noticed the curves of her breasts peeking through her blouse. I stared, and she knew it but didn't seem to care. In fact, she leaned over the table even more. When I noticed the other boys noticing me looking at her, I averted my eyes.

"Just want to make sure you're doing okay," she said. "We can't have the newest member of our family feeling left out."

"I'm okay," I answered, in a tone meant to convey my boredom. Suddenly, my nose started bleeding.

Alarmed, Tina stepped back, grabbed a napkin, and tried handing it to me.

"I don't need your help!" I rudely shot back. "Leave me alone!"

She scowled and returned to her friends.

Before the party ended, Mom walked into the restaurant and said hello to Tina and found me at the end of a long table sitting by myself.

"I have some sad news for you. Your dad needs to leave for a while. Papa Tony needs him. With just having baby Sal and now Dad leaving, I need a break. I want you to stay with cousins Becky and Preston while he's away. I know you'll have fun. When your dad gets back, we'll come get you. You remember Preston and Becky?" she asked.

"I met him a few times. Preston is the guy who has the gutter business. He always talks about it."

"They don't have any children of their own. You will like living with them. They have a nice big house and will be able to provide whatever you need. I've already taken your clothes and schoolbooks to their house."

I realized, once again, I was being kicked out of the family for something to do with Dad. First, it was his parents visiting and now this. This time, however, part of me wanted to get away from them too. I wanted to see the world.

After the party that evening, Mom dropped me off at Becky and Preston's house. They were standing under the arch of their large, white and gray painted townhome. Their home looked like the other hundred homes in the neighborhood: nice and kempt.

After mom drove away, we went inside. Becky said, "Benji we want to take care of you and want to be your parents now. Would you like that?"

I stood there in their big kitchen thinking about how I began living with the Vasquez family after Grandma Susie died and about how many other families they had asked me to live with. It had seemed normal before, but now it didn't. This was the second time my Vasquez family had done this, and it was obvious to me they did not want me. And, I didn't really want to be with them all the time either. I secretly wanted to watch R-rated movies without getting into trouble. And even though I had a long way to go to feel socially comfortable, I knew I wanted to spend more time with girls and boys my age.

"Do you have TV? What about MTV?" I inquired of them.

Not expecting such an easy transition, the couple looked at each other with both surprise and relief and simultaneously said, "We have that. Come inside. We'll get you settled."

My large room had a big bed, a basketball, a football, and a baseball glove and ball in the corner. The metal desk had a card on it. When I opened it, a Target gift card fell out of it. It had a hundred dollars on it, more money than I had ever had in my life. The card read:

*Welcome to the family, Benji!*
*Use this card for whatever you want.*
*Love,*
*Becky and Preston Houghton*

Becky brought popcorn into the living room while Preston grabbed some bean bags. We watched MTV and then the movie "Arachnophobia" like a family. Before I knew it, a month went by and I had gotten a dirt bike, remote control cars, and fishing gear. I got to watch hours of MTV and hours of watching scrambled porn. We didn't go to church, but I noticed God didn't smite this family for not going. I watched as much MTV as I possibly could because it taught me about the world.

One night, Preston caught me watching the scrambled porn. I think he probably heard it. But he didn't whip me or beat me. He just asked me to keep the volume down. That was it. I was embarrassed he caught me, but ecstatic that I was not beaten or made to fast, or even worse, forced to reveal this shame to my peers in a public setting in total embarrassment.

Some of the male cousins in the family came over on the weekends or I went to their homes. We played baseball in each other's backyards and swam. The dad of one of the cousins was a high school football coach. One day he told me, "You should really try out for the football team. I'm pretty sure you'll make the squad."

For the first time in a long time, I had a fun life, one worth living. And for the first time in my life, the outside world was making more sense. I was even beginning to feel normal again, like how I felt before Grandma Susie died.

After two months of living with Becky and Preston, Dad and Mom came to retrieve me, thanking Becky and Preston. Becky exited the home crying with Preston after her. "We're going to miss you," she said as I was ushered into the van.

I was angry that I was being forced to leave this new life. I felt the anger in my chest and forehead. It took the form of a boiling feeling, but I knew I couldn't show it too much. I was afraid how Dad Miguel would react if I said what was on my mind. The only thing I could muster to say was, "What about all my stuff?"

"You left it all once on The Ridge. You can leave it again. Let's go," Mom said.

So, I boarded the van with only the clothes on my back. Once the doors to the van were closed and the Houghtons could not hear him, Dad looked directly at me and said, "We're going back to Arkansas. You and I are going to be working for a family member until November, so we can save up for a house for the family. They caught Papa Tony and he's in jail."

"Papa Tony is in jail? Why is he in jail?"

"Papa Tony was captured in Tampa, Florida, using a fake ID posing as one of the other brothers. He was charged with threatening to kidnap a federal judge, interstate flight, and felony child abuse. It's in all the newspapers."

"He threatened a federal judge? Are you talking about the time he said he would take Judge Arnold out to the woods and hold court in the forest? He was just kidding, wasn't he?"

But Dad didn't answer.

Then I remembered hearing about Sebastian getting one hundred forty swats and seeing him on TV. The news episode showed his blurred butt on the TV saying that the bruising on it was too graphic for the evening news.

"Is the felony child abuse for when Sebastian got beaten?" I thought it probably was but wanted to hear them finally acknowledge that the beatings were too much for us kids.

Mom and Dad looked at each other but refused to answer me. We drove on in silence to Grandma and Grandpa's trailer home.

# CHAPTER THIRTEEN

A Search for Truth

In November 1991, my family drove out of cold New York to frozen Fort Smith, Arkansas, to try to rebuild the community we had left behind. The Ridge had been seized by the government and the Spec House was for sale, along with all our homes and property, at government auction. We drove to the Freeway dorm but were blocked by a chained gate and a "No Trespassing" sign.

A few of the adults who had grown up in the Fort Smith area settled with their parents in their homes. There were three to five homes in the area like these where members could find refuge for short periods of time. Although these properties were not church owned, they were church friendly.

No longer in possession of any church-owned real estate in Arkansas, Papa Tony ordered that the Vasquezes and a few other families rent homes in Fort Smith. Between my family, the church-friendly families, and the other families who were renting, there were still between forty to sixty followers in the Fort Smith area. Anyone over the age of eleven was supposed to be working and donating a hundred percent of their income to the church. We continued to pass out tracts. Eventually, after a few months of returning to Arkansas, we rented a small church building where we congregated on Sundays and listened to Papa Tony's recorded sermons.

We rented a small L-shaped, ranch style, three-bedroom home in a quiet Fort Smith neighborhood. All the church records were stored in the office of our house, therefore our home served as the church office.

The return to Arkansas was depressing. We had to keep the windows of the house covered by curtains and blinds. There was no cable TV either. I slept on the floor with my Walkman and a blanket, but I had no pillow. My only solace was an occasional song on the radio by Madonna or Michael Jackson. I would go to sleep with them and wake up to them every chance I got, which was often interrupted by me clicking off the radio and pressing the play button to play the Bible on tape when anyone came near me.

A few friends migrated back to Arkansas from wherever they were dispersed after the raid. I looked forward to seeing them on Sundays when they came for services. They usually left shortly after unless there was a special event like a birthday. Life was torture at a turtle's speed because I had been given a taste of the normal social life in the world, but here the church rules were back in force: no talking to girls, no walking outside the property without a witness, and no anything unless it was biblical. The daily Bible and prayer hours were reinstated. Not being able to talk to girls again was the most difficult part of life.

I missed the New York family. I missed Grandma's meatballs and spaghetti. I missed playing football with the boys at the trailer park and the few girls who came around to watch. I missed Tina. Now I was confined to spending time with only the family inside the small property.

In order to earn money, I asked Dad if I could mow lawns during the day. Dad said I could, but only if I answered the church phones at night. So, I answered the phones for the church at nights, but that didn't pay anything.

"The Tony and Susie Alamo Foundation," I said one night when answering phones. "This is Benji. How can I help?"

"Benji, is that you?" asked Papa Tony in a raspy baritone.

I knew it was him. There was no other voice in the world like his. It sent shivers down my spine when I heard it.

"Yes, Papa Tony. It's me."

"How old are you now?" he asked.

"I just turned sixteen."

"Praise the Lord! It's been awhile since I've seen you. How tall are you?"

"I'm about 5'5"."

"Did you know they locked me up?"

"Yes."

"They locked me up for doing the Lord's work," Papa Tony bellowed. "The one-world government hates me because I've been exposing their lies. The Vatican has infested our government. And she's got the White House, Congress, the U.S. Department of Labor, the IRS, the FBI, and the Supreme Court kissing her ring. They are taking the liberties of the American people and trying to destroy the true soldiers of Christ."

If my life was a teeter-totter, the world was on one side of the beam and Papa Tony was on the other. I sat in between what he told me and what I now knew to be true. The world was so different than what he preached. Maybe the government was doing these things to us, but I did not see a devil on the outside. The ground didn't open and swallow me either. And I knew that the beatings we kids received were wrong. Families protected their children as best they could in the world. Grandma and Grandpa Vasquez, Preston and Becky, and all the Vasquez uncles and aunts showed that to me.

Papa Tony's lecture against the Vatican devolved, and he asked, "Have you been reading and praying every day?"

"Yes. Every morning, noon, and at night, I pray and read the Bible," I replied. My lie was now automatic and came easy to me. I wasn't afraid because it was a self-preserving act to not get beaten or to be forced to go without food for a week. I had to lie.

"I have a surprise for you, to reward you for the good work you've been doing. What size are your feet?"

"Size nine."

"I have a pair of rattlesnake-skin cowboy boots just your size. How would you like it if I sent them to you?"

"I would like that. Are they your boots?"

"Yes, they are mine. I don't need them anymore. I'll send them to you soon," Papa Tony answered.

I thanked him and asked him if there was a message I could take.

"Tell the congregation to read and study Proverbs 3:5: 'Trust in the Lord and lean not on your own understanding.' Have your dad call me in the morning," Papa Tony told me.

I hung up the phone, glad to have spoken to him, but immediately began rummaging through the files, looking for the muscle magazines I remember Papa Tony telling me he was in. I hoped there would be a few cute girls in bikinis. I found a few, but I also found an article about a man named Craig Culler.

In the 60's and 70's, the church sent the local newspapers a picture and an essay about its new converts. Doing so gave the church a sense of legitimacy, and it was free advertising. Above this article, there was a picture of a handsome, bright-eyed, blond-haired man. He was described as a college dropout who, prior to joining the Church in 1969, was a drunkard and marijuana abuser.

The last name Culler struck me. Someone once told me my mom had left the Church with this man. I made a copy of the document and hid it in a manila file folder.

After finding the first article, I continued rummaging through the files. After several days, I had looked through nearly every article regarding every new convert who had joined the Church since the sixties. Some were OCs I had known since childhood. Others I did not recognize who were no longer members. One night I opened a file full of birth certificates. I read the names to myself. Each name was one of the children with whom I was reared. They were my friends, the closest people to me, but ninety-nine percent of them were no longer around.

One birth certificate was mine.

I had never seen my name on an official document. It never even occurred to me that such a document existed. I read through it, noticing an infant footprint in ink on the bottom. My birth date, my father's name, where I was born, and where my father was born came next. Under "Mother," I read an unfamiliar name ... Bethany ... with the maiden name of Scheine.

In amazement, I stared at the document for a while. I inspected the official state seal. For the first time in my life, I was holding and looking at something that defined and recorded something about my own mother, a woman about whom I knew nothing.

As I stared at my birth certificate, questions coursed through me. Who is she? Why don't I remember her? Where is she? Why did she leave? Why didn't she take me with her?

Then the realization of what the certificate meant came to me. The document proved who I am, and who my parents are. This was my mother, my father, and me together. The union of all three of us on my birth certificate seemed like it should be the most normal thing in the world and yet it had eluded me my entire life. This moment reignited the search I had started four years ago but was thwarted from completing when all the beatings and upheaval began. But now, I was holding an official document with my mother's name printed on it. My real mother who gave birth to me.

I placed the certificate in my hiding place next to my cash from mowing lawns and the article about Craig Culler. After finding my birth certificate, I searched the files methodically, like a detective poring over the details of a case. I did not miss a thing. Within a week, I found an article about Bethany Scheine and her conversion to the church. It said she was originally from New York and had moved to California, where she learned of the church. There were hundreds of articles of church members with their pictures stapled to them. This article, like all the others, had a picture stapled to it—except this one was of my mother with the two children in the photo that my friend showed me years ago.

For the first time in my sixteen years of living, I saw a picture of my mother. I was fixated on the photo, taking in every detail: her brown eyes and closed mouth, neither smiling nor frowning. Her long, flowing brown hair and petite size. I remained like that, studying the photo for quite some time.

I decided I had her eyes, her nose, and maybe even her hair. She looked at the camera with a gentle, ambiguous intensity, which I interpreted as saying, "I am tired, but I am happy." I had never seen anything like it, but her face glowed on the page. I felt a tingle in the back of my head, and I kissed the photo and held it to my cheeks.

I said her name softly, struggling with the pronunciation of her last name. I mouthed the 'S-c-h' and settled on making the 'C' silent so that when I said it out loud it sounded like "shine." I liked the sound and thought it appropriate that my mom looked like she shone in the photograph and her name sounded like "shine."

As I sat hunched over the box, I looked around the office to make sure no one had seen me. I looked at the nearby clock and realized it was almost 3:00 AM. Feeling safe, I let go of my tears which flowed uncontrollably. I fell to the ground between the boxes and sobbed, drenching the upper half of my shirt.

I grieved what I had missed: having my own mother, just one mother in my life who gave birth to me and raised me. I cried because I never knew her. I cried because I did not understand why she left me and my father. I was told she was dead, a sinner, an adulterer, and was burning in hell forever. But I had been told so many lies, I wondered if these were lies as well. Suddenly, I was compelled to know the truth. I had to find out if she was still alive and where she lived.

I began thinking again about the beatings and the forced fasting and wondered if she was ever beaten by Papa Tony or Grandma Susie? Was she ever forced to fast? Over the next couple weeks, my mind ruminated daily with questions about my mother's existence. By the second week in April of 1992, I could not take it any longer and I decided I had to look for her.

With unlimited access to the phones, the old Commodore computer in the office, and no adult supervision, I looked up area codes for Brooklyn, New York, and Uniontown, Pennsylvania, the birthplaces shown for my mother and my father on my birth certificate.

I dialed directory assistance, using a Brooklyn area code followed by 555-1212.

I did the same with each of the area codes I found for Brooklyn and Uniontown, but each time had the same results: no Scheines listed. Finally, I found a list of every area code in the US stored on the computer's database, and I tried every single one in New York, but I still didn't have any success.

With no results in New York, or Uniontown, Pennsylvania, I looked at my list of area codes and decided to focus on Arkansas, Florida, and California. I was terrified of being caught, but I had to make these calls. I had to know if she was dead or alive. I called all the area codes around Little Rock and Fort Smith, Arkansas, but had no luck. I called a few area codes in Florida, but still no matches. I was feeling dejected and tired after calling so many area codes, so I decided to stop for the time being, with a plan to start looking for my dad the next day.

With the rest of the night ahead of me, I opened the newspaper to the back, where the personal ads were located. Down a column were pictures of women dressed in sultry lingerie. I did not have the foresight or experience to know that the phone numbers would show up on the phone bill. It never even crossed my mind as I proceeded to call the first number.

"Are you over eighteen and want to enjoy the hottest, steamiest, and most erotic conversation with a beautiful young woman? If so, dial one. If you want to talk to a hot stud, then dial two."

The answering message was sexual and enticing, but the following recording: "$5.99 for the first minute and .99 cents for each minute thereafter to be billed to your telephone provider," was rapidly stated.

I dialed one.

"Hello handsome, where are you calling me from?" said a woman with a voice as soft as velvet.

"I'm in Arkansas."

"Ohhhh … Arkansas … is it cold out there?"

"Yeah, it's cold but starting to warm up."

"Ohhhh … well, let's see if we can warm it up some more," she responded in a lusty, seductive voice.

"Make me happy," I blurted out like a child sitting on Santa's lap.

There was a pause.

"Make you happy?" she asked. "Make you happy? How old are you? Are you even eighteen?"

"Ummm … yes," I said nervously, before swiftly hanging up the phone.

The call had lasted only a few minutes, but I felt such a rush that I picked up the phone and dialed the next ad. I had similar conversations with several women telling them to make me happy.

None did. Instead, they told me to stop calling.

Though I was not thinking at the time of the phone bill revealing what I had been doing, thankfully it was not due for another few weeks. Had it arrived while I was still there, I would have been in big trouble.

That night I dreamed of my parents. They stood at the end of a long lawn overgrown with weeds. My dad was wearing a carpenter's belt over his jeans and he waved me over with a hammer in his hand. My mom's face floated behind him. With my lawn mower, I cut the grass between me and them, trying to get closer. The lawn stretched two steps with each step I took in their direction. The more steps I took in their direction, the further away from me they moved. In the dream, the weeds got thicker and my mower got stuck. I never made it to them.

I started the next day's search by calling an operator in a different Pennsylvania area code who gave me four phone numbers that seemed to match. I called them all, but no one answered. Almost ready to give up, I decided to try the operator in Brooklyn, New York, once more, and again asked for the last name of "Scheine." Unlike the other operators, this operator asked me to spell the last name. I spelled out S-c-h-e-i-n-e.

"There is one Scheine in Brooklyn. Do you want that number?" she asked.

"What did you say?" I asked, half thinking I must be dreaming. I got goosebumps on my arms when she replied. It was then that I realized the other operators had undoubtedly been looking for the wrong spelling, probably by using the spelling of S-h-i-n-e.

"There is one Scheine in Brooklyn. Do you want that number? Her name is Jean Scheine. Is that who you want?" she asked.

"Do I want it? Of course, I want it."

"Here's the number …."

I quickly dialed the number and it rang several times before I heard a frail sounding voice of an elderly woman with a New York accent answer in a hushed tone.

"Hello, who is this and why are you calling me at such a time?" She asked the last part with some irritation, but also with genuine curiosity.

"I'm sorry," I said, suddenly thinking about it being 3:00 AM in Brooklyn. "I am Benji Risha. I am looking for my mom, Bethany Scheine. Do you know her?"

"Who are you? What do you want from me?" she asked, still irritated. "Leave me alone."

The next sound I heard was a dial tone as she hung up the phone.

The disappointment dissipated quickly. I was too excited to get down about being hung up on. I was exhilarated. I felt like I had genuine hope for the first time in my life. Unlike when I hoped I would be changed by saying the sinner's prayer at age five. And, unlike the hope I had of not being caught for the stuff I did with the girls, this hope was fresh and revitalizing to me. This hope was like the hope a bird has in its wings. This hope came from following my own heart and daring to escape the cage of someone else's rules. This hope was liberating.

I waited until the next night before I tried the number again. "I'm sorry to bother you, but I am looking for my mom."

"I am not your mom. Why are you calling me?"

"You have the same last name as her."

"I'm sorry, but it's three in the morning. Can you call me at a better time?"

She again abruptly hung up the phone.

I returned to work the following night to find Kiona sitting in my chair with his big feet resting right on top of the desk. He was leaning back as if he planned on staying for a while.

"What are you doing here? It's almost 10:00 PM and time for my shift."

"Benji, why don't you like me?" he asked. "When Papa Tony married my mom, I thought we were gonna be brothers. Instead, you mad dog me every time you see me."

"Kiona, you told me that Papa Tony was no longer my dad. You remember that? Well, that wasn't cool," I said. "It was very uncool of you. Plus, you're ugly and you have zits."

"Hahaha ... I'm a tall, handsome African prince. And you know it."

"If that phone rings, I'll have to answer it. So, I need you to move your tall African prince butt out of my seat."

"I'm not going anywhere until we're friends."

"Your mom left Papa Tony too, so how would you feel if I now told you that you were not his son? You need to recognize that it was mean to say that to me."

"It was the truth then and I'm not sorry."

I flared my nostrils at him and all he did was roll his eyes.

"Okay ... let's see how you like it. Papa Tony has three spiritual wives and you are no longer his son."

"That's messed up, brother," he said in a goofy manner.

"I'll be your friend if you let me do my shift without interruption tonight," I answered. "That's all I want."

For what seemed like forever, Kiona sat motionless just staring at me, then he finally extended his hand. When I shook it, he pulled me toward him causing me to collapse into his lap and he hugged me.

"That's all I wanted," he said, laughing. "Papa Tony is and was my dad. And I guess he is and was your dad too. You sure you don't want any help around here? Must get lonely."

"Just leave so I can get my work done," I said, walking over to the day's newspaper. "I need to go through these."

A few hours after Kiona left, when I knew for sure the house was quiet, I dialed Jean Scheine's number again.

"Hi, Jean. Please, don't hang up on me, please?" I softly pleaded. "My mother is Bethany Scheine. Your last name is Scheine. Isn't it? Well, I am trying to find her. She is my mom and you are the only person in all of New York who has the same last name as her maiden name. I beg you. Please tell me if you are related to her or if you know where she is."

The pause on the phone went on for what felt like an eternity.

"Benji, is that you?" she asked, in a tone that could only be called loving and caring.

Another long pause while I sobbed without restraint.

"Benji! Beth's baby boy? Is that you?" she asked again.

"Yes, it is me," I said, wiping away the tears and sniffling as I tried to get myself under control.

"I have pictures of you, but your mom got all caught up with that religious group in California," she said. "Where are you?"

"I'm in Arkansas. Can you help me find her? I don't even remember her. She left me here with my dad when I was little. Do you know where she is?"

"The last time I heard from her she was married and living in California. I'll have to look in my records for her contact information. Can you call me back in a few days? I'll have her contact information for you. Are you okay right now? Do you need anything? Maybe some money?"

"I'm fine, but I have to hang up. If they catch me, I will get in trouble. They'll beat me."

"When you called me the other day I was sleeping and didn't know who you were," she said. "I'm an old woman. Do you understand why I hung up on you?"

"Yes. I'm sorry for waking you up, but I must find her. My life depends on it."

"Well, I am your great aunt Jean. Call me in a few days, and I'll have your mom's phone number for you."

# CHAPTER FOURTEEN

## Hope Keeps a Man Alive

As I hung up the phone, I found myself looking at it in awe before setting it in its cradle. As if it were an Aladdin's lamp and had granted me my deepest wish. My hand levitated over it for a few seconds, its energy still pulsing through me.

I was filled with mixed feelings of hatred, rage, and contempt for Tony Alamo and the Vasquez family for lying to me for all these years. At the same time, I was filled with optimism, hope, and the new conviction to find my mom. The emotions were at war within me and for the first time I understood what it meant to have a war going on inside of me as so many adults had told me.

I ran to the back of the room where I had hidden my personal documents in a box and pulled the picture of my mom from the folder and kissed her forehead.

Then, I retrieved the phone numbers the operator had given me for "Risha" in Uniontown, Pennsylvania.

I dialed the first number for a Talib Risha, and a man picked up the phone.

"This is Talib, and this better be good," the man said rather curtly.

"Do you know Ed Risha?"

"Yeah, I know Ed. Who is this?"

"I'm Ed's son, Benji. I'm looking for him. Do you know where he is?"

"Benji? I'm your uncle Talib. I've been wondering about you ever since your dad left that religious group. Where are you?"

"I'm in Arkansas and I need to find my dad. Do you know where he is? Do you have his phone number?"

"Yeah … hold on …."

Right away I dialed the number my uncle gave me, and a woman picked up the line.

Her voice was groggy, and she sounded a bit irritated. "Hello?"

"This is Benji Risha. Is my dad there?"

"Your dad? You mean Ed? Yeah, hold on."

"There is some boy on the line asking for his dad," I heard her say.

Ed took the receiver.

"Benji, is that you?"

"Yes, it is. I've been looking for you and my mom. I want to leave the church and live with you."

"Okay. Are you alright? Is there anything wrong right now?"

"No, I'm alright. I just want to leave as soon as possible. Will you help me?"

"Yes, of course, I'll help you. Where are you?"

"Fort Smith, Arkansas."

"Okay, I'll get you a plane ticket. Go to the airport ticket counter one week from today and there will be a ticket waiting for you, Son. What time do you want to leave?"

"Early in the morning before the sun comes up. I want to talk to you now, but if they catch me, they will punish me."

"I understand."

"I'll see you in a week."

The next day, my brothers and I dribbled the basketball on the concrete slab in the back yard. I played hide-and-seek with Nicole and the boys. As I hid from them, I thought about everything else I was hiding from them ... that I knew my parents were alive, that my father had purchased an airline ticket, and that I was planning on running away.

I tried to act as if everything was status quo. I went to church that night. I continued mowing lawns, but instead of drearily pulling the lawn mower along, I often pushed it while running in excitement behind it. However, when I returned home each evening and was around my family, the pressure to keep my secrets nearly boiled over.

One morning at the breakfast table, Nicole asked me, "Why aren't you eating all your food? You never leave food on the plate."

I scowled at her for a minute before I snapped at her, "I just don't want to eat right now. Why do you care?"

"Jeez. What's wrong with you? I just think it's weird that you're not finishing your breakfast."

That night when Dad came in, he said, "Don't you move. We've got a surprise for you!"

It was now the last week of April 1992. Apparently, Papa Tony, who had been out of jail for six months, sent me a gift. He had kept his promise.

Sal carried the package, which was almost half his size, and dropped it at my feet. Nicole stood by my side smiling and I could tell by the look in her eyes that she was excited for me. I hoped that meant she forgave me for my breakfast outburst.

She put her hand on my shoulder and said, "Is this why you've been acting so strange? You've been waiting for Papa Tony's gift?" Raising her eyebrows, she picked up Sal and put him on her hip.

Mom chimed in, "Well, what did you get? Are you going to keep us waiting?"

The cardboard box was sealed with brown packaging tape. I ripped the brown package open to reveal a pair of maroon-colored, snakeskin cowboy boots. A slight foul smell hit my nostrils when I lifted them out of the box and my nose twitched when the smell hit me. The left side of my lip began to tic uncontrollably and I put my hand to my face to stop it. When they looked at me, I averted my eyes by looking down and away from them. I did my best to act pleased by smiling and opening my eyes wide.

They did not know I was feeling angry with them and did not want to be around them because of the lies they had been telling me and the cover up they were involved in. I had uncovered a lifetime of lies. Did Mom and Dad Vasquez know that they were lies? I wasn't sure, but I had already said goodbye to them in my heart, but I had to make sure to not show it.

I struggled to prevent my eyes from revealing my secret: I was someone different now. I was no longer their son or brother. I wasn't Benji Vasquez. I was Benjamin Risha. I had my own identity now. Inside my heart I had become Benjamin Risha, my newly embraced identity, but with little money, resources, and worldly knowledge to support my new self.

Yet when I looked over at Nicole, I felt my new mask begin to fade. I looked at little Miguel and my mask faded even more. When I looked at Sal, my mask melted away completely. I loved them too much to hide my new self and I began crying.

The day before I got the boots from Papa Tony, we had played basketball as a family. I let Sal dribble the ball past me. I helped little Miguel dunk the ball by picking him up so he could make a basket. I held him a little longer than was really needed for him to dunk and let go before he noticed. Benjamin Risha was not strong enough to be completely present yet. At that moment, I had to admit to myself I was still there with them as Benji Vasquez.

There in the Vasquez living room that day, as I thought about all of that, is when I started crying.

Dad reassured me, "It's okay to cry. It's not that often someone gets a present from Papa Tony. Are you going to be all right? You better write him a thank-you letter."

"I'm not writing ..." my words trailed off when I realized what I was saying.

"What do you mean you're not going to write to Papa Tony?"

"I mean, I'll thank him when calls into the office. I'll thank him on the phone instead of writing to him."

The next day I walked to a post office and mailed the boots to my dad. I liked the boots and hoped they would be there when I arrived. I had one more night of lying and hiding my thoughts and feelings. One more night before this life was completely over. One more night before I'm in my dad's arms. Dad's arms: so big and strong. Dad's hands: calloused and scarred. Arms I hadn't seen in eight years.

"There will be a ticket waiting for you at the airport when you get there, Son," he'd said on the phone.

Son. Son. Son ... I'm his son. He's my father. He's alive. He's alive. He's alive. Will he explain why he left me?

What about my mom? I wondered the same things about her. What if she left me because she is an evil person? What will I do if she tells me she does not want to talk to me or even worse, if she does not want to meet me?

My plan was that after staying with my dad for a few days, I would search for my mom. Hopefully my great aunt Jean would come through and find her phone number or address for me. I thought about the photo Lonny had shown me fours year earlier. Did I really have a brother and sister too? Did they live with my mom? Would they accept me into their family? I hoped they were still alive. I looked at the young smiling brunette, my only image of my mother, and it settled me. She did not look evil to me. She looked like a woman who would love me.

During my shift that night, I sat counting the money I had earned and had been stockpiling for mowing lawns.

I had one hundred twenty dollars. I filled a manila folder with my newly-found birth certificate, Aunt Jean's phone number, my father's address and phone number, and my flight number, which my father had given me when I called back a few days after our initial contact. I felt assured that I had everything I needed to run away.

Using the Yellow Pages, I called a taxi from an ad. I picked that one because it had a picture of the fastest looking car. A few hours later, I heard gravel grinding under the taxi's tires as it approached, getting louder and louder. I hurriedly stuffed my money into my pants pocket and grabbed my manila folder and the toiletry bag Dad Miguel had given me when I was eleven. I opened the sliding glass door to exit, while the sunrise's colors of orange, yellow, and red rays greeted me as I climbed into the cab.

The driver asked, "Is that all you have? No luggage?"

"It's all I need," I replied. If he knew the significance of the items I possessed, he wouldn't have asked such a question. I knew it was exactly what I needed to escape this life and start a life out in the real world.

"To the Fort Smith Regional Airport as fast as you can," I said anxiously, taking a final glance back at the still-dark office and main house.

The driver wore a T-shirt which had the sleeves cut off, revealing a tattoo on his shoulder of a horse's head under a horseshoe inscribed with the name Secretariat. The top of his head revealed a balding pattern that reminded me of the horseshoe in his tattoo. The thick smells of cigarette smoke and body sweat in the air of the taxi filled my nostrils.

But the taxi driver had business to take care of first, before he was going to get me out of there. "How you gonna pay, kid?" he asked with a southern twang, looking back over his shoulder at me, his bare arm extended across the front seat.

"You got cash?"

I showed the driver my cash and he immediately put the Chevrolet in reverse just as the lights in the main house lit up.

Silhouettes moved around in the now-lit main house. The taxi reached the end of the driveway, just as I saw my dad, his hair disheveled as one who has just woken up, standing on the front porch wearing only his sweatpants. He stepped off the porch onto the gravel turning his head as if attempting to hear something more clearly.

I watched nervously as he turned and walked a few feet back toward the sliding glass door of the office. He stood there for a moment, staring inside before returning to the porch. Much like someone who just put the final piece of a puzzle together, he turned his attention to the taxi. My dad then appeared to panic, pacing back and forth, as he yelled to the taxi, demanding that it stop. He raised his hands and waved them back and forth wildly above his head. Finally, he placed his middle fingers into his mouth, whistling and running after the car. Realizing the uselessness of his efforts, he turned around and went back inside.

I turned back facing forward, for the first time looking at the road before me. Like Lot's wife, I turned to look back in the rear again, not believing redemption was at hand, and saw the headlights of the family's beige van behind me. I knew it well. It followed us, gaining on us with flashing headlights and a loud horn. Sweat rolled down my back as a knot swelled in my stomach.

"Keep going. Please keep driving," I begged, never taking my eyes off the van behind us as the sun opened up before my eyes.

"When we get to the airport, I'll give you money to get out of the car and stop the guy in the van from coming after me. I have to get inside the airport."

"Whadda ya mean? Stop the guy?" the driver asked, just now noticing the van with flashing lights behind us. "I ain't getting involved in no disputes with your dad, boy."

"He's not my dad! I promise you; he is not my dad. If I don't get to the airport I will get in a lot of trouble and will most likely get beaten badly. Do you know what I mean?"

"No, I don't. Explain yerself," the driver demanded.

I was not prepared to tell this story, not to a stranger with a horseshoe tattoo and reeking of cigarettes. But I saw the van headlights nearing and my freedom fading.

"Last week I just found out that my mom and dad are alive and the place where I just came from has told me my entire life that they are dead. They are alive, and I am running away to see my dad. My real dad."

"What kind of place do you come from?" the driver asked as he looked at me in the rearview mirror.

"It's the Tony and Susan Alamo Christian Foundation. Have you heard of it?"

"What? You from there? The driver asked. "Ha! Everyone around here knows about you guys. You guys are a damn crazy group. Damn. I just saw you guys on the news a while ago."

"Well, if they catch me, they will beat me," I said softly.

"Well, if he ain't your dad and he'll put a hurtin' on you, then I'll see what I can do."

With that, the driver accelerated, increasing the distance, until the van was little more than a spec on the highway.

At the airport I leaped out of the taxi and ran into the terminal, turning once to look at the balding taxi driver who was pacing back and forth in anticipation of my dad who was presumably behind us. As I ran to the door an elderly woman stepped in front of me. I held the door open for her, smiled and said, "Good morning."

After she ambled through the door, I ran up to the first airline employee I saw standing behind a ticket counter.

"Hi. My name is Benji Risha. My dad said there was a ticket here for me," I said stammering while looking around.

"How do you spell your last name, Benji?" asked the man behind the counter in the crisp blue uniform.

"R-I-S-H-A."

"I see your ticket right here. Your flight is leaving soon. Do you have ID?"

I showed the agent my birth certificate. The agent examined it, saying, "It's not every day I see one of these. It's a good thing you got here when you did. Do you see that door right there?" he asked while pointing about fifty feet to his right. "That's the door to your flight. Here's your ticket."

I took the ticket and my birth certificate from the agent, the involuntary shaking now spreading from my leg to my hands. I looked around for any sign of Dad Miguel. Not seeing him, the quaking of my limbs finally began to subside. But I looked again and suddenly I saw the taxi driver yelling and circling right in front of Dad Miguel who was at the entrance to the small airport.

I kept walking toward the door and turned my head back and spotted him standing only thirty feet away, looking in the opposite direction. The small airport was sparsely populated. Dad Miguel turned around and faced in my direction, making eye contact before I could get through the door and onto the tarmac. My heart raced as I moved toward the gate. Handing my ticket to the agent, I held my hands together with my belongings to steady my hands to conceal my nervousness.

"Through this door, please," said a gate agent, with a smile that was reassuring and kind, as she pointed me to a door on her right.

"Benji! Benji! What are you doing? Where are you going? Benji, stop! Stop!" Dad Miguel voice bellowed after me.

I momentarily felt disoriented and stopped. I was supposed to obey my elders. But this elder had lied to me about my own mom and dad and plenty of other things. I no longer felt I could trust him.

As I stood there and evaluated the situation for that moment, a newly-found sense of confidence washed over me and helped me to find the courage I needed to walk through the gate and onto the tarmac where the plane seemingly waited for me.

As I began my trek in that direction, handed my ticket to the gate agent, and walked onto the tarmac, I turned around and saw Dad Miguel trying to squeeze through the door I had just exited. The gate agent, with her kind smile and soft voice, placed her body in front of him, blocking his passage and preventing him from stepping onto the tarmac.

"Benji!" he called after me, "Papa Tony wants to talk with you! Tony Alamo wants to talk with you! He said you can marry any girl you want and live anywhere you want! Just come back!" he yelled, holding a cell phone in his hand."

He repeated, "Any girl you want and any place you want to live … just come back!"

I walked back toward the door I had exited moments earlier. I realized that I was not the same person I was just moments ago inside the airport. Seeing Dad Miguel standing there, begging me to return, reassured me that I made the right decision. I understood in that moment that his and Papa Tony's desperation for me to return had nothing to do with what was best for me.

Even though Dad Miguel and I were a mere two feet away from each other at that point, the disconnect when it came to where we were in our lives was increasingly widening. I was moving toward freedom while he remained enslaved to Tony Alamo.

I looked directly into Dad Miguel's eyes and was surprised to realize that I wasn't afraid anymore. Dad Miguel had stopped struggling to get past the gate agent and looked back at me with what seemed to be kindness and acceptance. His shoulders relaxed, one hand on his hip, the other holding the cell phone.

There weren't very many travelers and the gate agent did not resist my return toward her, nor had the plane started its engines. Unlike the quiet airplane that now sat behind me, a roar was rumbling inside of me.

I heard Tony's voice on the phone barking an order. "Tell him he's a liar!" I yelled loudly toward the phone, once again surprising myself and undoubtedly alarming or at least confusing my fellow travelers. "I found my mom and my dad. And they are both alive. I am going to live with them. He's a liar. He's lied to me about them all these years."

The agent placed her hand on my shoulder and said, "We're boarding, sir. You need to get on the plane."

And with that, I was on my way.

# CHAPTER FIFTEEN

### Freedom

When I landed at Lake Placid, I immediately spotted my dad in the airport waiting for me right at the gate. As the passengers unloaded, they filed in around him. He was smiling but was not the man I remembered. The man I saw before me was a thinner and seemingly shorter version of the man I had known as my father. As I approached, I could see he had tears in his eyes. He reached out and shook my hand firmly. I recognized his calloused hands. When he hugged me, his five-o'clock shadow bristled against my cheek, chafing like sandpaper. That I also remembered from my younger years.

While we drove, my father kept looking at me and saying, "Wow! You are so big. You grew up." He told me about his work as a handyman and carpenter. He also said he had a few surprises for me, but I would have to wait a few days to see them.

The drive was short, and we arrived at a one-bedroom cabin located in the woods. A portable toaster oven sat on the counter of a small kitchen with a single sink. A few plastic plates, silverware, and cups were neatly stacked next to it. A couch, which doubled as a pull-out bed, sat in the center of the room, positioned in front of an old TV which used rabbit ears as an antenna.

"Is this your house?"

He must have seen the look of disappointment on my face because he said, "It was tough for me to get on my feet when I left you at the church. And no, it's my boss's cabin so don't break anything. He lets me stay here when I do work down here."

"Why did you leave me there?"

He sat down slowly on the couch as if he was moving under a tremendous weight.

"Have a seat, son," he said, patting the cushion next to him.

I sat down and he turned to me, taking my hand in his.

"Do you see the bathroom door there and the bedroom door over there?"

"Yes, I see them, but what's that got to do with you leaving me?"

"What if you had to walk through one of those doors and I told you behind one was a pit full of venomous snakes and behind the other was a starving tiger that would eat you alive the moment you walked in? But you had to go into one of them. No matter what, you had to go into one of them. What would you do?"

"Well, I know how to kill snakes so I would choose the door with the venomous snakes. But what does that have to do with you leaving me?" I persisted.

"I didn't have any real choice but to leave you, son. My life in the church was like living with a crazy tiger on my back. Tony Alamo was a crazy tiger and leaving you was like going into a den of vipers. No matter what I did, stay at the church or leave you, I was going to die from my actions. I really didn't have a choice. Life doesn't always give you the choices you want."

I pulled my hand away from his as I tried to process what he had just said.

The next morning was cold and gray. I woke up to see my dad looking at me, smiling. "I have a big surprise for you. You have a brother and two sisters in Saranac Lake where I live." I was surprised to hear this. The pace at which my new life was unfolding—news of another brother, two sisters, seeing my father and, hopefully soon, my mom, and maybe even more siblings—overwhelmed me.

We drove for hours the next day, eventually pulling into the driveway of an old home where a barking chocolate lab greeted us at the gate. Inside, three dark-haired kids sat on a dark-colored couch, mesmerized by a television program they focused on intently.

"This is Kay, Melody, and Will. They are your sisters and brother," he said. "Will there is two. Melody is four. And Kay is five."

They only momentarily looked up from the television screen in a brief acknowledgement of my presence. I mumbled "Hi," but received no response.

This was not how I imagined meeting my siblings. Where was their mom? Why weren't they in school? I wondered all these things, but I wasn't comfortable asking these questions to my dad because I didn't want to seem like I was being nosy.

"Where is their mom?" I asked.

"She went to the grocery store. She knew I would be coming here so she left them alone for a bit," Dad replied.

After the brief introduction to my young siblings, I followed Dad back outside. He lit up a cigarette, something I had never seen him do before. In the distance, I could see an old barn at the end of the property that looked like it could be haunted. He began to talk about various improvements he wanted to make to the property but kept talking about needing money. I offered him my hundred twenty dollars, but he refused it, saying, "You might need that for an emergency."

While he talked, I felt as if the cold of the day had forced itself between him and me. I wasn't feeling the close connection to him I had enjoyed when I was a child. I stood there, my gaze focused on the smoke swirling through the air, as if the gray of the smoke and the gray of the day collaborated to erase whatever bonds we had shared during my childhood. I was so aware of myself being aware of myself that it was like I was looking down on my own body while we were standing there talking. I thought about those times we worked together on the church homes in Arkansas. My thoughts moved to my siblings sitting in the house watching television and I wondered what kind of connection they shared with Dad.

That night I called my great aunt Jean and she gave me my mom's number like she had promised she would. I felt a rush of both excitement and fear as I dialed my mother's number. The phone rang several times, and my heart sped up with each ring. Finally, a woman's voice answered.

"Hello."

I could hear the Indigo Girls playing in the background and I was transfixed right away.

"Hello? Hello?" the woman repeated impatiently.

"I'm Benji Risha. I'm looking for Bethany Scheine."

At first, all I heard was silence, but then she hesitatingly spoke.

"I'm Bethany, but I don't go by that last name anymore. What did you say your name was?"

"Benji Risha. You're my mom. Jean Scheine gave me your number. I've been looking for you."

More silence but then I heard her sobbing.

I wished I could reach through the phone line and comfort her. Turning her mouth away from the phone, she yelled out to somebody else who was with her.

"Craig ... honey ... it's Benji on the phone!"

She returned her attention to the phone.

"Where are you? Are you ok?" she said breathlessly, her speech interrupted by her sobs.

"I'm okay. I'm with Dad in Lake Placid."

"I can't believe you're calling me! Do you know how many times I tried to find you? Do you know how many times I tried to get you?" she asked through her tears. "I did everything in my power to find you. I contacted the sheriff's department. I hired a detective and he called the sheriff in Crawford County. They must have called the church looking for you and inadvertently tipped them off. I guess Tony and Sue moved you around quite a bit. Did you move around a lot when you were young?"

"I did," I replied, remembering all the places I visited as a child and the families with whom I lived.

My mother, with the meager income she and her husband earned, had scraped enough together to hire a detective to try to find me. The church moved me around from family to family and location to location and lied to the deputy sheriffs to thwart her efforts.

She continued, "Dorian and Kendra Yale also tried to grab you from Nashville once, but they were seen by some of the church brothers. I can't tell you how happy I am to hear your voice. You must be seventeen now. Do you know that you have two brothers and a sister here in California?"

"I knew I had one brother and a sister."

"You have another brother. He lives with us in the house we just bought. Can I talk to your dad, sweetie?"

They spoke for about twenty minutes and I watched my dad's face light up. He glanced over at me a few times while speaking to her. "Yeah, he's a young man now. Big and strong."

He handed the phone back to me.

"We just bought a house a month ago, and we are still moving in. We have a room for you if you want to stay with us," she said softly, as if she was unsure how I would respond.

"I want to see you," I said.

We all devised a plan that I was to stay with Dad for a month before I flew out to California to live with my mom. During that month, I worked with my dad, picking up debris, and cleaning the houses and tools when he was done working. One day while working, Dad threw a lit cigarette butt on the ground and walked away toward the trench. The still-burning cherry lit the grass and quickly became a fast-moving flame in a matter of seconds. There was no water in sight.

"Fire!" I yelled. "Fire!"

Dad came running back and we both kicked and stomped at it. Then he panicked and got into his jeep and drove away, leaving me with the fire. This time, I didn't just stand there watching him drive away, I took two large pieces of cardboard and laid them on the fire's edge, leapfrogging one piece over the other, until it was extinguished. Worn out, I sat down in the charred field and waited for his return. Eventually he did, along with his boss who yelled at me, asking me how I managed to almost burn down Lake Placid.

"Look, I didn't start the fire, I put it out!" I told him. "It was my dad's cigarette in the dry grass."

My dad didn't accept responsibility or protect me; instead he ran away, just as he had done before. I was tired of adults who failed to take responsibility and certainly wasn't going to defend him to his boss. His "tiger and den of vipers" analogy sprang up in my mind. He could have stayed in the church and stayed here fighting the fire with me, but he didn't do either. What had happened to him? Where was his fighting spirit?

The boss, I guess appreciating my honesty and maybe a little sorry he had accusingly yelled at me, pulled out a twenty-dollar bill and handed it to me.

That night, we slept in yet another house instead of going back to Dad's house. Dad said it was a real beauty. It wasn't. I fell asleep on a sheetless twin bed in a tiny room.

I was awakened in the middle of the night by the sound of music. When I opened the bedroom door to leave the room, I saw a topless woman gyrating on my dad's lap. There was a skunky odor, something I would later recognize as the smell of marijuana, a smell I also remembered coming from the bathroom when Papa Tony used it. Empty beer bottles, half-emptied liquor bottles, and two full ashtrays were on the coffee table next to the couch.

Neither of them saw me and I didn't know what to make of the scene. I didn't judge them or have any negative feelings about them. I was surprised to see a woman in the house and to see her topless. I guess I was just happy to be with my dad and I didn't care who else was with him.

Dad spent eleven years in the church, and it had been nine since he left. He obviously never broke the initial addiction of the pain meds he was given after his childhood surgery. I sadly realized it must have led to other addictions.

A few days later, it was time for me to go live with my mom. After hugging my dad goodbye, I looked back at him as I moved toward the boarding gate and saw him wiping tears from his eyes. I could still feel where his arms had wrapped around me on my back. His signature bear hug stayed with me for most of the flight, but the excitement I felt anticipating seeing my mom for the first time eclipsed the sadness I felt when I left my dad. I now knew where to find him whenever I wanted to.

When I first landed, I was somewhat disoriented and searched the many faces around me but did not see the smiling woman from my photo. Finally, a short, chubby, gray-haired woman screamed my name as I was walking right past her. I felt astonished. I simply could not believe that this was my mom. I had not considered how time would certainly have changed her. I stared into her eyes, trying to find the woman in the photo, just to make sure it was really her.

"Take a picture. It will last longer," she said sarcastically.

I pulled the photo from my pocket, pointing at it.

"I thought you were this person."

"Hmm ... I used to be," she said, glancing at it. "That was a long time ago and a different world."

She reached out to me and hugged me for what seemed like a long time. I breathed into her hug trying let go of my worries and concerns, but I had too many questions. I hugged her back uneasily and then heard her say, "We have a lot to talk about. That picture of me was taken during a time in my life that was confusing, to say the least. I'll explain it all once we get on the road. We have a long drive ahead of us."

Initially, I felt a lot of unease and distrust toward her. I listened closely as she told me why she left the church, trying to find answers to the unasked question that burned in me: why did she leave me?

"You see, Ben, or do you go by Benjamin?"

"No one ever calls me Ben, but I like how it sounds."

"You see, Ben, I joined the church because of what I thought it was. I thought it was a place that wanted to save the world, but over the course of six or seven years, I forget how long I was in it, I realized the place was just a place for Tony and Susan Alamo to express their egos. I loved the brothers and sisters who were there because they had real love in their hearts. They cared for me and I cared for them, but what Tony and Sue did was unspeakable. They essentially tortured me, spiritually speaking, and in some ways the work they made me do was torture."

"What do you mean? How did they torture you?"

"Well, to begin with, they blamed me for Randall's death. Randall was my first husband there and I loved him more than my own life. I had two children with him. I loved him so much and still do. They convinced the entire congregation that I killed him. They claimed that I did not have enough faith to heal him. His death was unavoidable. We took him to numerous doctors and none of them could heal him. Then there was the pressure to marry your dad. I was still mourning the death of Randall when they started their Jewish-Arab peace campaign on me. The pressure was too much for me. I just wanted to worship the Lord, help people who needed help, and make sure I got into heaven. I haven't even told you about how they worked me to exhaustion. I had three children and was working eighteen hours a day. Can you imagine that? You were only an infant and they made me work overnight shifts in addition to attending all of the church services, church functions, and prayer hours."

"Oh, ok. I didn't know any of that."

"And you need to know," she said, slowing the car's speed and turning toward me, "you need to know that I did not want to leave you. It was not part of my plan." Refocusing her attention on the road, she continued to explain, "You were my little prince. That's what I called you. Before I left, I tried to find you to take you with me, but your dad had hidden you where I couldn't find you. It was unexpected for him to get you that early in the morning. I can't tell you how bad I felt to leave you. I spent a lot of nights crying for you and praying to God that he would bring you back to me. And, here you are. I guess he answered my prayers." She was smiling, but tears were rolling down her face.

"I didn't know any of this."

"That's not all of it. I tried to come get you three times. Each time the sheriff's deputies would tip off the church simply by reporting that they were looking for you and the church would move you. I even hired a private detective, but we didn't have enough money to keep paying him to find you. Plus, the church had a lot more money and could have made our lives miserable."

As time and miles passed, some of the unease passed. About thirty minutes passed quietly, each of us in our own thoughts, while I mulled over what she had told me and allowed her words to sink in.

"Your other brother and sister are driving up from university just to see you," she said as we drove along a winding row of olives trees, pulling up to a ranch-style house.

Inside the home, I was even more overwhelmed. I walked around in a daze, looking at photographs of the life I was robbed of, inspecting albums I was not a part of, and books I had never had the opportunity to read. There were a few photos of me as a three-year-old and I wondered how she had managed to get them.

I later learned that Dorian and Kendra Yale found my mom after they left the church and they gave her the photos.

Shortly after our arrival, a young woman with long brown hair, kind eyes, and a big smile, who my mother introduced to me as my sister Chelsea, walked through the front door. I greeted her with an awkward kiss on the cheek.

"Oh … how European," she responded, giving me a hug and presenting me with an empty journal as a gift. "Your sister's an artist," Mom said.

My younger brother, Carter, came in soon after. He measured me up, looking me directly in my eyes, and embraced me in a big hug. As he stepped away to go wash his hands in the kitchen, he asked, "Do you want a beer?"

Mom interjected saying, "No. He does not want a beer. Neither do you."

"And he's the party animal, if you can't tell," Chelsea said, with a gentle warning.

Unlike Chelsea and me, Carter was tall and husky.

Samuel arrived later, just before dinner. He dropped a cotton knapsack of dirty clothes on the ground and walked past me to hug Mom. He then turned his attention to me and grabbed me firmly by the hand, pulling me in close for a bear hug. He appeared naturally self-confident and was lean and athletic looking.

The four of us sat down on the fireplace hearth together so that mom could take some photos. They made small talk about university life and Carter talked about his friends who were in town. There was a party in the orange groves, and he wanted me to go with him.

My mother's husband, Craig, was also quite kind. Watching him and my mother make dinner together was like watching two dancers move through the kitchen with well-practiced steps and maneuvers. They joked with each other, but when his path got in her way near the hot stove, she made it known by playfully slapping his hand.

In the fall, I enrolled in high school. My grades were surprisingly quite high, despite missing half of the tenth grade and the entire eleventh grade, but it was a social disaster for me. I did not grasp the idiomatic jargon and cultural references that other teenagers used effortlessly. I was terribly awkward with girls; I couldn't have gotten laid even if I had a pound of marijuana in a women's prison.

I went to bed every night filled with anxiety and questions about how to navigate this new world. I saw the way the girls looked at the letterman jacket-wearing jocks. Their clothes said they had money, an area I certainly couldn't compete in. Realizing I was going to need more than my personality in this new world, I tried out for the football, baseball, and wrestling teams and made football and wrestling which I enjoyed very much. I made some good friends, some not-so-good friends, and met a few party animals.

One day, two of the cutest girls in school walked with me to the cafeteria.

"You're new, right? Where did you come from?" asked the blonde.

The cult story was clearly not going to work.

"New York. I lived there with my dad."

"That explains it then," she answered.

"Explains what?"

"The attitude. People talk, you know."

"Shit, no one is talking about me."

Just then, someone grabbed my shoulder from behind.

"You're not allowed to use that language here!" I heard.

I was startled ... and immediately imagined seeing myself suspended in the air and whipped with a board. My instinctive reflexes kicked in and, without thinking, without even asking or caring who he was, I swiftly looped my arm around his and pinned him down on the floor in front of all the students who looked on in shock. No one could lay their hands on me without my consent. Unfortunately, the person I was pinning to the floor turned out to be a teacher. A few kids snickered, knowing I was in big trouble. The girls I had been talking with drew back in disgust. I was expelled and not allowed to return the following day.

Mom highly encouraged me to enlist in the Army, which is to say she insisted because I needed "discipline," as she put it. I enlisted in the Army in the summer of 1993. I had just turned eighteen. My preference was the Marines over the Army, but I did not receive my high school diploma because all my high school records were at the church somewhere and I did not graduate. Instead, I received my GED.

While in boot camp, I received a phone call telling me my father's liver had failed so the doctors had put him in a medically-induced coma. The nurse held the phone to my father's ear so I could speak to him one last time.

Struggling to keep it together, I said, "I love you, Dad. I have missed you. Remember the day you taught me to ride a bike? Don't brake when you hit the curve, lean into it, and let it carry you through. Right, Dad, right?" I knew he couldn't respond, and I told him I would pray for him before I hung up. For the next several weeks, I did just that. On my knees at night before going to bed and again in the morning when I awoke. I cried and prayed for my dad when I said the blessing before meals. A month after that phone call, I received a phone call telling me he had died. He died on his forty-fifth birthday, and the thought of him dying on his birthday really grabbed me and made it seem even sadder. I never got to see him again after I left Lake Placid, which had been two years prior.

I grieved for him and for the three young children he left behind. I never met the mother of his children, so I didn't know what she was like and how she treated my siblings on my dad's side because they lived separately from my father. I grieved for all my friends who were still in the cult. I grieved for all the friends for whom I did not know how they were doing. Were they on the streets? Did they get hooked on drugs? Were they still alive? But when I retreated into those dark places of my past, it was my mother who pulled me out.

No, she was no longer the thin, young brunette in the photo. She was real, a woman who had endured pain and had regrets yet grew wise as a result of them. "Every last one of these gray hairs I've earned," she once told me, before hugging me long and hard. We have openly talked and shared our experiences and made our peace. Today, my mom is one of my best friends. I turn to her when I need advice and I know I can trust it.

People have told me to "Forgive, but never forget." Forgiveness for me requires understanding those who have acted against me. Forgetting involves the self-protecting mechanism of the mind and body to block out traumatic events for the purposes of self-preservation. It also involves remembering things so that we learn things to protect ourselves. So yes, I have forgiven them, but I will never forget.

# PHOTOS

*The picture Ben saw when he found his mom's picture in files.*

*Me sitting on Tony Alamo's lap next to Susan Alamo*

*Me in red shirt, age 3 or 4*

*Me showing off the biggest catch*

*Children's church service*

*For More News About Benjamin Risha,
Signup For Our Newsletter:*
**http://wbp.bz/newsletter**

*Word-of-mouth is critical to an author's long-term success. If you appreciated this book please leave a review on the Amazon sales page:*
**http://wbp.bz/sevenmothersa**

**AVAILABLE FROM CARL DENARO, BRIAN WHITNEY, AND WILDBLUE PRESS!**

THE 'SON OF SAM' AND ME by CARL DENARO and BRIAN WHITNEY

http://wbp.bz/sonofsama

**AVAILABLE FROM STEVE KOSAREFF AND WILDBLUE PRESS!**

SATIN PUMPS by STEVE KOSAREFF

http://wbp.bz/satinpumpsa

**AVAILABLE FROM JONI ANKERSON
AND WILDBLUE PRESS!**

TO KILL OR BE KILLED by JONI ANKERSON

http://wbp.bz/tkobka